Street by Street

BOURNEMOUTH
CHRISTCHURCH, POOLE, WIMBORNE MINSTER

Bransgore, Brockenhurst, Corfe Mullen, Ferndown, Lymington, Milford on Sea, New Milton, Ringwood, Verwood, West Moors

1st edition May 2001

© Automobile Association Developments Limited 2001

This product includes map data licensed from Ordnance Survey® with the permission of the Controller of Her Majesty's Stationery Office. © Crown copyright 2000. All rights reserved. Licence No: 399221.

Published by AA Publishing (a trading name of Automobile Association Developments Limited, whose registered office is Norfolk House, Priestley Road, Basingstoke, Hampshire, RG24 9NY. Registered number 1878835).

Mapping produced by the Cartographic Department of The Automobile Association.

ISBN 0 7495 2617 3

A CIP Catalogue record for this book is available from the British Library.

Printed by Edicoes ASA, Oporto, Portugal

The contents of this atlas are believed to be correct at the time of the latest revision. However, the publishers cannot be held responsible for loss occasioned to any person acting or refraining from action as a result of any material in this atlas, nor for any errors, omissions or changes in such material. The publishers would welcome information to correct any errors or omissions and to keep this atlas up to date. Please write to Publishing, The Automobile Association, Fanum House, Basing View, Basingstoke, Hampshire, RG21 4EA.

Ref: ML002

Key to map pages	ii-iii
Key to map symbols	iv-1
Enlarged scale pages	2-3
Street by Street	4-85
Index – towns & villages	86
Index – streets	87-102
Index – featured places	102-103

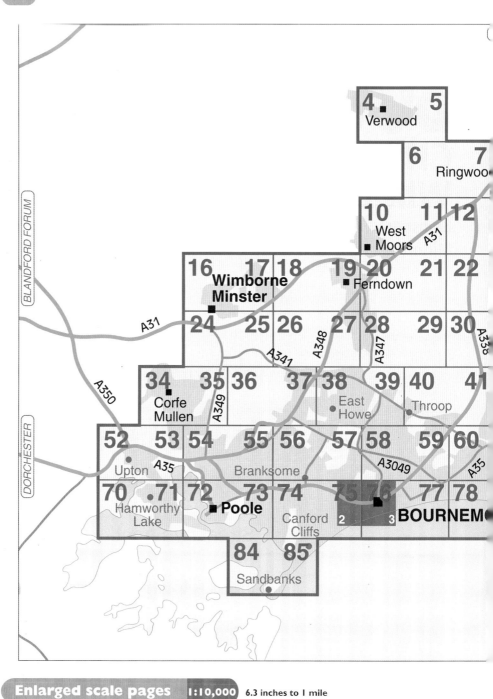

							4 Verwood	5
							6	7 Ringwood
						10 West Moors	11 12 A31
16 Wimborne Minster	17 18		19 20 Ferndown	21 22				
A31 24	25 26	A341	A348 27 28 A347	29 30 A338				
A350 34 Corfe Mullen A349	35 36	37 38 East Howe	39 40 Throop	41				
52 Upton A35	53 54	55 56 Branksome	57 58 A3049	59 60 A35				
70 71 72 Hamworthy Lake	73 74 Poole	Canford Cliffs 2	75 76 3 BOURNEM 77 78					
	84 85 Sandbanks							

DORCHESTER   BLANDFORD FORUM

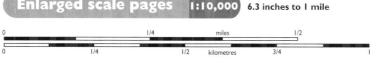

Enlarged scale pages   **1:10,000**   6.3 inches to 1 mile

0		1/4	miles	1/2
0	1/4	1/2	kilometres 3/4	1

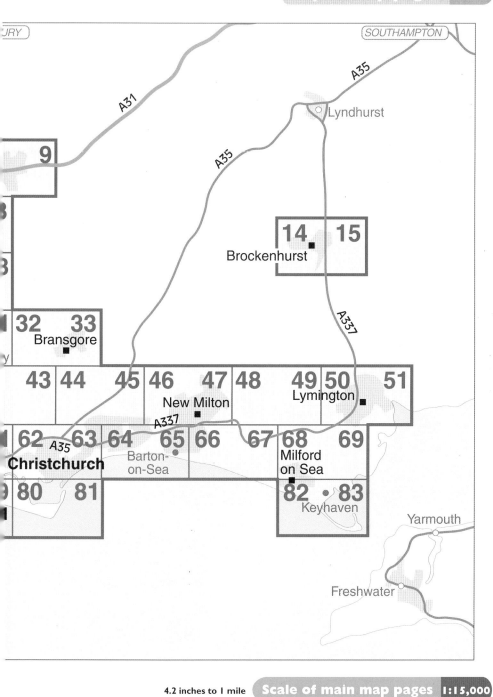

JRY

SOUTHAMPTON

A31

A35

Lyndhurst

9

A35

14 15

Brockenhurst

32 33
Bransgore

A337

43 44 45 46 47 48 49 50 51
New Milton   Lymington

A337

62 63 64 65 66 67 68 69
A35
Christchurch   Barton-on-Sea   Milford on Sea

80 81   82 83
Keyhaven

Yarmouth

Freshwater

4.2 inches to 1 mile   **Scale of main map pages** 1:15,000

0   1/4   miles   1/2   3/4   1

0   1/4   1/2   kilometres 3/4   1   1 1/4   1 1/2

Junction 9	Motorway & junction	P+R	Park & Ride
Services	Motorway service area	🚌	Bus/Coach station
	Primary road single/dual carriageway		Railway & main railway station
Services	Primary road service area		Railway & minor railway station
	A road single/dual carriageway	⊖	Underground station
	B road single/dual carriageway	⊖	Light Railway & station
	Other road single/dual carriageway	+++++++++	Preserved private railway
	Restricted road	*LC*	Level crossing
	Private road	•—•—•—•	Tramway
← ←	One way street	-----------	Ferry route
	Pedestrian street	·············	Airport runway
-------------	Track/ footpath	— · — · — · —	Boundaries- borough/ district
	Road under construction	▼▼▼▼▼▼▼▼▼	Mounds
⊢ = = = ⊣	Road tunnel	**93**	Page continuation 1:15,000
P	Parking	**7**	Page continuation to enlarged scale 1:10,000

	River/canal, lake, pier	&#9855;	Toilet with disabled facilities
	Aqueduct, lock, weir		Petrol station
465 ▲ Winter Hill	Peak (with height in metres)	PH	Public house
	Beach	PO	Post Office
	Coniferous woodland		Public library
	Broadleaved woodland	i	Tourist Information Centre
	Mixed woodland		Castle
	Park		Historic house/ building
	Cemetery	Wakehurst Place NT	National Trust property
	Built-up area	M	Museum/ art gallery
	Featured building	†	Church/chapel
⊓⊓⊓⊓⊓⊓⊓	City wall	Y	Country park
A&E	Accident & Emergency hospital		Theatre/ performing arts
	Toilet		Cinema

4

A3
1 Beech Cl
2 Haywards Fm Cl

A2
1 Churchfield

A1
1 Bakers Farm Rd
2 Forest La

B1
1 Manor Wy

B2
1 Manor Ct
2 Manor Gdns
3 Pennine Wy

B3
1 Cotswold Cl
2 Mendip Cl
3 Purbeck Dr
4 St Michaels Cl
5 Woodpecker Cl

C1
1 Starlight Farm Cl

C2
1 Acorn Wy
2 Heathlands Cl
3 Oaks Mead
4 Shires Mead

C3
1 Nightingale Cl
2 Orchard Ct

D2
1 Foxhills
2 Noon Hill Dr

Stephen's Castle

Wild Church Bottom

VERWOOD

BH31

Hillside County First School

Verwood Town Council

Verwood Leisure Centre

Verwood Industrial Est

Verwood Sports Cen

Police Station

Manor Road Surgery

Verwood C of E School

Verwood C of E First School

The Surgery

River Crane

Manor Farm

Crab Orchard

1 grid square represents 500 metres

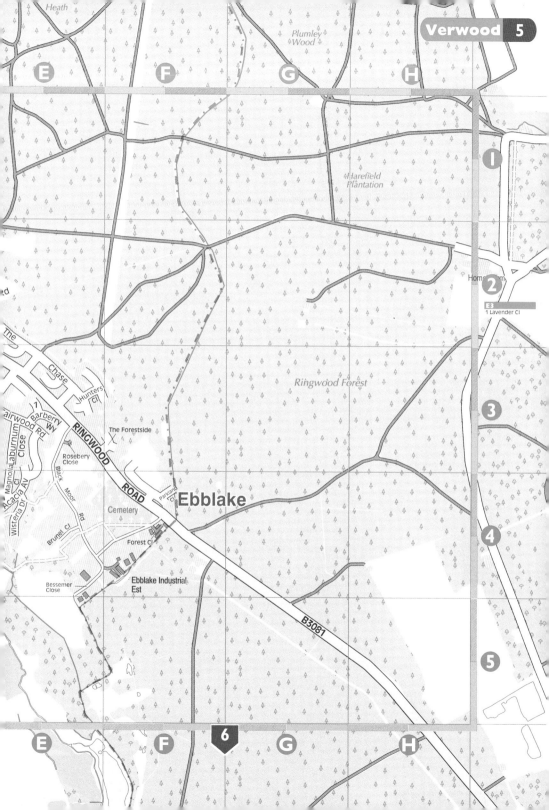

Heath

Plumley
Wood

E   F   G   H

Harefield
Plantation

I

Hom...

2

E3
1 Lavender Cl

Ringwood Forest

3

The
Chase

Hunters
Cl

1

Barberry
Wa

Fairwood Rd

Laburnum
Close

Magnolia Cl

Acacia Cl

Wisteria Dr

Black Moor Rd

Rosebery
Close

The Forestside

Parkland Cl

Ebblake

Cemetery

Brunel Cl

Forest Cl

Bessemer
Close

Ebblake Industrial
Est

4

B3081

5

E   F   6   G   H

6

5

I

2

3

4

5

A B C D

Hampshire County
Dorset County

⛲ Moors Valley
Country Park

Moors River

Ashley Heath
Industrial Est

Woolsbridge
Industrial Est

Victory Cl

Liberty Cl

Azura Cl

Ringwood Rd

Wools Bridge

Horton Road

Forest Edge Dr

Webbs Cl

Mnr Rd

Castleman Trailway

Grosvenor

Dryden Cl

Evans

Emore Cl

Cs Lane

DS
1 High St

Horton Rd

1

Peveril Cl

Ashley Drive W

The Spinney

Struan

Monkworthy Dr

The Glad Road

Hill Wy

A B 11 C D

1 grid square represents 500 metres

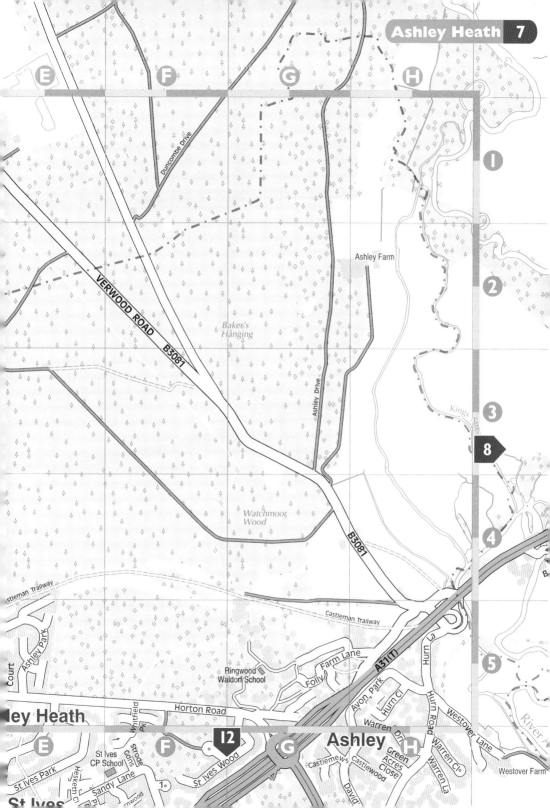

E F G H

I

2

3

8

4

5

Duncombe Drive

Ashley Farm

VERWOOD ROAD B3081

Baker's Hanging

Ashley Drive

Kings Acres

Watchmoor Wood

B3081

Castleman Trailway

Castleman Trailway

Ringwood Waldorf School

Farm Lane

Folly

Avon Park

A31(T)

Hurn La

Hurn Road

Westover Lane

River

Court

Ashley Park

ley Heath

Horton Road

Whitfield

Stroude Gdns

Warren Dr

Hurn Cl

Green Acres Close

Warren Cl

Warren La

Westover Farm

E F I2 G Ashley H

St Ives Park

St Ives CP School

Hesketh Cl

Sandy Lane

St Ives Wood

Castlemews

Castlewood

David

St Ives

8

1 Manor Gdns B3

Blashford Farm

Ivy Lane

Snail's Lane

Snail's Lane

Woolmer Lane

Avon Va Pth

Headlands Business Park

Avon Valley Path

North Morant Road

1

B4
1 Centre Pl
2 The Close
3 Cottage Ms
4 High St
5 Kings Arms Rw
6 Meeting Ho La
7 The Sweep

Waterside Close

Wansitead

2

C3
1 Somerley Vw

River Avon

Gouldings Farm

SALISBURY ROAD A338

Hurst Rd

Northfield Road

Broadshard Lane

Meadow Cl

Meadow Road

Seymour

Hampton Dr

Meadow Wy

Cyspy La

Oak La

Beechcroft

Fieldway

Wessex Rd

Stream

3

RINGWOOD

Salisbury Road

Gravel Lane

Farm Cl

Highfield Drive

Orchard

Pound La

Highfield Avenue

Highfield Rd

Middleton Rd

George Rd

Lilac Cl

Winston

Kestrel Ct

Southampton Rd

7

C4
1 Bishop Ct
2 Clark's Cl
3 Frampton Pl
4 Middle La
5 Mount Pleasant
6 The Quomp

A31(T)

Stallards La

Linden La

Gravel La

Gdns

Parsonage

Ringwood School

Green La

Barn

Cadogan Rd

Keppel Cl

Clough's

4

C5
1 Charing Cl
2 Duck Island La
3 Harry Barrow Cl
4 Nursery Rd
5 Southfield
6 Southfield Ms
7 Victoria Gdns
8 Waterloo Wy
9 Woodstock La

The Furlong

West St

Market Pl

Strides La

The Bridges

Lynes La

Kings Arms La

Kingsbury's La

MANSFIELD RD

Christchurch Rd

Dr Hughes & Partners

Carvers Trading Est

Carvers La

Collins La

School La

Ringwood Recreation Centre

College Road

Kingsfield

Top La

Manor Rd

Redwood Cl

East View Rd

Hilton Rd

Poplar

Redwood Rd

5

Hurn La

Riverside

Bickerley

Bickerley Gdns

CHRISTCHURCH RD

New Forest District Council

Limestone La

C of E Infant School

Hampshire Co Council

Ringwood Town Council

Ringwood Town Council

Hightown Road

Co Junior School

Ringwood Trading Est

Cemetery

Castleman

Pullman Way

Euston Way

Addison Square

Embankment Wy

New

Crow

Joyce Dickson Cl

Books

Hightown Industrial Est

Hurn Road

Westover Lane

Hotel

Parkside

Police Station

Warren Cl

Green

River Avon

Avon Valley Path

Westover Farm

1 Lumby Drive Pk D3

Stag Business Park

Willow Dr

1 Coniston Rd D5

ch Lane

Industrial Est

ch

Moortown

I grid square represents 500 metres

Highwood Lane

Lin Brook

Corley Road

Old Farm Close

North Poulner

Cowpitts Lane

Lin Brook Dr

Road

Shaw Rd

Ross Rd

Lawren Rd

Junior & Infant School

Forests de Gdns

Dene Cl

Croft Road

Holm

Denholm

Butlers La

Fairlie

Poulner Pk

Linford

Drake Cl

Narrow La

Grenville Cl

Chester Rd

Chi Cl

Corley

Link Rd

Somer ville Rd

Anson Cl

Beatty Cl

The Mount

Narrow La

Southampton Road

Eastfield La

Audemer Ct

Chaffel

jubilee Cl

Hangersley

St Aubyns Lane

Poulner

A31(T)

POULNER HILL

Novale Lane

Hightown Hill

Hill

Eastfield Lane

Ash Gv

Gdns

stfield se

Hightown

Hightown Road

Hightown Hill

Forest Lane

Lakeview Dr

Holmwood Garth

Ashburn Garth

Forestake Av

Ashley Cl

Forest Lane

Crow Lane

Pelican Md

Lakeside

Merlin Cl

Ship Dr

Waterm

Swan Md

Crow

Crow

Forest End Rd

Forest Rd

Hurn Farm

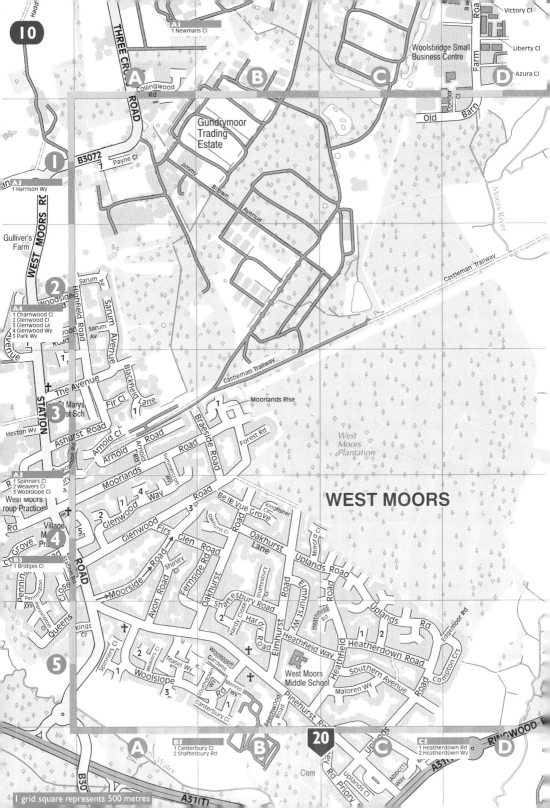

West Moors

10

A B C D

Victory Cl
Liberty Cl
Azura Cl

Woolsbridge Small
Business Centre

A1
1 Newmans Cl

THREE CROSS ROAD

Collingwood Rd

Old   Barn

Gundrymoor
Trading
Estate

1 B3072   Payne Cl

A3
1 Harrison Wy

Jimmy Brown Avenue

Gulliver's
Farm

WEST MOORS ROAD

Woodside   Sarum Av

2

A4
1 Charnwood Cl
2 Glenwood Cl
3 Glenwood La
4 Glenwood Wy
5 Park Wy

Highfield Road

Wood Road

Sarum Av

Sarum Avenue

Blackfield Lane

Castleman Trailway

Castleman Trailway

West
Moors
Plantation

Moors River

Avenue

The Avenue

St Marys
1st Sch

Fir Cl

3

STATION

Heston Wy

Ashurst Road

Arnold Cl

Arnold Road

Arnold Rd

Arnold Rd

Braeside Road

Road

Moorlands Rise

Forest Rd

A5
1 Spinners Cl
2 Weavers Cl
3 Woolslope Cl

West moors
roup Practice

Moorlands   Way

Summercroft Wy

Glenwood Way

WEST MOORS

Road

Belle Vue Grove

Kingfisher Cl

Milford Cl

Village
M
Pra

Grove

4

Glenwood

Glenwood Firs

Glen Road

Oakhurst Cl

Oakhurst
Lane

Oakhurst Road

Uplands Road

Uplands Road

B3
1 Bridges Cl

ROAD

Station Rd

Close

Shirley

Moorside Road

Avon Road

Fernside Rd

Oakhurst Road

Shaftesbury Road

Shaftesbury Cl

Hardy Cl

Elmhurst Road

Heathfield Rd

Uplands Rd

Edgemoor Rd

Pennington Crs

Pennington

Queens

Kings Cl

Spinners Cl

Weavers Cl

Teasel Wy

Woolslope
Gardens

Hardy Cl Road

Elmhurst Wy

Heathfield Way

Heathdown Road

Compton Crs

5

Woolslope
Road

Southdown Rd

Merino Wy

Canterbury Cl

West Moors
Middle School

Heathfield Road

Southern Avenue

Maloren Wy

Road

Pinehurst Rd

Beechwood Road

A B **20** C D

B5
1 Canterbury Cl
2 Shaftesbury Rd

C5
1 Heatherdown Rd
2 Heatherdown Wy

RINGWOOD R

Cem

B30

A31(T)

Uplands Rd

Priory Rd

Abbotts Wy

1 grid square represents 500 metres

Wools Bridge

Horton Road

Horton Rd

The

Peveril Cl

E **F** **6** **G** **H**

Ashley He

Ashley Drive

Badgers Dr

Pine Mnr Forest Edge Dr

Burton Cl

Lions Lane

Shore

Sir Evans

Evergreens

Ashley Drive W

Monkworthy Dr

St Ives Park

I St Ives Park

St Ive

Castleman Trailway

Grosvenor Cl

Dryden Cl

Shelley Cl

The Glade

Woolsbridge Road

Hill Wy

Langley

1 Forest Edge Cl

Lions Lane

St Leonards Way

Fernlea Cl

Bushmead Drive

Norris Cl

Lane

Gainsborough Road

Windsor Cl

Paddock Cl

Sandy Lane

Coppice

School Lane

7

St Ives End La

Greenwood Way

Lions

Bracken Close

Willow Cl

Sylvan Cl

John Cl

Craig

Braeside

Lions Wd

Cornerways Surg

Woodlands Wy

Pine Drive

Knoll Gdns

Pinewood Rd

Glenives Cl

2
1 Cedar Av
2 Garden La

Garth Cl

Heath

Conifer Cl

Ivy Cl

Spinney

Gorse Rd

Road

St Leonards

Drive

Acorn Cl

Heather Cl

Rd

Laurel Close

Laurel Lane

Haslemere

Hobbs Park

King Cl

RINGWOOD ROAD

A31

Rowan Cl

Oaks

Birch Close

Cedar Avenue

Malmesbury

Road

2

Brocks

Pine

3

12 ath
Country Park

Oaks

Cherry Tree Cl

Fir Tree Cl

RINGWOOD ROAD

Beech Lane

4

Eucalyptus

East Moors Farm

Grange Road

Barnsfield Rd

Boundary La

5

A31 (T)

GWOOD ROAD

St Leonards Hospital

Boundary Lane

Ways

Road

Foxbury Road

E **F** **21** **G** **H**

**Grange
Estate**

Moortown

District Council

Ringwood Trading Est

Castleman

Pullman Way

Highfown Gdns

Highfown Industrial Est

Crow Lane

Hotel

New

Police Station

8

E   F   G   H

Millstream Trading Est

Crow Arch Lane Industrial Est

Stag Business Park

Willow Dr

Crow Arch

Lane

Crow Lane

I

Westover Farm

River Avon

Avon Valley Path

Moorland Ga

CHRISTCHURCH

Moortown

Lane

Moortown

Lane

Streets La

Snires Cl

Hampshire Hatches Lane

ROAD

Long Lane

2

Green

Upper Kingston Fa

3

Lakes Farm

North Kingston

4

Avon Valley Path

Brixey's Farm

5

Kingston

23

E   F   G   H

B3347

Avon Valley Path

Wilkins Farm

Lane

14

A B C D

1

Ober Water
Highland Water

Black Knowl

2

Butts Lawn

Beachern Wood

D3
1 Culverley Cl
2 The Paddock
3 Wide Lane Cl

Oberfield Rd
Whitemoor Road
New Forest Drive
Broadlands Rd
Knowle Rd
Forest Park Road
Hotel
Ober Rd
Rhinefield Close
Meerut Butts Paddock
Brookside Road
Carey Cotta

The Coppice
Moorlands Cl
New Forest Dr
BROCKENHURST
Fibbards Rd
Fath

Ober House

3

New Forest Clade Close
Forest Drive
Forest Vw
Broadlands Rd
Armstrong Lane
Armstrong Cl
Armstrong Road
Wilverley Road
Brookley
Brookley Road
The Rise
PO 3

North Weirs

North Weirs

Brockenhurst Primary School
Av

4

Burley Road

South Weirs

The Surgery
Partri Rd
Highwood Road
Tattenham Rd

South Weirs

Addison Road
Collvers Rd
Woodlands Road

5

ROAD
SWAY

A B C D

Blackhamsley Ho

Brockenhurst Manor Golf Club

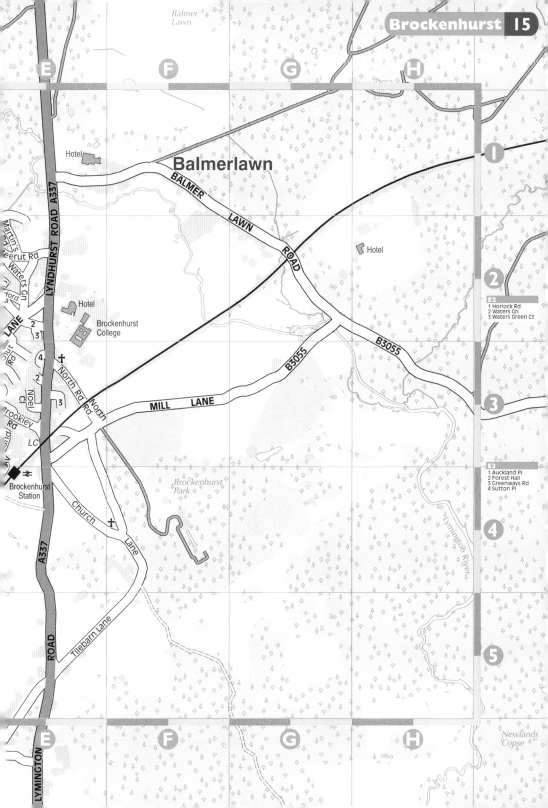

Balmer
Lawn

E   F   G   H

1

Hotel

Balmerlawn

BALMER

LAWN

Hotel

ROAD

2

Martin's
Meerut Rd
Waters Gn
ford

LANE

Hotel

Brockenhurst
College

LYNDHURST ROAD A337

B3055

B3055

4
2
3

North Rd

MILL   LANE

3

Noel
Cl
rookley
Rd

North Rd

LC

Brockenhurst
Station

Brockenhurst
Park

Church

Lane

4

Lymington River

A337

Tilebarn Lane

ROAD

5

E   F   G   H

Newlands
Copse

LYMINGTON

Furzehill

B3
1 Cowdrys Fld
2 Culverhayes Pl
3 Farmers Wk
4 Sheppards Fld

C3
1 Chaucer Cl
2 Courtenay Dr

C4
1 Crown Mead
2 Hanham Rd

C5
1 Crown Mead

D4
1 Oakdene Cl
2 Royston Dr

D5
1 Chas Keightley Ct
2 Cromwell Rd
3 Cuthburga Rd
4 Harleston Vls
5 Ingram Wk
6 Richmond Rd

1 grid square represents 500 metres

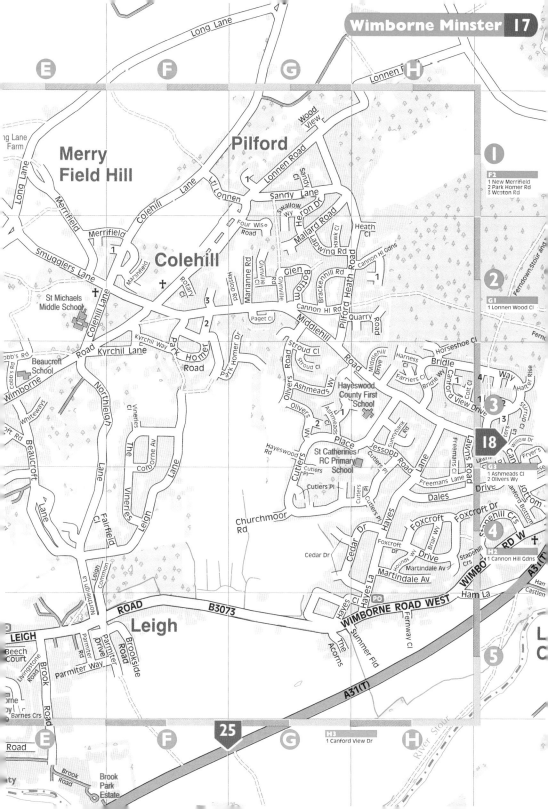

E   F   G   H

Long Lane

Lonnen R

I

Wood View

ng Lane Farm

Pilford

Lonnen Road

Sandy

Merry Field Hill

Lane

Lit Lonnen

Colehill

Swallow Wy

Heron Dr

Sandy Lane

Four Wise Road

Mallard Road

Hawk Cl

Heath Cl

Merrifield

Colehill Lane

Colehill

Marsnfield

Glynville Rd

Glynville

Glen Bottom

Brackenhill Rd

Haslop Rd

Marianne Rd

Cannon Hi Gdns

Pilford Heath Road

1

St Michaels Middle School

†

Smugglers Lane

Merrifield

†

Rotary

3

Cannon Hi Rd

Paget Cl

Middlehill

Quarry Road

2

Ferndown Stour Rd

Fern

Cobb's Rd

Beaucroft School

Kyrchil Way

Kyrchil Lane

Park Homer Road

Park Homer Dr

Stroud Cl

Stroud Cl

Olivers

Ashmeads

Middlehill Drive

Harness Cl

Farriers Cl

Bridle

Horseshoe Cl

Bridle Wy

Canford View Drive

Colt Cl

Way

Halter Rise

4

Wimborne Road

Northleigh Lane

Whiteways

Beaucroft Rd

Vineries Cl

Colborne Av

The Vineries

Olivers

Ashmeads Wy

Hayeswood County First School

1

Ashmeads

2

Olivers

Summbank Rd

Lawns Road

Burton

3

2

Willow Dr

Canf

Fryer's

Hayeswood Rd

Cutlers Place

St Catherines RC Primary School

Cutlers Pl

Jessopp Road

Cutlers Pl

Lawns Road

Freemans Cl

Freemans Lane

18

Leigh Lane

Fairfield

Churchmoor Rd

Cutlers Pl

Cutlers Pl

Hayes

Cedar Dr

Foxcroft Dr

Foxcroft Dr

Foxcroft Drive

Briar Wy

Dales

Canford Bottom

Stapehill Crs

Stapehill Crs

4

A31(T)

Leigh Common

Northleigh Lane

Cedar Dr

Hounds Wy

Martindale Av

Martindale Av

Hayes La

WIMBO

RD W

†

LEIGH

Beech Court

Livingstone Road

Brook Road

Parmiter Drive

Parmiter Way

Parmiter Rd

Brookside Road

ROAD

B3073

Leigh

Hayes Cl

WIMBORNE ROAD WEST

Ham La

PO

Fernway Cl

5

Barnes Crs

Road

The Acorns

Summer Fld

A31(T)

River Stour

Brook Road

Brook Park Estate

E   F   **25**   G
H

18

A   B   C   D

Copse Farm

Ferndown, Stour and Forest Trail

Uddens Plantation

Castle

1

Bedborough Farm

Maple Bus

Uddens Drive

2

Ferndown, Stour and Forest Trail

Cannon Hill Plantation

Castleman Trailway

Nimrod Way

Nimrod Way

A3
1 Hunter Cl
2 Saddle Cl
3 Spur Cl
4 Suffolk Cl

Dors Cou

Ferndown, Stour and Forest Trail

A31(T)

Uddens Drive

Old Forge Rd

Horseshoe Cl

Bridle

Way

3

Bridle Wy

Canford

Halter Rise

Suffolk

Chestnut Grove

17

Porters

Willow Dr

Fryer's Copse

Lawns Cl

Dales Cl

Canford Bottom

Stapehill

Freemans Lane

Drive

Dales

Canford Bottom

Stapehill

Wimborne Road West

Abbey Gdns

Stapehill Road

Foxcroft

Foxcroft Dr

Stapehill Crs

Fox La

Wyelands Avenue

Stapehill Abbey

Keepers Lane

4

Briar Wy

Drive

Stapehill Crs

WIMBORNE RD W

A31(T)

Fox Lane

HAM LANE

Martindale Av

dale Av

Ham La

Ham La

Castleman Trailway

OAD WEST

Fernway Cl

5

Little Canford

Old Ham Lane

Stour Close

B3073

River Stour

A   B   **26**   C   D

Stapehill Road

HAM

1 grid square represents 500 metres

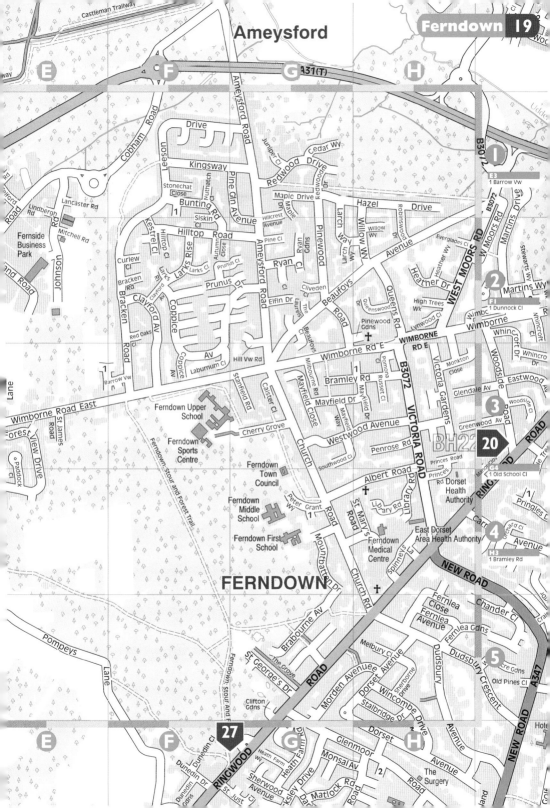

A31(T)

NGWOOD ROAD

Boundary Lane

Boundary La

St Leonards
Hospital

E

F

II

Wayside Road

G

H

Foxbury Road

**Grange
Estate**

I

Foxbury Road

2

Foxbury

Road

3

22

Moors River

Heath

Road

West

B...field

4

Waterma

Fir Grove
Farm

Heath Road West

5

Moors River

Hurn
Forest

E

F

29

G

H

I grid square represents 500 metres

E **Kingston** F **13** G H

I

Wilkins Farm

Dragon Lane

B3347

Avon Valley Path

Dragon Lane

Avon Valley Path

Upper
Bisterne Farm

2

Bisterne
Manor

3

Bisterne

B3347

Ripley
Wood

Lower
Bisterne Farm

4

Avon Valley Path

5

Anna Lane

Hotel

E F **31** G H

B3078

River Stour

A

B

16

C

D

Grammar School Lane

Deans Ct La

ST

LEIGH RD

The Quarter
Jack Surg

St Johns School

2

Millstream Close

Poole Rd

RODWAY

Crescent Fds

Stevensons Close

St Catherines

Grove Road

St John's pa

Avenue Road

Grenville Rd

6

Allens Rd

Osbo

Ashmore

Ethelbert Rd

Market

Day

Welland Rd

Hardy Cl

Leigh Gardens

S Cr

New Borough Rd

Eden Gv

POOLE ROAD

Stour Valley Way

Station Road

Do

1

A31(T)

Willett Road

Stour Valley

Way

Merley Ways

OAKLEY HILL

Whitehouse Road

Oakley Rd

B3073

Lake Farm

Willett Road

Ullswater Rd

Derwentwater

Silver

2

Poole Lane

Dorset County

Ashington Lane

Harrie

A341

3

Ashington

Merley House

Oakley

reen

La

Merley Lane

M

hington ardens

Road

Merley Park Road

de Montf

Rempstone Road

PINE

4

Rose Lawn Coppice

GRAVEL HILL A341

Castleman Trailway

Ivy Road

Delph Road

5

Blackwater Drive

A

B

35

C

D

ensleeves Avenue

Castleman Trailway

Woodleaze Cl

Merrifield Close

1

Port e Close

A349

GRAVEL HILL

OFC

grid square represents 500 metres

LEIGH

PO

Beech
Court

Gordon Road

Livingstone

Parmiter
Rd

Parmiter
Drive

Brookside
Road

Parmiter Way

Brook Road

borne
ugby
Club

Barnes Crs

E

F

17

G

A31(T)

H

ll Road

nty

Brook
Road

Brook
Park
Estate

River Stour

I

A31(T)

Stour Valley Way

Castleman Trailway

Canford School

Lane

Oakley Lane

Cobham Wy

Sopwith
Crs

Sopwith Crs

Walk

Sopwith Crs

Sopwith Crs

De Havilland Cl

Mountjoy Cl

Floral Farm

Oakley Lane

Stour Valley Way

✝

2

Chichester

Sopwith Crs

✝

Cockerel Cl

Brabazon Road

Hawker

School

Cemetery

Canford Magna

3

PO

The Harvey
Practice

Merley Lane

Selkirk Close

Merley

Gardens

Huntington Dr

Countess Close

Moorlyn Cl

Harvey Road

Drive

Lynwood Dr

ANNE

DRIVE

Stour Valley Way

Moortown Dr

Moortown

26

Rosa Av

Egdon Dr

cute Wy

QUEEN

Harvey Road

Drive

Drive

Longfleet

Moortown Drive

MAGNA

4

Moorto Farm

E4
1 Longespee Rd

Arrowsmith La

Arrowsmith Road

5

E

F

36

G

H

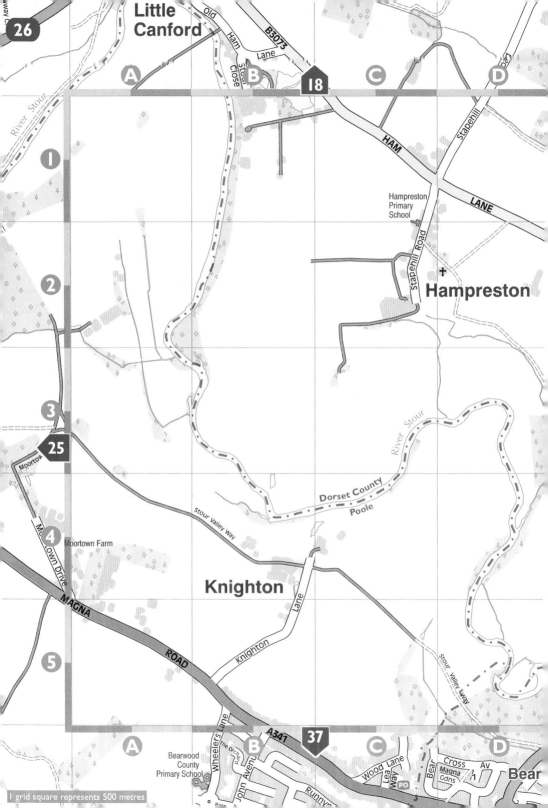

26

Little
Canford

Old
Ham
Lane

B3073

A **B** **18** **C** **D**

River Stour

HAM

Stapehill

I

Hampreston
Primary
School

LANE

2

Stapehill Road

✝
Hampreston

3

River Stour

25

Moortow

Dorset County
Poole

4 Moortown Farm

Stour Valley Way

McLown Drive

Knighton Lane

Knighton

MAGNA

5

Stour Valley Way

ROAD

A Wheelers Lane **B** A341 **37** **C** Wood Lane **D**

Bearwood
County
Primary School

The Orchard

John Avenue

Runnyn

Lea Way

PO

Bear
Cross
Magna
Gdns

Av

Bear

1 grid square represents 500 metres

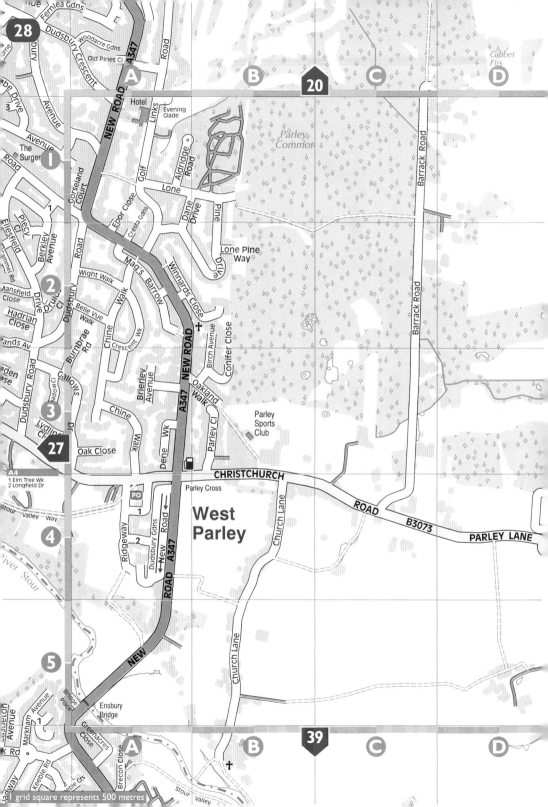

E F **21** G H

Moors River

Hurn
Forest

I

2

3

30

Bournemouth
International
Airport

4

Bournemouth
Sports Club

Chapel Lane

Dorset
County
Police

McIntyre

Brackley
Ci

Theobold Rd

Pussex

**East
Parley**

PARLEY LANE

B3073

Merritown
La

5

PARLEY LANE

B3

Merritown

arley
reen

Dales
Lane

River Stour

E F **40** G H

West
Hurn

Hurn Cou

30

A   **B**   **22**   C   D

Hurn
Forest

Plantation Ro

Matchams Lane

A338

Christchurch
Ski & Leisure
Centre

I

2

Avon
Common

3

29

Matchams Lane

Pitl

Bournemouth
International
Airport

Pithouse Lane

4

McIntyre Rd

Brackley
Cl

Theobold Rd

Dorset
County
Police

Pussex

A338

✝

Moors Cl

Matchams Lane

Moors Drive

Hurn

Avon Causeway

Sopley
Common

5

Lane

ARLEY LANE

B3073

PO

**West
Hurn**

A   **B**   **41**   C   D

Hurn Bridge

Mill

B3073

1 grid square represents 500 metres

Anna Lane

Hotel

E F 23 G H

I

Avon Tyrrell Farm

2

London Lane

London Lane

Avon

R

Avon Valley Path

Sop
CP S

B3347

Parsonage Farm

3

32

River Avon

4

Court Farm

B3347

Avon valley path

Priest Lane

Causeway

B3347 RINGWOOD

Meadow Cl

5

ROAD

Sopley

PO

E F 42 G H

B3347 SAL

Avon Valley P

Sopley Park

A **B** **C** **D**

North Ripley

I

Martin's Copse

Thatchers Lane

2

Ripley

Sopley CP School

Thatchers Lane

3

Parsonage Farm

◄ **31**

4

Derritt Lane

Wilts

Wilts

Derritt Lane

Hampshire County

Dorset County

Burley Road

5

Priest Lane

Sopley

North Bockhampton

A **B** **C** **D**

Lr Clockhouse Farm

Avon Valley Path

B3347

BH23

1 grid square represents 500 metres

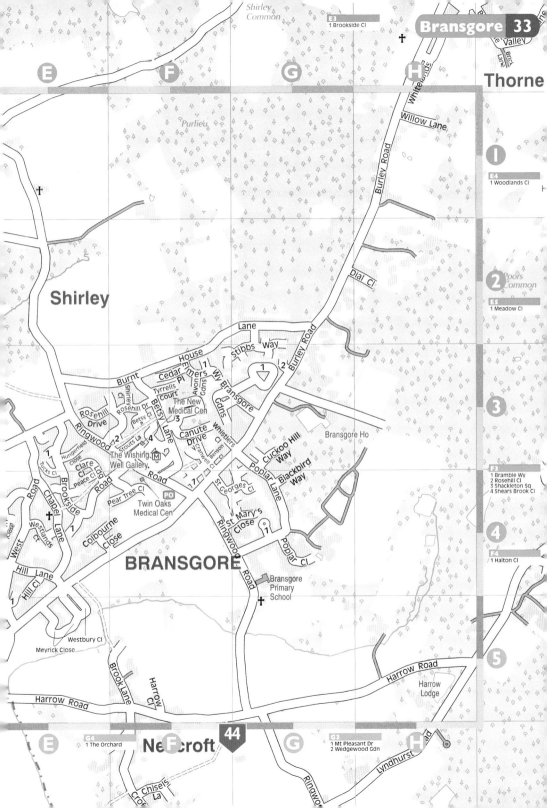

Thorne

Shirley Common

1 Brookside Cl

Purlieu

Willow Lane

Whitelands

Burley Road

Dial Cl

Shirley

I

E4
1 Woodlands Cl

2 Poors Common

E5
1 Meadow Cl

3

Lane

Stibbs Way

House Burnt

Cedar Pl Palmers

Tyrrells Court

Avon Gdns

Wy Bransgore Gdns

Burley Road

Rosehill Drive

Shirley Dr

Rosehill Dr

Betsy Cl

Betsy Lane

The New Medical Cen

Canute Drive

Whistlers Rd

Cranwell Benson Cl Cl

Bransgore Ho

Ringwood

Stouts La

Hungerfield Close

Clare Cl

Peace Cl

Ducks Cl

The Wishing Well Gallery

Road

Cuckoo Hill Way

Poplar Lane

Blackbird Way

F3
1 Bramble Wy
2 Rosehill Cl
3 Shackleton Sq
4 Shears Brook Cl

4

West Road

Chapel Lane

Brookside

Westlands Ct

Pear Tree Cl

Twin Oaks Medical Cen

PO

St Georges

Colbourne Close

St Mary's Close

Ringwood Road

Poplar Cl

F4
1 Halton Cl

BRANSGORE

Hill Lane

Hill Cl

Bransgore Primary School

5

Westbury Cl

Meyrick Close

Brook Lane

Harrow Cl

Harrow Road

Harrow Lodge

Harrow Road

Netcroft

G4
1 The Orchard

G3
1 Mt Pleasant Dr
2 Wedgewood Gdn

Lyndhurst Rd

Ringwo

Chisels La

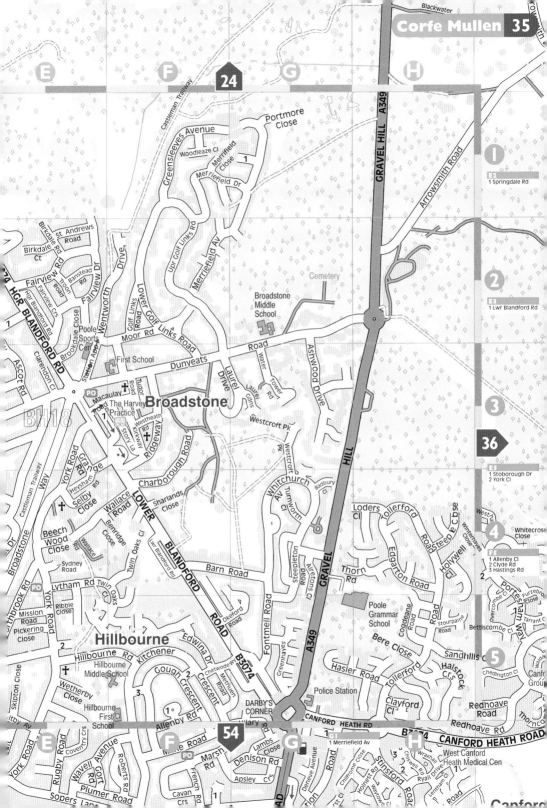

E F **26** G H

Bearwood

Bear Cross A341

Bear Cross

Bearwood County
Primary School

Eastlands Farm

Bearwood
Medical Cen

BH11

Oakmead
College of
Technology

Elmrise
Junior &
Infant School

**West
Howe**

Dorset County
Council

West Howe
Industrial
Estate

Knighton Heath
Industrial
Estate

Drewitts
Industrial
Estate

Police
Station

38

Heathlands

**Turbary
Common**

Alderney
Alderney
Community
Hospital

E F **56** G H

Winchelsea
School

E2
1 Ross Gdns

F2
1 Anjou Cl
2 Marquis Wy
3 Steph Langton Dr

F4
1 Todber Cl

F5
1 Cleeves Cl

G2
1 Deepdene La

Christ the King
Primary Scho

G3
1 Cranwell Cl
2 Gaydon Rd
3 High Howe Gdns
4 High Oaks Gdns
5 Holly Green Ri
6 Knighton Hth Cl
7 Maidment Cl
8 Ringwood Rd
9 Wescott Wy

Draper Road

G4
1 Bexington Cl
2 Holworth Cl

H1
1 Magna Cl
2 Marpet Cl
3 Quayle Wy

H4
1 Kimber Rd

1 Cherrett Cl

H2
1 Lydwell Cl

A3049

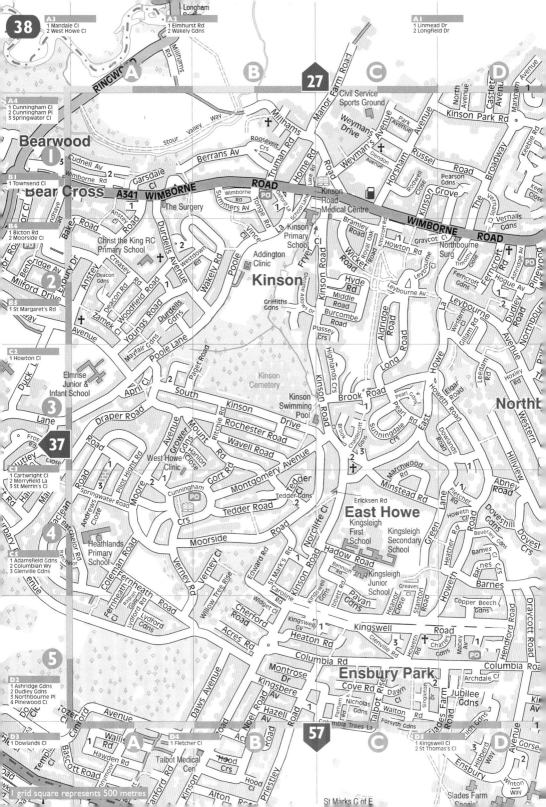

E1
1 Austen Av
2 Old Vicarage Cl

E2
1 Heads Farm Cl
2 Saxonhurst Cl

E3
1 Headswell Gdns
2 Saxonhurst Gdns

E4
1 Broughton Cl
2 Romney Cl

E5
1 Parkside Gdns

F3
1 Georgian Wy

F4
1 Old St John's Ms

G3
1 Castle La West
2 Portswood Dr
3 Redhill Ct
4 The Circle

G4
1 Franklin Rd
2 Malvern Cl
3 Redbreast Rd N
4 Webster Rd

G5
1 Derwent Cl
2 Forest View Cl
3 Mcwilliam Rd
4 Minterne Rd
5 Rosebud Av

H5
1 Charminster Cl
2 Luckham Cl
3 Luckham Pl
4 Luckham Rd East
5 Oakwood Cl

H4
1 Charnwood Av
2 Chickerell Cl
3 Knowlton Gdns
4 Shillingstone Dr

H3
1 Bosworth Ms
2 Cerne Cl
3 Iwerne Cl
4 Sturminster Rd

Ensbury
Bridge

Ensbury

Mus(cliff

Red Hill

Moordown

28

40

58

E F G H I
2 3 4 5

1 grid square represents 500 metres

Hurn

Sopley
Common

Avon Causeway

Moors River

Match Cl

Lane

E 3073

F PO

30

G

H

I

Hurn Bridge

Mill Lane

B3073

CHRISTCHURCH ROAD

Hurn Court Lane

Blackwater

B3073

B3073

Hurn Court

2 Own Common
H3
1 Valencia Cl
2 Whitby Cl

Orford Cl

Heston Cl

Foreland Close

Hillside

Blyth Close

Dreswick

Ave

3

River Stour

HURN ROAD

Hurn Rd

Durlston Crs

Tees

7

2

Lynton Crs

Kendal Cl

42

New Bridge

A338

River Way

Chalfont Av

Grasmore

Ambleside

Highview Cl

Hill

Marina Cl

Woodbu

Cl

4

H5
1 Old Barn Cl
2 Squirrels Cl

Holdenhurst Road

Holdenhurst

Conifer Cl

St Catherines's Way

Glendale Cl

2

Old Barn Rd

HURN ROAD

Watton Cl

Gdns

Jewell

Tyrrell Gdns

Hopkins Cl

Road

Birch Dr

Swansbury Dr

Noyce Gdns

Wilkinson Dr

Vickers Cl

Cheshire Dr

Throop Rd

Cl

PO

E

WESSEX WAY

F

60

G

Bournemouth
Crown & County
Courts

H

Royal
Bournemouth
Hospital
A&E

Deansleigh

Rivers

Stour

Dukesfield

River Way

Springfield Av

Hurn

Rivermead

Gdns

Bosley Way

Stourcroft Dr

Way

Links Dr

Cross Way

The Elm Av

5 Katterns Cl

A B 31 C D

Sop

ROAD

PO

I

2

Town
Common

B3347 SALISBURY

Dudmoor Farm

Orford
Cl

Heston
Cl

land

3

Hillside Drive

4 I

Durlst

Lees
Cl

Lynton Crs

Chalfont
Av

Grasmere
Cl

Ambleside

Marlow

Highview Cl

Aston Rd

Rydal Cl

River Way

4

1 Lincoln Av

B5

Woodbury
Cl

Hillside Dr

Valley Cl

**St Catherine's
Hill**

Dudmoor Lane

Dudmoor Farm Road

Winkton
Common

Glendale
Cl

Old Barn Rd

2

HURN ROAD

Hillside Dr

B3073

Sandy

5

Hurn Way

Katterns
Cl

Rivermeadow
Gdns

Bosley

Bosley Way

Springfield
Av

Stourcroft

our

Way

Grove

B3073

Apple Gv

Pippin Cl

Marsh Lane

Hampshire

Huntingdon
Gdns

Surrey

Marsh Lane
Avenue

Norfolk Av

Essex

Suffolk

Cambridge
Gdns

Av

Avon Valley Park

Cross

Way

The

Elm Av

Melbourn

Road

Darwin Av

anton

PO

B

Rutla

Rd

FAIRMILE

dia

Walcot

Fa **6I** le

Flambard Avenue

C

Haworth Cl

Villette

Wildfel
Close

D

I grid square represents 500 metres

Derritt La

Hampshire Cou
Dorset County

Burley Road

E

F

32

G

H

North Bockhampton

Harr

Lr Clockhouse Farm

Avon Valley Path

opley Park

lands
ge

Harpway Lane

Burley Road

BH23

Bockhampton Road

Middle Bockhampt

I

E4
1 Avon View Rd
2 Harrison Cl
3 Heathlands Cl
4 Kath Chance Av
5 Kirkham Av
6 Pittmore Rd

Winkton

Hotel
PH

Burley Road

Hawthorn Road

Middle Bockhampton

2

E5
1 Barlands Cl
2 Summerfield Cl

Homefield School

Lyndhurst Road

Avon Valley Path

South Bockhampton

3

44

Waterditch F

F4
1 Burton Hall Pl

Jopps Cnr

Burton Croft

Salisbury Road

Waterditch Road

Chestnut Wy

Campbell Park

Primary School

Farwell Cl

Birch Rd

1

Winkton Cl

Brinsons

4

1

The Lindens

Lane

Preston

4

F5
1 Woodstock Rd

Cowleys Rd

Redcliffe Cl

6

Rd

3

Moorcroft Av

2

1

7

Pittmore Rd

1

Burnham Rd

Vinneys Cl

Burton Medical Cen

Vicarage Way

Meadow La

Priory

Fern Cl

Crabtree Cl

Lane

PO

Hawthorn Road

Hill Lane

Dorset County

Hampshire County

5

Footners

Whitehayes Cl

Whitehayes Road

Bodowen Rd

LANE

E

Burton

Treeby

F

62

Holli

Sumr

ane

G

H

Whitehayes Rd

Martins Cl

Hill

Gordon

Alder Cl

Medlar

Martins Wy

E   F   G   H

A35

1

2   B

Beckley Farm

B3055

Hinton Park

✝

3

Hinton

46

Hinton House

Dark   Lane

4

A35

LYNDHURST RD

GS
1 Beckley Copse

Station Road

Hintonwood La

nton Admiral
Station

5

e Road

Buckland Grove

Rossley Cl

odhayes

Cranemoor Cl

Crane moor Av

Cranemoor Gdns

Thursby

Talbot Drive

Dunbar Crescent

Amberwood Dr

Amberwood Gdns

Pinewood Road

Pinewood Cl

Southwd

Marlpit Dr

William

Plantation Dr
1

Glenville
Cl

Glenville
May
Gdns

Heather

Tresillian Wy

Solent
Road
1
2

Road

Wyndham Rd

Broa

lands Cl
3

Hurst Cl

Walkford

Avenue Roa

E   F   64   G   45   H   **Walkford**

2 Wy
Chantry
Close

ood Latimers
Cl

Brookside Road

Hinton Wd Av

Pinewo

Glenavon
Road

Rotherfield
Road

1 Clinton Cl
2 Nicholas Cl
3 Wyndham Cl

2

Fields
Road

Jacobean
Close

Seaview Rd

Chewton

Ar

Ashmore
Gv

Marston
Grove

Hurstb

Terring

Smugglers La N

Avenu

La Larg

Holmhurst
Avenue

Shepherd
Close

Lakewood Rd

Drive

mar

A　　　B　　　C　　　D

Ossemsley
Manor

45

Hinton

C2
1 Cherry Tree Dr

C3
1 The Hyde

B3055

Beckley

Birch Av

Forest View

Robin Cl

Lawn View

BASHLEY

CROSS

NEW

Smithy Lane

Lane

ROAD

Stem Lane

Vintage
Motorcycle Museum

Bashley
Manor Farm

New Milton

C4
1 Breamore Cl
2 Hatfield Ct
3 Stratfield Pl
4 Thoresby Ct

D3
1 Deer Park Cl
2 Rosecrae Cl

Velvet Lawn

Antler

Hartley Cl

Fawn Gdns

Road

Stag Cl

Doe Copse Way

Hazelwood

Beechwood Av

Rosewood
Gardens

Avenue

Kennard

Avenue

Marley

Cabot

Marley Cl

Marryat

Kenn Co

Kennard Road

Blair Cl

Cadnay Cl

Drake Close

Raleigh

Hardy Close

Nelson
Close

Longleat
Gate

Cadnam Cl

Cardbrooke

Carbrooke

Arundel

Chatsworth

Way

Queensway

Brownsea
Cl

LC

LC

Walkford Lane

Stem Lane

Walkford Brook

Wick 1
Industrial
Est

Wick 2
Industrial
Est

Wick 3

Nova
Business Park

Chaffinch
Close

Fawcett
Road

Jowitt Dr

Davis

Albert

Pleasance

Robin Gv

Jowitt

Gore Road

New Milton
Recreation
Centre

Milton Md

Culver
Rd

Cemetery

Cemetery

Holly
Lane

Broadlands Cl

Walkford

Road

Avenue Road

Road

Wyndham Rd

Hurst Cl

Solent Rd

Seaview Rd

Walkford

A　　　B　　　65　　　C　　　D

D4
1 Balmoral Wk
2 Brooklyn Ct
3 Foxcote Gdns
4 Linnet Ct
5 Wilton Gdns

D5
1 Goldfinch Cl
2 Magpie Gv
3 Wagtail Dr
4 Wren Cl

Arnewood
School

OLD
MILTON
GN

Southlawns
Walk

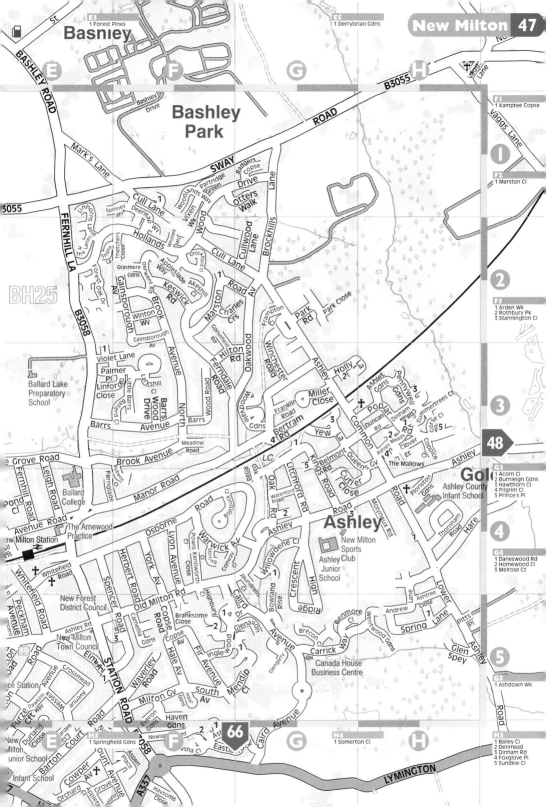

48

Northover Lane

ARNEWOOD BRIDGE

Linnies Lan

Barrows Lane

Vaggs Lane

A B C D

Little Arnewood House

1

Arnewood
Court

Hordle
Grange

2

Agar's Lane

Silver Street

The
Surgery

Summertrees Ct

Gorse Cl

5

Coppice

3

Laurel Cl

Ashley La

Blenheim
Crs

Holes
Cl

Sycamore Rd

Monteray Dr

Everton Road

Lane

Cottagers

Sheldrake
Gdns

Hordle

47 Lane

Windsor

Stoneleigh
Av

Elvin Cl

Stoples
Lane

1

Acacia Rd

2

Slade
Cl

Woodcock

Mallard
Cl

Golden Hill

Aniston Gdns

Pinewood
Road

Firtree Cl

2

Stopples La

Charnock

Yerville Gdns

White
Barn Crs

Heather
Close

Everton Rd

Ashley County
Infant School

Thornham

4

Lavender Rd

Heath Road

3 1

Wisbech Wy

Primary
School

2

Longfield Road

Ashtree
Close

1

Lower Lane

Pitts Pl

Danecrest
Rd

Dudley Av

Stopples Lane

Hordle Lane

Vicarage Lane

Berryfield Rd

St Marks

Elizabeth
Crs

7

Pegasus Av

Sylvan
Cl

5

Ashley
Road

Danes Stream

End

La

Sky

A **B** **67** **C** **D**

Hordle Lane

ROAD

TON

Yeatton Ho

Mill Lane

E F G H

Flexford Lane

Hazelhurst Farm

South Sway Lane

Sway Road

Bowling Green

I

SW

Gordleton Industrial Estate

Hotel

Gordleton Farm

Silver Street

2

H3
1 Upr Common Rd

ver Street

Ramley Road

Ramley

Ramley No

3

50

Haze

Avon Water

Batchley Fm

Upr Common Rd

Middle common Rd

Up enni

4

Arnewood Ho

Wainsford Ho

Wainsford Road

5

Everton Rd

Wainsford Road

Efford Ho

E F G H

68

Greenm Avenue

Buckstone Cl

Everton

Manor Ho

Frys Lane

Everlea Cl

Centre L East La Firmoun

Everton F

Golden Crs

Beacon Cl

Hart

Forest W

Golden

2

Southlands
School

E2
1 Campion Cl
2 Fromond Cl
3 Seaton Cl
4 William Rd

Hundred Lane

ROAD

E

F

G

H

Undershore

B3054   MAIN

Snooks Lane

I

E3
1 Jasmine Ct

WALHAMPTON HL

MARSH

Undershore

Monument Lane

2

SEE
1 Bramley Cl
2 Gold Mead Cl
3 Peartree
4 Peartree Ct

LANE B3054

2
3
Colborne
4
Canton Rd
Ellery Gv

Lower Buckland

Brickfield La

S041

Walhampton

Solent Way

Baddesey

Tithe Barn

BRIDGE RD

LC

Monument Lane

Solent Way

South

Undershore

3

Broomfield
Fairlea
East HL

North Close

Waterloo Rd

Lymington
Town Station

Lisle

Court

F1
1 Mill La

Lymington
Community
Hospitals

Gosport St

Riverside
Business Park

Station Rd

New

Brunswick

North Rd

School La

Cannon St

Emsworth Rd

Anchor
Mews

Our Lady &
St Joseph RC
Primary Sch

Quay St

Lymington
Pier Station

Ferry
Terminal

F4
1 Winton Cl

St Barbe
Museum

M

Ashley La

St

Hotel

Captain's Rw

Nelson

Solent Way

Bath

4

Chawton
House
Surg

High

W Hayes

Grove Road

Qu Katherine Road

Fluchards

Solent
Close

Road

Church
Wykeham

Gv
Pastures

South Gv

Waterford Cl

Solent Av

5

Grove Pl

Springfield
Cl

Mayflower

PH

Fairfield
Cl

Webb Peploe
House Surgery

Lane

Bingham
Dr

Waterford Lane

Brook Rd

Spring Rd

PO

Spring Road

Westfield Road

King's Saltern Road

Courtenay Pl

Daniell's Walk

Daniell's
Cl

Ambleside Rd

Broad Lane

Russet Cl
3
Orchards

Burrard Gv

Stanley Road

Purford Ms

Victoria Gdns

Old Pippin

3

Vitre Gdns

Oaklands

Lane

Tranmere
Close

Lockerley Cl
Newenham

4

2

Normandy

Waterford

All Saints Road

Church Mead

Woodside

Woodside
Av

G5
1 Kingsfield

Viney

E

F

G

H

G5
1 Brackens Wy
2 Conference Pl
3 Worcester Pl

Race Farm

A   **B**   ROAD   **C**   **D**

Beacon Hill

Old Ware

NORTH

1

Huntick Road

Randalls Hill

Blandford Rd N

Green Road

Cemetery

2

Lytchett
Minster
Upper School

Redwood

2   1

Cedar

Ash

Road

Kestre
Cl

War
Cl

Beacon Pk Crs

Beacon

Park

St Anne's Rd

St David's Rd

Stuart

5

BLANDFORD

New Road

3

A35

Marsh La

DORCHESTER ROAD

Oakley Gdns

Pinewood Rd W

Way

Pinewood Rd

Franklyn

Cl

Upton

Policemans La

Holm

1   2

Barn Cl

Greenway
Crs

St Martins
Rd

Sea View Road

Seabank

Moora

Upton Infant
School

3   4

Guest
Rd

Moorland

Yarrells
Preparat
School

Watery
Lane

Watery La

**Lytchett
Minster**

Lane

Beach

Chelmsford Rd

Upton Junior
School

Pearce Rd

1

Holcombe Rd

Birchwood
Rd

Woodcote

Cherry Hl

4

Slough

Lane

Rd

Sandy Lane

Otter Cl

Saltings
Rd

Lytchett Wy

Furzey
Rd

2

Furzey Rd

5

Sherford River

Lytchett
Ba

Set County

Poo

Turlin

Egmont
Rd

l grid square represents 500 metres

E F 34 G H

Upton Heath

Spindl
Sorrel
Close

Sundew Rd
Gdns

wood
Road

Witchampton Rd
Whitby
Crescent
Skipton Clos

Broadstone

Keighley Av
Cannon Cl
Whitby Av

Renault
Dr
Mea
York Road

Castleman Trailway

Dorset County
Poole

Larch
Rowan Dr
Spruce Close
Hawthorn
Dr
Sycamore
Longmeadow
Honeysuckle La
Bluebell Lane

Primrose
Gdns
Creekmoor Lane
Clover Dr

1 Meadows Cl
2 Turbary Ct

Broadstone
Brownsea
Open Air Thea

Creekm

Goldfinch Rd
Linnet Rd

Meadowsweet
Rd
Blackbird Cl

Woodpecker Drive
Nightjar La
Grebe Cl

Swallow Cl
Swift
Northmead
Drive

Tarn Dr
Priors Rd
Pinetree
Wk
Birchwood
Medical Cen

Petersham Rd

Benmoor Road
Creekmo
Balen

Petersham Road
Millstream

Castleman Trailway

Martin Close
Nuthatch Close
Nuthatch Close

2

Millfield

3

Heights
Road
Llewellin
Cl
Hibbs
Cl
th
re
Upton
Heights
Ap
5
Barlam
Ct
Meadows
Dr
Dacombe
Drive
Da
Combe
3
2
1
Gorse La
Palmerston Rd
Upton Heath
Estate
Stirrup
Bridle
Martingale Cl
Road
1

POOLE RD
A35
A350
UPTON ROAD

54
W RO

1 Briarswood Rd
2 Davenport Cl
3 Meadows Dr
4 Preston Cl
5 Upton Ct

PO
The
Crossways
Poole
Ropers La

Old Kiln Road

Ventura Pl

Factory
Road

Upton House
Upton
Country Park

4

1 Palmerston Cl

wenlyn
Rd
acre Cl
Lane
Yarrells
Cl
Pine Vw
Sandy Lane
Shore
Cl
Border Dr
Peters
Cl
Oak
Rd
Old
Bound
Border
Road

BLANDFORD ROAD
Factory
Road
Factory
Rd
Allens
Rd
Allens
Rd
B3068
Willow
Cl
Allens Lane
Border
Road

Pergins
Island

5

E F 71 G H

Turlin
Moor First
School
Turlin Moor
Middle
School
Keysworth
Road
Turlin
PO
Ship
Maryl

Symes
Rd
Cl
Symes
2
Symes

Hamworthy
Station
Middlebere
Crs
Galloway
Rd
Carters
Road

Hewitt
Rd
Falconer
Dr
Hewitt Road
Falconer

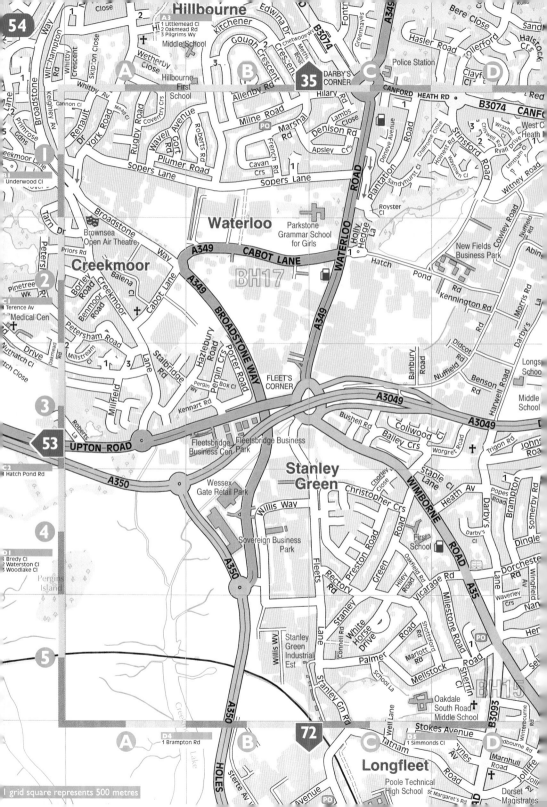

I grid square represents 500 metres

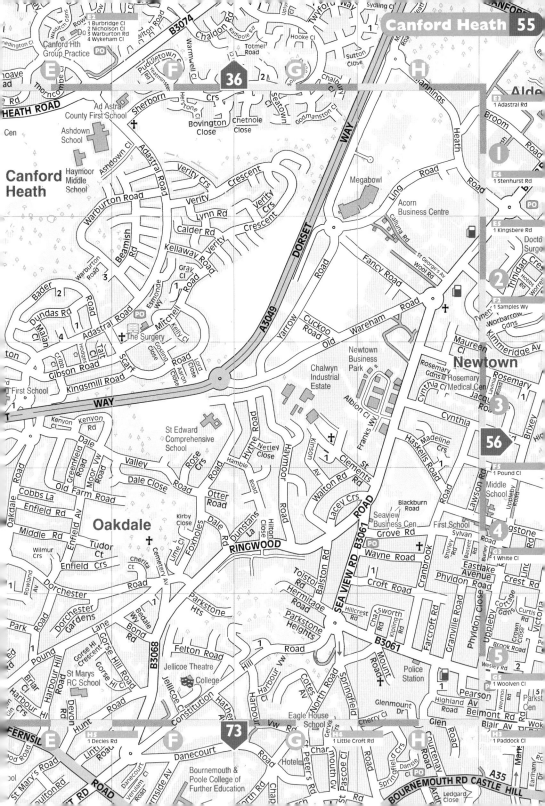

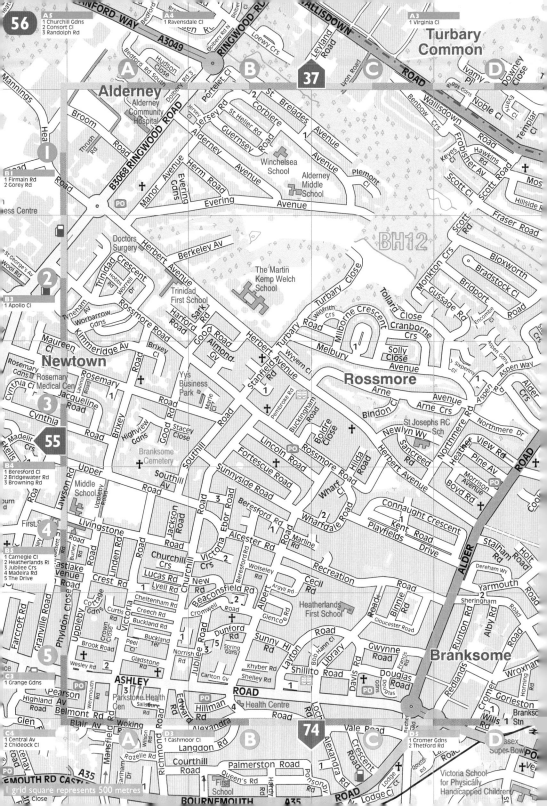

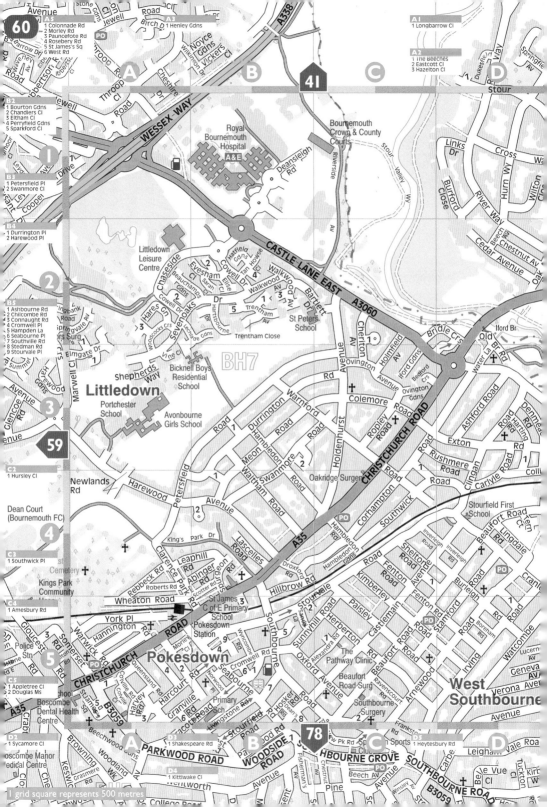

A5
1 Colonnade Rd
2 Morley Rd
3 Pauncefote Rd
4 Rosebery Rd
5 St James's Sq
6 West Rd

A3
1 Henley Gdns

A1
1 Longbarrow Cl

A2
1 The Beeches
2 Eastcott Cl
3 Hazelton Cl

B2
1 Bourton Gdns
2 Chandlers Cl
3 Eltham Cl
4 Perryfield Gdns
5 Sparkford Cl

B3
1 Petersfield Pl
2 Swanmore Cl

B4
1 Durrington Pl
2 Harewood Pl

B5
1 Ashbourne Rd
2 Chilcombe Rd
3 Connaught Rd
4 Cromwell Pl
5 Hampden La
6 Seabourne Pl
7 Southville Rd
8 Stedman Rd
9 Stourvale Pl

C2
1 Hursley Cl

C3
1 Southwick Pl

C4
1 Amesbury Rd

C5
1 Appletree Cl
2 Douglas Ms

D2
1 Sycamore Cl

D3
1 Shakespeare Rd

D4
1 Kittiwake Cl

D1
1 Heytesbury Rd

41

59

78

WESSEX WAY

Royal Bournemouth Hospital A&E

Bournemouth Crown & County Courts

CASTLE LANE EAST A3060

Littledown Leisure Centre

BH7

Littledown

Bicknell Boys Residential School

Portchester School

Avonbourne Girls School

Dean Court (Bournemouth FC)

Newlands Rd

CHRISTCHURCH ROAD

Oakridge Surgery

St Peters School

Stourfield First School

Pokesdown Station

St James C of E Primary School

Kings Park Community

Cemetery

Police Stn

Pokesdown

Boscombe Dental Health Centre

West Southbourne

The Pathway Clinic

Beaufort Road Surg

Southbourne Surgery

PARKWOOD ROAD

WOODSIDE ROAD

SOUTHBOURNE GROVE

SOUTHBOURNE ROAD

B3059

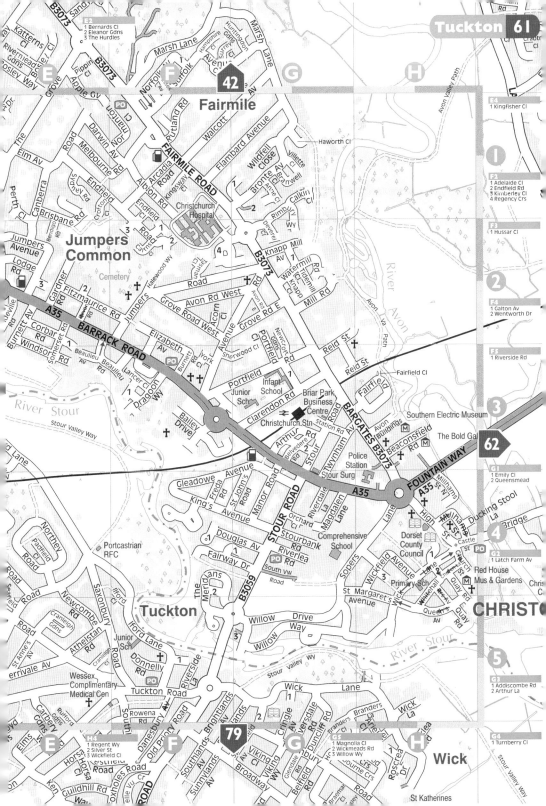

B2
1 Sarah Sands Cl

B1
1 Martins Hill La

A1
1 Burton Cl

B3
1 Amsterdam Sq
2 Cameron Rd
3 Chant Cl
4 Delft Ms
5 Haking Rd
6 Livingstone Rd
7 Utrecht Ct

B4
1 Addington Pl
2 Asquith Cl
3 Grafton Cl

C2
1 Bonington Cl
2 Hillary Rd

C3
1 Bingham Cl
2 Court Cl
3 Wolfe Cl

61

C4
1 Alexander Cl
2 Buccaneers Cl
3 Groveley Rd
4 Johnstone Rd
5 Rosedale Cl
6 Stroud Gdns

C5
1 Harbour Crs

D2
1 Charles Rd
2 Coleridge Gn

D3
1 Amethyst Rd
2 Marmion Gn
3 Southey Rd

D4
1 Drake Cl
2 Frobisher Cl
3 The Hawthorns

D5
1 Mudeford Gn Cl

A B 43 C D

Burton

Whitehaves Road
Whitehaves Cl
Bodowen Rd
Treebys
Holly Gdns
Summers Lane
Priory Vw
Crabtree Cl
Fern Cl
Medical Cen
PO
Whitehaves Rd
Martins Cl with sports ctr
Hill Cl
Gordon Wy
Alder Cl
Medlar Cl
Lane
Salisbury Road
Martins
Lane
B3347
Sandy Plot
Linesiding

CHRISTCHURCH   BY-PASS
Ambury Lane
Staplecross La

Purewell
B3059
PUREWELL CROSS RD

Irvine Wy
Everest Road
Hunt
Druitt Rd
Dorset Road
Edward Road
Scott's Gn
Southey Rd
Amethys
Grange Comprehensive School

Battens Cl
Normandy Drive
Oak Cl
Vickery Wy
Knowles Cl
Redvers
Burton Road
Slinn Road
Draper Road
Junior School
Somerford
ROAD
Miller Rd
Marabout
Meredith Cl
Le Patourel
Norton Cl
Bingham
Infant
Scherford Rd
Somerford Rd
Silver Business Park
New
Pennant Wy
Croft Cl

Southern Electric Museum
Orchid Wy
Stony Lane
Tilburg Ms
Haarlem Ms
Rotten Row
Scotts
Moffat Rd
The Buttery
Dairy
Christchurch Medical Centre
Somerford
Somerford Wy
Stroud Cl
Beresford Gdns
Stroud
Blackberry La
Meadowlands
Dennistoun Av
Campion La
Crossley side
Rodney Dr
Elderberry
Elderberry La
Jellicoe Dr

Ducking Stool La
Bridge Street
Civic Offices
Stony La South
Monkswell La
Purewell
Purewell Cl
PO
Groveley Business Cen
Mudeford La
Sandown Rd
Primary Sch
Mudeford Junior School
Anson Cl
Nelson
Warre

Red House Mus & Gardens
Christchurch Castle
Two Riversmeet Leisure Centre
Pelham Close
Palmerston
Russell Drive
Baldwin Cl
Queen's Road
Stanpit
Caroline Av
Lingwood
Foxwood Avenue
Mudeford
Warren Av
Pinehurst Av

CHRISTCHURCH
Gladstone Close
Disraeli Rd
Stanpit
Paulnley
Victoria Rd
Minterne Rd
Ledbury Road
Argyle Rd
PO

Stour
Stanpit Marsh
Shermin's Bank

80

Coastguard Way
Rushford Warre
Waters

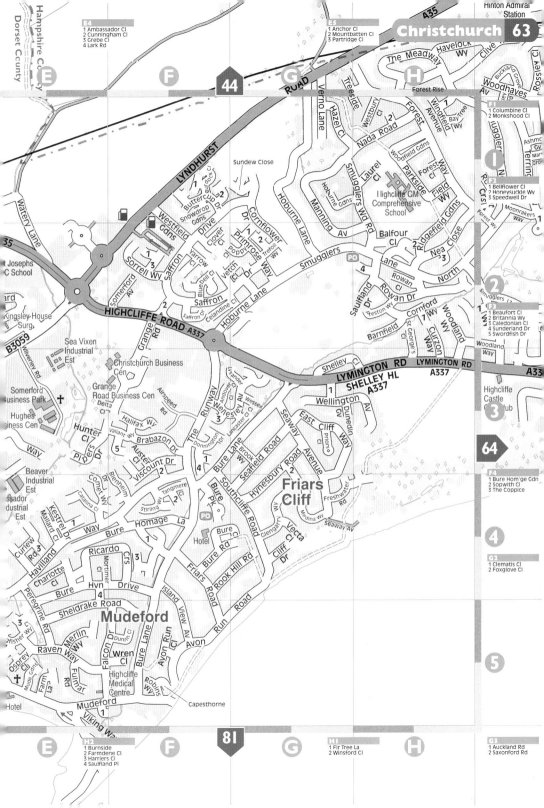

Old Milton

Barton on Sea

Gore Road

Industrial Est

Nova Business Park

New Milton Recreation Centre

Police Station

Cemetery

Cemetery

Culver Rd

Well Cl

Church La

Arnewood School

New Milton Junior School

Infant School

OLD MILTON ROAD

Southlawns Walk

Southern Oaks

Bouveri

Barton Surgery

F2
1 Rockb'rne Gdns
2 Sellwood Wy
3 Studley Ct

Albany Cl

Moat La

Friars Walk

Farm Lane

Highland

Park Rd

Christchurch Rd

Southern Drive

Parkland Drive

Chiltern

Moorland Av

Lawn Close

Wood

CHRISTCHURCH

A337

Glen Cl

East Cl

Byron Road

Western

Barton

Studley Ct

Burley

Ramshaw Wy

Sopley

Millyford

Neacroft

Knight Park

Sea

Connaughtcl

Penn

Chiltern

Eldon

Eldon Cl

Three Acre Dr

Heathwood Av

Wavendon Avenue

Seacroft Av

Pine Cl

Hengistbury Road

Carlton Av

Seafield Road

Avenue

Fairfield Road

Keysworth

Avenue

Heathy Close

Barton Way

Arnolds Close

Barton

Barton Dr

Homeopathic Surgery

G2
1 Christchurch Rd
2 Dunford Cl

Dilly

Mitchell

Farm Lane

Field Place

The Crescent

Cul-De-Sac

Bartonside Rd

Glendrive

Glendrive

The Dell

Ellingham

ngdon Drive

Pinecliffe Road

Seaview Rd

Southcliffe Rd

The Park

East Av

Island Road

VeiW Rd

Island Vw Rd

Vectis Road

Naish Road

Cleveland Cl

Purbeck Rd

Powerscourt Rd

Cliffe Rd

Marine Drive

Barton Rd

WEST

Seaward

Woodlands Rd

Christchurch Bay

Beach Avenue

Seafield Close

Avenue

Barton Court

Lyric Cl

White Knights

First Marine

Marine

Hotel

Marine Drive

Sandmartin

Marine Prospect

Cliff Cts

Cliff

H1
1 Manor Farm Cl
2 Moore Cl
3 Prestwood Cl
4 Wendover Cl

H3
1 Blythswood Ct

Dorset County

Hampshire County

Walkford Road

Avenue

Chewton Farm Road

VIEW Rd

Hotel

46

2

3

66

4

5

1

Bartsh

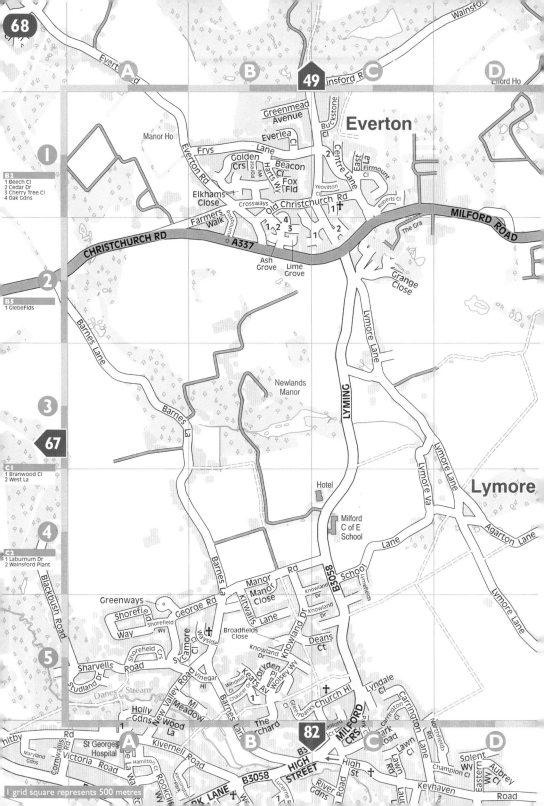

68

49 insford Rd

A   B   C   D

Elford Ho

Greenmead Avenue

Everton

Manor Ho

Everlea

Frys   Lane

Everton Rd

Golden Crs

Beacon Cl

Fox Fld

Harts Wy

Buckstone Cl

Centre Lane

East La

Firmount Cl

Yeovilton Rd

Elkhams Close

Crossways

Old Christchurch Rd

Roberts Cl

The Gra

MILFORD ROAD

Farmers Walk

Redbourne La

4

1   3

1   2

2

1

B2
1 Beech Cl
2 Cedar Dr
3 Cherry Tree Cl
4 Oak Gdns

I

CHRISTCHURCH RD   A337

Ash Grove   Lime Grove

Grange Close

2

B5
1 GlebeFlds

Barnes Lane

Lymore Lane

3

Barnes La

Newlands Manor

LYMING

Lymore Lane

Lymore Va

67

Lymore

C1
1 Branwood Cl
2 West La

4

Hotel

Milford C of E School

Agarton Lane

Lymore Lane

C2
1 Laburnum Dr
2 Wainsford Plant

Blackbush Road

Barnes Rd

Manor Close

Kitwalls Lane

School Lane

B3058

Lymefields

Greenways

Shorefld Way

Shorefield Wy

George Rd

Wayside

Broadfields Close

Knowland Dr

Knowland Dr

Deans Ct

Knowland Dr

5

Shorefield Crs

Sycamore Cl

Vinegar Hl

Keats Av

Lyden Pl

Windmill Dr

Chaucer Dr

Nosey Wy

Lyndale Cl

Carrington Lane

Sharvells Road

Studland Dr

Danes Stream

Holly Gdns

New Valley Road

New Wood La

Ml Meadow

Barnes Lane

Greenbanks

Church Hl

Lynden Cl

Carmton Cl

Park Cl

Northfields

Whitby

Cornwallis Rd

Victoria Road

De La Wa

Hamilton

St Georges Hospital

The Orchard

82

Milford CRS

MILFORD CRS

Lawn Cl

Lawn Rd

Solent Wy

Aubrey Cl

Maryland Gdns

Kivernell Road

Rookcliff Wy

Kensington

B3058

Lucerne Rd

HIGH STREET

B3

High St

River Gdns

Champion Cl

Eastern Cl

Keyhaven Road

1 grid square represents 500 metres

Broomhill Cl

Broadly Cl

Meadow Rd

Widbury Rd

Forward Dr

Street

MIL

E

F

50

G

A337

H

Gilbert Close

Court Close

Curzon

Rookes

Deneside Copse

Deneside Gdns

Harford Cl

ROAD

Elm Avenue

Fox Pond Lane

Lee Lands

Ridgeway Lane

Forest Gate Gdns

Woods

MILFORD

Genoa Cl

Grafton Gdns

Clausen Way

Newbridge Wy

Lower Pennington Lane

I

1 Saracen Cl

Lower Woodside

Poles

Avon Water

Experimental
Horticulture Station

**Lower
Pennington**

2

PH

Lwr

3

Iley Lane

Lwr Pennington Lane

Pennington

ton Lane

4

nington shes

Avon Water

5

Van Farm

E

Lane

F

83

Keyha Marsh

G

H

Sherford Tower

Lytchett
Bay

Dorset County

Poole

Turlin

I

D1
1 Peverell Rd

Egmont
Rd

Egmont Road

Peverell
Rd

Patchins
Rd

South Hvn Cl

Egmont
Road

Holton
Point

**East
Holton**

2

Rockley
Viaduct

3

Rockley
Sands

Wood
Bar
Looe

4

Wareham Channel

WAREHAM

5

Shag Looe
Head

1 grid square represents 500 metres

E

1 Redhorn Cl

F

G

H

53

Turlin Moor First School

Turlin Moor Middle School

Keysworth Road

Turlin

PO

Middlebere Crs

Russel

Shipstal Cl

Fitzworth

Maryland Rd

Avenue

Junction Road

Road

Goathorn

Galloway

Carters Avenue

Galloway Rd

Hamworthy Station

Symes Road

Symes Road

Symes Rd

Hewitt Road

Hewitt Rd

Ingleshame Road

Falconer Dr

Falconer

Way

Harkwood Dr

Harkwood Dr

Beckhampton Road

Woodlands Av

I

Dawkins Rd

Dawkins Rd

Dawkins Business Cen

Freshwater Dr

Carisbrooke Crs

Aimer Rd

Freshwater Dr

Upwey Av

Winspit Cl

Hamworthy

Hamworthy Community Clinic

Woodlands Av

Woodland Rd

Woodlands Avenue

Woodlands Crs

2

Walcheren Pl

Walcheren Pl

Walcheren Pl

Napier

Road

Hoyal Road

BH15

Samson Road

Goliath Rd

Delilah Dr

Reuben Wy

Solomon

Normandy Wy

David Wy

Jacobs Rd

Benjamin Rd

Annet Cl

Lake Road

Caversham Cl

Halter Pth

Lake Crs

Dean

PO

Burngate

Hamilton Road

Hamilton Crs

Coles Gdns

Coles

Avenue

Rockley Cl

Legion Road

Legion Cl

Legion Close

Legion

Albany Gdns

Hounslow Cl

BLANDFORD

Hinchliffe Cl

Hinchliffe Road

Avenue

Carter Community School

Beccles

Blandford Cl

ROAD

72

3

rs Road

Nor

IVO

PO

Lake Drive

Lake Dr

Lake Drive

Lake Av

Lake

Lulworth Cl

Lulworth Crs

Branksea Cl

Lulworth

Purbeck Av

Branksea

Avenue

Avenue

Hamworthy First Sch

The Old Rope Wk

Ashmore Av

Hamworthy Middle Sch

Shapw Rd

4

5

Gold Point

oint h

E

F

G

H

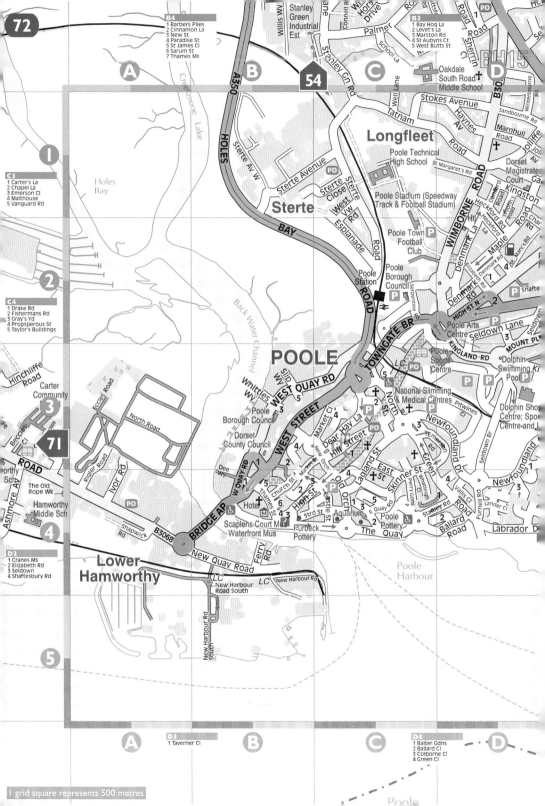

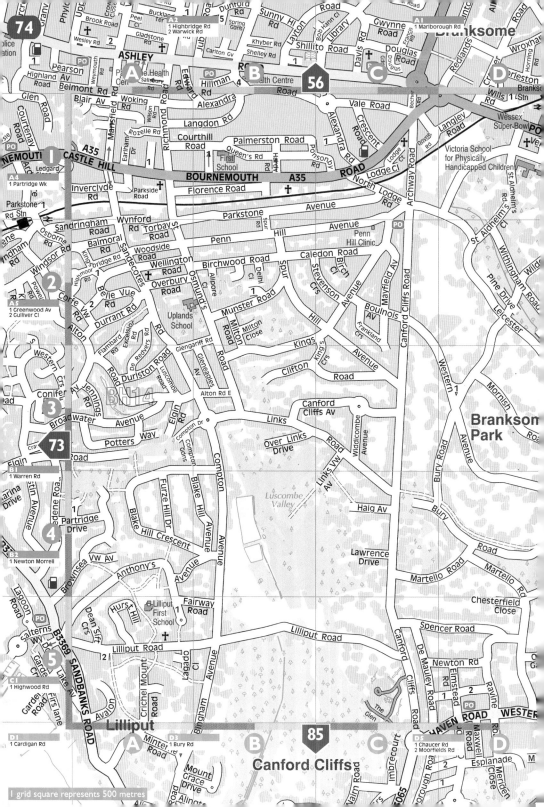

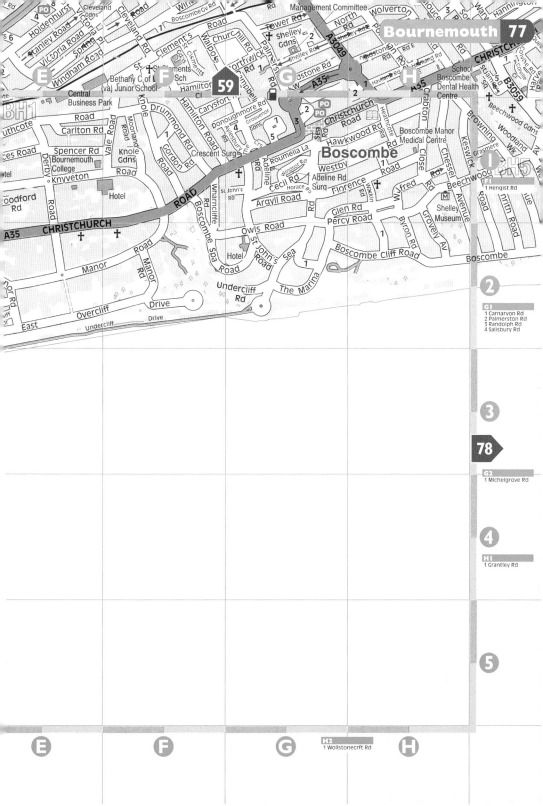

62

A   B   C   D

Stanpit
Marsh

Shermin's Bank

Coastguard Way

Water
Rushford Warre

Wick

St Katherines

1 Hamilton Cl
Primary School

1

Stour Valley Way

Christchurch
Harbour

Dorset County
Bournemouth

2

Broadway

3

79

Stour Valley Way

Hengistbu
Head

4

5

A   B   C   D

1 grid square represents 500 metres

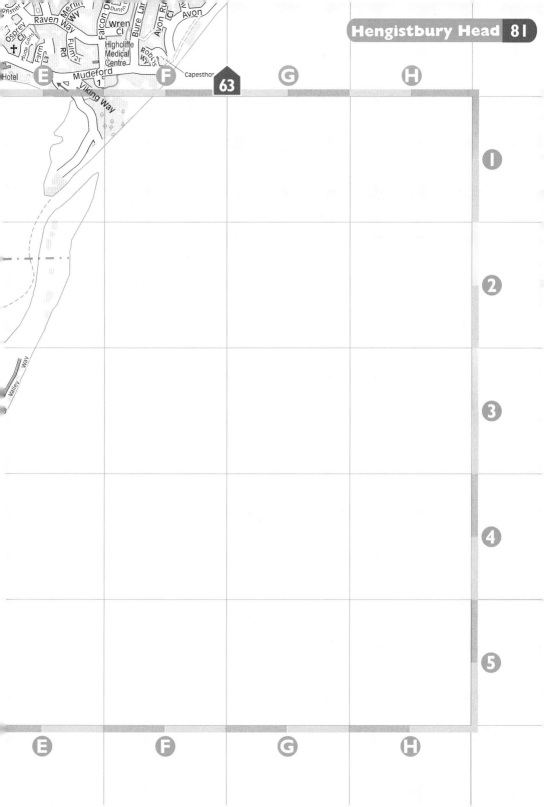

Raven Way

Osprey Cl

Farm La

Wren Cl

Falcon Cl

Merlin Wy

Fulmr Rd

Dunl

Bure La

Avon Cl

Avon

Highcliffe Medical Centre

Robins Wy

Mudeford

Hotel

Viking Way

Capesthor

63

Valley Way

E   F   G   H

I

2

3

4

5

E   F   G   H

MILFORD ON SEA

1 grid square represents 500 metres

E
F
69
G
H

Van Farm

Lane

Keyhaven
Marshes

Keyhaven

Harewood
Gn

Road

New
Rd

Aubrey House

Keyhaven

Salt
Grass

Lane

Solent Way

Solent Way

Saltgrass

Solent Way

I

2

3

Solent Way

Hurst
Beach

4

Solent Way

Solent Way

5

E
F
G
H

A   B   **73**   C   D

Salterns
Wy
Gardens
Crs
Hotel
Gardens Road

Marina

I

Poole
Dorset County

Main
Channel

2

3

The
Villa

Middle   street

Brownsea
Island (NT)

BH13

4

†

Coastguard
Road

North
Haven Point

Grasmere
Seacombe
Road

Brownsea Road

5

FERRY
WY

Ferry
WY

A   B   C   D

South Haven Point

Lilliput Road

Lagado Cl

Avalon

Cricket Mount Road

Bingham Avenue

Lilliput Road

De Mauley Road

Newton Rd

Elmstead Rd

WESTERN RD

B3065 PINECl

E

F

74

G

PO

HAVEN ROAD

H

Lilliput

Minterne Road

Mount Grace Drive

Alington Road

Alington Close

Alington

Canford Cliffs Road

Glen

Imbrecourt

Maxwell Road

Esplanade

Martello Park

Meriden Close

Canford Cliffs

Brudenell Av

Dornie Rd

Nairn Road

Canford Crs

B3065

Bessborough Road

Flaghead Rd

St Clair Rd

Cliff Dr

Promenade

I

Canford Cliffs Chine

F2
1 Harbour Cl

SHORE ROAD

B3369

Brudenell Road

HAVEN ROAD

Hotel

Chaddesley Pines

Flaghead Chine Rd

Cliff

Drive

2

G3
1 Chadd'sley Wd Rd

Chaddesley

St Anns Hospital

Glen

Flag Head Chine

Shore Road

Hotel

Poole Head

3

BANKS ROAD

B3369

H1
1 Beaumont Rd
2 Bodley Rd
3 Macandrew Rd

4

PO

ROAD

B3369

Sandbanks

5

E

F

G

H

Ashley ... 12 C1	Ebblake ... 5 F4	Lower Buckland ... 51 E2	Sandbanks ... 85 E5
Ashley ... 47 G4	Everton ... 68 C1	Lower Pennington ... 69 G2	South Weirs ... 14 B4
Ashley Heath ... 6 D5	Ferndown ... 19 F4	Lymington ... 50 D3	Stapehill ... 18 C4
Balmerlawn ... 15 F1	Golden Hill ... 47 H4	Lymore ... 68 D4	Trickett's Cross ... 20 B2
Barton on Sea ... 65 H4	Grange Estate ... 21 H1	Lytchett Minster ... 52 A4	Turlin Moor ... 70 D1
Bashley Park ... 47 F1	Hamworthy ... 71 G2	Merry Field Hill ... 17 E1	Upper Pennington ... 50 A4
Beckley ... 46 A2	Hangersley ... 9 G1	Moortown ... 13 G1	Upton ... 52 D3
Bisterne ... 23 F3	Highcliffe ... 64 C2	New Milton ... 46 C3	Verwood ... 4 B2
Bournemouth ... 3 J4	Hightown ... 9 F5	North Poulner ... 9 F1	Walhampton ... 51 G2
Bowling Green ... 49 H1	Hill View ... 34 B3	North Weirs ... 14 A3	Walkford ... 64 D1
Brockenhurst ... 14 C3	Hinton ... 45 G3	Old Milton ... 65 G1	Waterford ... 51 G5
Buckland ... 50 C2	Hordle ... 48 C3	Pennington ... 50 C5	West Cliff ... 2 D6
Canford Cliffs ... 85 F1	Keyhaven ... 83 E2	Pilford ... 17 G1	West Moors ... 10 C4
Colehill ... 17 F2	Kingston ... 13 E5	Poulner ... 9 F3	Westbourne ... 2 A5
Corfe Mullen ... 34 A1	Lake ... 71 F4	Ringwood ... 8 A3	Wimborne Minster ... 16 C4
Downton ... 67 F3	Leagreen ... 67 G2	St Ives ... 12 A1	
East Holton ... 70 A2	Lilliput ... 85 E1	St Leonards ... 11 G2	

USING THE STREET INDEX

Street names are listed alphabetically. Each street name is followed by its postal town or area locality, the Postcode District, the page number, and the reference to the square in which the name is found.

Abbots Cl *CHCH/BSGR* BH23 ... **64** B3 ▯

Some entries are followed by a number in a blue box. This number indicates the location of the street within the referenced grid square. The full street name is listed at the side of the map page.

GENERAL ABBREVIATIONS

ACC ... ACCESS	EMB ... EMBANKMENT	LK ... LOCK	RDG ... RIDGE
ALY ... ALLEY	EMBY ... EMBASSY	LKS ... LAKES	REP ... REPUBLIC
AP ... APPROACH	ESP ... ESPLANADE	LNDG ... LANDING	RES ... RESERVOIR
AR ... ARCADE	EST ... ESTATE	LTL ... LITTLE	RFC ... RUGBY FOOTBALL CLUB
ASS ... ASSOCIATION	EX ... EXCHANGE	LWR ... LOWER	RI ... RISE
AV ... AVENUE	EXPY ... EXPRESSWAY	MAG ... MAGISTRATE	RP ... RAMP
BCH ... BEACH	EXT ... EXTENSION	MAN ... MANSIONS	RW ... ROW
BLDS ... BUILDINGS	F/O ... FLYOVER	MD ... MEAD	S ... SOUTH
BND ... BEND	FC ... FOOTBALL CLUB	MDW ... MEADOWS	SCH ... SCHOOL
BNK ... BANK	FK ... FORK	MEM ... MEMORIAL	SE ... SOUTH EAST
BR ... BRIDGE	FLD ... FIELD	MKT ... MARKET	SER ... SERVICE AREA
BRK ... BROOK	FLDS ... FIELDS	MKTS ... MARKETS	SH ... SHORE
BTM ... BOTTOM	FLS ... FALLS	ML ... MALL	SHOP ... SHOPPING
BUS ... BUSINESS	FLS ... FLATS	ML ... MILL	SKWY ... SKYWAY
BVD ... BOULEVARD	FM ... FARM	MNR ... MANOR	SMT ... SUMMIT
BY ... BYPASS	FT ... FORT	MS ... MEWS	SOC ... SOCIETY
CATH ... CATHEDRAL	FWY ... FREEWAY	MSN ... MISSION	SP ... SPUR
CEM ... CEMETERY	FY ... FERRY	MT ... MOUNT	SPR ... SPRING
CEN ... CENTRE	GA ... GATE	MTN ... MOUNTAIN	SQ ... SQUARE
CFT ... CROFT	GAL ... GALLERY	MTS ... MOUNTAINS	ST ... STREET
CH ... CHURCH	GDN ... GARDEN	MUS ... MUSEUM	STN ... STATION
CHA ... CHASE	GDNS ... GARDENS	MWY ... MOTORWAY	STR ... STREAM
CHYD ... CHURCHYARD	GLD ... GLADE	N ... NORTH	STRD ... STRAND
CIR ... CIRCLE	GLN ... GLEN	NE ... NORTH EAST	SW ... SOUTH WEST
CIRC ... CIRCUS	GN ... GREEN	NW ... NORTH WEST	TDG ... TRADING
CL ... CLOSE	GND ... GROUND	O/P ... OVERPASS	TER ... TERRACE
CLFS ... CLIFFS	GRA ... GRANGE	OFF ... OFFICE	THWY ... THROUGHWAY
CMP ... CAMP	GRG ... GARAGE	ORCH ... ORCHARD	TNL ... TUNNEL
CNR ... CORNER	GT ... GREAT	OV ... OVAL	TOLL ... TOLLWAY
CO ... COUNTY	GTWY ... GATEWAY	PAL ... PALACE	TPK ... TURNPIKE
COLL ... COLLEGE	GV ... GROVE	PAS ... PASSAGE	TR ... TRACK
COM ... COMMON	HGR ... HIGHER	PAV ... PAVILION	TRL ... TRAIL
COMM ... COMMISSION	HL ... HILL	PDE ... PARADE	TWR ... TOWER
CON ... CONVENT	HLS ... HILLS	PH ... PUBLIC HOUSE	U/P ... UNDERPASS
COT ... COTTAGE	HO ... HOUSE	PK ... PARK	UNI ... UNIVERSITY
COTS ... COTTAGES	HOL ... HOLLOW	PKWY ... PARKWAY	UPR ... UPPER
CP ... CAPE	HOSP ... HOSPITAL	PL ... PLACE	V ... VALE
CPS ... COPSE	HRB ... HARBOUR	PLN ... PLAIN	VA ... VALLEY
CR ... CREEK	HTH ... HEATH	PLNS ... PLAINS	VIAD ... VIADUCT
CREM ... CREMATORIUM	HTS ... HEIGHTS	PLZ ... PLAZA	VIL ... VILLA
CRS ... CRESCENT	HVN ... HAVEN	POL ... POLICE STATION	VIS ... VISTA
CSWY ... CAUSEWAY	HWY ... HIGHWAY	PR ... PRINCE	VLG ... VILLAGE
CT ... COURT	IMP ... IMPERIAL	PREC ... PRECINCT	VLS ... VILLAS
CTRL ... CENTRAL	IN ... INLET	PREP ... PREPARATORY	VW ... VIEW
CTS ... COURTS	IND EST ... INDUSTRIAL ESTATE	PRIM ... PRIMARY	W ... WEST
CTYD ... COURTYARD	INF ... INFIRMARY	PROM ... PROMENADE	WD ... WOOD
CUTT ... CUTTINGS	INFO ... INFORMATION	PRS ... PRINCESS	WHF ... WHARF
CV ... COVE	INT ... INTERCHANGE	PRT ... PORT	WK ... WALK
CYN ... CANYON	IS ... ISLAND	PT ... POINT	WKS ... WALKS
DEPT ... DEPARTMENT	JCT ... JUNCTION	PTH ... PATH	WLS ... WELLS
DL ... DALE	JTY ... JETTY	PZ ... PIAZZA	WY ... WAY
DM ... DAM	KG ... KING	QD ... QUADRANT	YD ... YARD
DR ... DRIVE	KNL ... KNOLL	QU ... QUEEN	YHA ... YOUTH HOSTEL
DRO ... DROVE	L ... LAKE	QY ... QUAY	
DRY ... DRIVEWAY	LA ... LANE	R ... RIVER	
DWGS ... DWELLINGS	LDG ... LODGE	RBT ... ROUNDABOUT	
E ... EAST	LGT ... LIGHT	RD ... ROAD	

POSTCODE TOWNS AND AREA ABBREVIATIONS

BDST ... Broadstone	BROC ... Brockenhurst	CHAR ... Charminster	LYMN ... Lymington
BKME/WDN ... Branksome/Wallisdown	BWD ... Bearwood	CHCH/BSGR ... Christchurch/Bransgore	MOOR/WNTN ... Moordown/Winton
BMTH ... Bournemouth	CCLF ... Canford Cliffs	FERN ... Ferndown/West Moors	NBNE ... Northbourne
BOSC ... Boscombe	CFDH ... Canford Heath	LTDN ... Littledown	NMIL/BTOS ... New Milton/Barton on Sea

87

PLE....Poole
PSTN....Parkstone
RGWD....Ringwood
SBNE....Southbourne
TWDS....Talbot Woods
UPTN....Upton
VWD....Verwood
WBNE....Westbourne
WCLF....West Cliff
WIMB....Wimborne Minster

Aar - Bar

A

Aaron Cl CFDH BH17 55 F3
Abbey Gdns WIMB BH21 18 B4
Abbey Rd FERN BH22 20 C1
Abbotsbury Rd BDST BH18 34 C2
Abbots Cl CHCH/BSGR BH23 64 B3
Abbott Rd MOOR/WNTN BH9 58 C2
Abbotts Wy FERN BH22 20 C1
Aberdare Rd NBNE BH10 39 E4
Abingdon Dr CHCH/BSGR BH23 65 E2
Abingdon Rd CFDH BH17 54 D1
Abinger Rd LTDN BH7 60 A4
Abney Rd NBNE BH10 38 D4
Acacia Av VWD BH31 5 E4
Acacia Rd LYMN SO41 48 B3
Acland Rd MOOR/WNTN BH9 58 D2
Acorn Cl CHCH/BSGR BH23 61 F2
NMIL/BTOS BH25 47 G3
RGWD BH24 11 G3
The Acorns WIMB BH21 17 G5
Acorn Wy VWD BH31 4 C2
Acres Rd BWD BH11 38 B5
Acton Rd NBNE BH10 57 F1
Adamsfield Gdns NBNE BH10 38 C5
Adastral Rd CFDH BH17 55 E3
Addington Pl
CHCH/BSGR BH23 62 B4
Addiscombe Rd
CHCH/BSGR BH23 61 G3
Addison Rd BROC SO42 14 D4
Addison Sq RGWD BH24 8 D4
Adelaide Cl CHCH/BSGR BH23 61 F2
Adeline Rd BMTH BH1 77 G1
Admiralty Rd SBNE BH6 79 F2
Agar's La LYMN SO41 48 D2
Agarton La LYMN SO41 68 D4
Aggis Farm Rd VWD BH31 4 A2
Airetons Cl BDST BH18 35 G4
Airfield Rd CHCH/BSGR BH23 62 D3
Airfield Wy CHCH/BSGR BH23 62 D3
Akeshill Cl NMIL/BTOS BH25 47 F2
Albany Cl NMIL/BTOS BH25 65 H1
Albany Gdns PLE BH15 71 H3
Albemarle Rd TWDS BH3 58 B3
Albert Rd BKME/WDN BH12 56 B5
BMTH BH1 3 G3
FERN BH22 19 H4
NMIL/BTOS BH25 46 D5
WIMB BH21 34 B2
Albion Rd CHCH/BSGR BH23 61 F1
Alby Rd BKME/WDN BH12 56 D5
Alcester Rd BKME/WDN BH12 56 B4
Alder Cl CHCH/BSGR BH23 62 B1
Alder Crs BKME/WDN BH12 56 D3
Alder Hills BKME/WDN BH12 57 E3
Alderley Rd NBNE BH10 38 D3
Alderney Av BKME/WDN BH12 56 B1
Alder Rd BKME/WDN BH12 56 D4
Aldis Gdns PLE BH15 71 G2
Aldridge Rd FERN BH22 28 A1
NBNE BH10 38 C2
Alexander Cl
CHCH/BSGR BH23 62 C4
Alexandra Rd LYMN SO41 50 C2
PSTN BH14 74 C1
SBNE BH6 60 B5
lford Rd TWDS BH3 57 H3
lington Cl PSTN BH14 85 E1
lington Rd PSTN BH14 85 E1
TWDS BH3 58 C4
lipore Cl PSTN BH14 74 B2
llenby Cl CFDH BH17 35 F5
llenby Rd CFDH BH17 54 B1
llen Ct WIMB BH21 16 C4
llen Rd WIMB BH21 16 C5
llens La UPTN BH16 53 F5
llens Rd UPTN BH16 53 E4
llenview Rd WIMB BH21 16 C4
l Saints Rd LYMN SO41 51 E5
ma Rd MOOR/WNTN BH9 58 C3
mer Rd PLE BH15 71 G2
mond Gv BKME/WDN BH12 56 B3
pine Rd RGWD BH24 12 C4
ton Rd NBNE BH10 57 F1
PSTN BH14 73 H2
Alton Road East PSTN BH14 74 B3
Alum Chine Rd WBNE BH4 75 F2
Alumdale Rd WBNE BH4 75 F3
Alumhurst Rd WBNE BH4 75 F3
Alverton Av PLE BH15 73 F2
Alyth Rd TWDS BH3 57 G4
Ambassador Cl
CHCH/BSGR BH23 63 E4
Amberley Cl CHCH/BSGR BH23 64 A2
Amber Rd WIMB BH21 34 A3
Amberwood FERN BH22 20 A2
Amberwood Dr
CHCH/BSGR BH23 45 G5
Amberwood Gdns
CHCH/BSGR BH23 45 G5
Ambleside CHCH/BSGR BH23 41 H4
Ambleside Rd LYMN SO41 51 E5
Ambury La
CHCH/BSGR BH23 62 D2
Amesbury Rd SBNE BH6 60 C4
Amethyst Rd
CHCH/BSGR BH23 62 D3
Ameys La FERN BH22 20 B2
Ampfield Rd CHAR BH8 40 B4
Amsterdam Sq
CHCH/BSGR BH23 62 B3
Anchor Cl BWD BH11 37 H2
CHCH/BSGR BH23 63 E5
Anchor Ms LYMN SO41 51 E3
Anchor Rd BWD BH11 37 H2
Andover Cl CHCH/BSGR BH23 63 F3
Andrew La NMIL/BTOS BH25 47 H5
Andrews Cl BWD BH11 38 A4
Angeline Cl CHCH/BSGR BH23 64 B2
Angel La FERN BH22 27 F1
NMIL/BTOS BH25 66 D2
Anjou Cl BWD BH11 37 F2
Anna La CHCH/BSGR BH23 23 G5
Anne Cl CHCH/BSGR BH23 61 G1
Annerley Rd BMTH BH1 77 E1
Annet Cl PLE BH15 71 G3
Anson Cl CHCH/BSGR BH23 62 D4
RGWD BH24 9 E3
Anstey Cl BWD BH11 38 A1
Anstey Rd BWD BH11 38 A2
Anthony's Av PSTN BH14 74 A4
Antler Dr NMIL/BTOS BH25 46 C3
Anvil Crs BDST BH18 34 C2
Apollo Cl BKME/WDN BH12 56 B3
Apple Cl BKME/WDN BH12 75 E1
Apple Gv CHCH/BSGR BH23 42 A5
Appleslade Wy
NMIL/BTOS BH25 47 F2
Appletree Cl NMIL/BTOS BH25 66 A1
SBNE BH6 60 C5
Apple Tree Gv FERN BH22 20 A4
Approach Rd PSTN BH14 73 H2
April Cl BWD BH11 38 A3
Apsley Crs CFDH BH17 54 C1
Aragon Wy MOOR/WNTN BH9 39 H2
Arcadia Av CHAR BH8 58 D3
Arcadia Rd CHCH/BSGR BH23 61 F1
Archdale Cl NBNE BH10 38 D5
Archway Rd CCLF BH13 74 C1
Arden Rd MOOR/WNTN BH9 39 F4
Arden Wk NMIL/BTOS BH25 47 F5
Ardmore Rd PSTN BH14 73 H1
Argyle Rd CHCH/BSGR BH23 62 C5
Argyll Rd BKME/WDN BH12 56 B4
BOSC BH5 77 G1
Ariel Cl SBNE BH6 61 H5
Ariel Dr SBNE BH6 79 H1
Arley Rd PSTN BH14 73 G3
Arlington Ct NMIL/BTOS BH25 66 B2
Armstrong Cl BROC SO42 14 C3
Armstrong La BROC SO42 14 C3
Armstrong Rd BROC SO42 14 C3
Arne Av BKME/WDN BH12 56 C3
Arne Crs BKME/WDN BH12 56 C3
Arnewood Rd SBNE BH6 60 C5
Arnold Cl FERN BH22 10 A3
Arnold Rd FERN BH22 10 A3
Arnolds Cl NMIL/BTOS BH25 65 H2
Arran Wy CHCH/BSGR BH23 64 D1
Arrowsmith La WIMB BH21 25 E5
Arrowsmith Rd WIMB BH21 35 H1
Arthur Cl WCLF BH2 58 B5
Arthur La CHCH/BSGR BH23 61 G3
Arthur Rd CHCH/BSGR BH23 61 G3
Arundel Cl NMIL/BTOS BH25 46 C4
Arundel Wy CHCH/BSGR BH23 64 B3
Ascham Rd CHAR BH8 58 D5
Ascot Rd BDST BH18 35 E3
Ashbourne Rd BOSC BH5 60 B5
Ashburn Garth RGWD BH24 9 F5
Ashburton Gdns NBNE BH10 57 H1
Ash Cl UPTN BH16 52 D2
Ashdene Cl WIMB BH21 16 D4
Ashdown Wk
NMIL/BTOS BH25 47 G5
Ashford Rd SBNE BH6 60 D3
Ash Gv LYMN SO41 68 B2
RGWD BH24 9 E4
Ashington La WIMB BH21 24 A3
Ashington Pk NMIL/BTOS BH25 66 B1
Ashlet Gdns NMIL/BTOS BH25 47 H3
Ashley Cl BMTH BH1 59 F4
RGWD BH24 9 F5
Ashley Common Rd
NMIL/BTOS BH25 47 G3
Ashley Dr RGWD BH24 7 G3
Ashley Dr North RGWD BH24 11 H1
Ashley Dr South RGWD BH24 11 H1
Ashley Dr West RGWD BH24 11 H1
Ashley La LYMN SO41 51 E3
NMIL/BTOS BH25 47 H3
Ashley Meads NMIL/BTOS BH25 47 H3
Ashley Pk RGWD BH24 7 E5
Ashley Rd BMTH BH1 59 G4
LTDN BH7 59 H5
NMIL/BTOS BH25 47 G4
PSTN BH14 56 A5
Ashling Cl CHAR BH8 59 E2
Ashmeads Cl WIMB BH21 17 G3
Ashmeads Wy WIMB BH21 17 G3
Ashmore WIMB BH21 16 D5
Ashmore Av NMIL/BTOS BH25 66 B2
PLE BH15 71 H4
Ashmore Gv CHCH/BSGR BH23 64 A1
Ashridge Av NBNE BH10 38 D2
Ashridge Gdns NBNE BH10 38 D2
Ashton Rd MOOR/WNTN BH9 39 F5
Ashtree Cl NMIL/BTOS BH25 47 H5
Ashurst Rd CHAR BH8 40 B4
Ashwood Dr BDST BH18 35 G3
Aspen Dr VWD BH31 4 D2
Aspen Gdns BKME/WDN BH12 56 D3
Aspen Pl NMIL/BTOS BH25 66 B1
Aspen Rd BKME/WDN BH12 56 D3
Aspen Wy BKME/WDN BH12 56 D3
Asquith Cl CHCH/BSGR BH23 62 B4
Astbury Av BKME/WDN BH12 57 E2
Aston Md CHCH/BSGR BH23 42 A3
Athelstan Rd SBNE BH6 61 E5
Aubrey Cl LYMN SO41 82 D1
Auckland Pl BROC SO42 15 E3
Auckland Rd
CHCH/BSGR BH23 63 G3
Audemer Ct RGWD BH24 9 E3
Aukland Av BROC SO42 15 E3
Austen Av NBNE BH10 39 E1
Auster Cl CHCH/BSGR BH23 63 F3
Austin Av PSTN BH14 73 H3
Austin Cl BMTH BH1 59 F5
Autumn Cl FERN BH22 19 F2
Autumn Rd BWD BH11 37 F4
Avalon PSTN BH14 74 A5
Avebury Av NBNE BH10 39 E1
Avenue La WCLF BH2 3 F4
Avenue Rd BROC SO42 14 D3
CHCH/BSGR BH23 61 F3
CHCH/BSGR BH23 65 E1
LYMN SO41 50 D3
NMIL/BTOS BH25 47 E4
WCLF BH2 3 F4
WIMB BH21 16 D5
The Avenue CCLF BH13 75 E4
MOOR/WNTN BH9 39 F4
Avon Av RGWD BH24 12 D3
Avon Buildings
CHCH/BSGR BH23 61 H3
Avon Castle Dr RGWD BH24 12 D2
Avon Cswy CHCH/BSGR BH23 30 B5
Avoncliffe Rd SBNE BH6 79 E2
Avon Cl BMTH BH1 59 F4
LYMN SO41 50 C4
Avon Gdns CHCH/BSGR BH23 33 F3
Avon Pk RGWD BH24 7 H5
Avon Rd CHAR BH8 59 E4
FERN BH22 10 A5
Avon Rd East CHCH/BSGR BH23 61 G2
Avon Rd West CHCH/BSGR BH23 61 F2
Avon Run Cl CHCH/BSGR BH23 63 F5
Avon Run Rd CHCH/BSGR BH23 63 F5
Avon Valley Pth RGWD BH24 13 F5
Avon View Rd
CHCH/BSGR BH23 43 E4
Award Rd WIMB BH21 18 D4
Axford Cl CHAR BH8 40 B4
Aylesbury Rd BMTH BH1 77 F1
Aysha Cl NMIL/BTOS BH25 66 B1
Azalea Cl RGWD BH24 12 A1

B

Badbury Cl BDST BH18 35 G4
Badbury Vw WIMB BH21 16 D4
Baden Cl NMIL/BTOS BH25 66 B1
Bader Rd CFDH BH17 55 E2
Badgers Cl RGWD BH24 11 H1
Badgers Copse
NMIL/BTOS BH25 47 G1
Badgers Wk FERN BH22 20 A2
Badger Wy VWD BH31 4 B3
Bailey Cl NMIL/BTOS BH25 47 H3
Bailey Crs PLE BH15 54 C3
Bailey Dr CHCH/BSGR BH23 61 F3
Baiter Gdns PLE BH15 72 D4
Baker Rd BWD BH11 37 H2
Bakers Farm Rd VWD BH31 4 A1
Balcombe Rd CCLF BH13 75 E2
Baldwin Cl CHCH/BSGR BH23 62 B4
Balfour Cl CHCH/BSGR BH23 63 H2
Balfour Rd MOOR/WNTN BH9 58 B1
Ballam Cl UPTN BH16 53 E3
Ballard Cl NMIL/BTOS BH25 47 F3
PLE BH15 72 D4
Ballard Rd PLE BH15 72 D4
Balmer Lawn Rd BROC SO42 15 F1
Balmoral Av CHAR BH8 59 G1
Balmoral Rd PSTN BH14 74 A2
Balmoral Wk NMIL/BTOS BH25 46 D4
Balston Rd PSTN BH14 55 G5
Bankhill Dr LYMN SO41 50 D2
Bankside LYMN SO41 50 D1
Bankside Rd MOOR/WNTN BH9 39 G4
Banks Rd CCLF BH13 84 D5
Bankview LYMN SO41 50 D1
Banstead Rd WIMB BH21 35 E2
Barberry Wy VWD BH31 5 E3
Barbers Piles PLE BH15 72 B4
Barfields LYMN SO41 51 E3
Bargates CHCH/BSGR BH23 61 G3
Baring Rd SBNE BH6 79 G1
Barlands Cl CHCH/BSGR BH23 43 E5
Barn Cl UPTN BH16 52 C3
Barnes Cl NBNE BH10 38 D4
Barnes Crs NBNE BH10 38 D4
WIMB BH21 17 E5
Barnes La LYMN SO41 68 A2
Barnes Rd NBNE BH10 38 D4
Barnfield CHCH/BSGR BH23 63 H2
Barn Rd BDST BH18 35 F4
Barnsfield Rd RGWD BH24 12 A5
Barns Rd FERN BH22 20 C3
Barons Rd BWD BH11 37 F1
Barrack Rd CHCH/BSGR BH23 61 E2
FERN BH22 28 C2
Barrie Rd MOOR/WNTN BH9 39 F4
Barrow Dr CHAR BH8 40 D5
Barrowgate Rd CHAR BH8 40 B3
Barrowgate Wy CHAR BH8 40 B4
Barrow Rd CHAR BH8 40 D5
Barrows La LYMN SO41 48 D2
Barrow Vw FERN BH22 19 E3
Barrow Wy CHAR BH8 40 D5
Barrs Av NMIL/BTOS BH25 47 E3
Barrs Wood Dr NMIL/BTOS BH25 47 F3
Barrs Wood Rd
NMIL/BTOS BH25 47 F3
Barry Gdns BDST BH18 34 D2
Barters La BDST BH18 34 D3

Bartlett Dr *LTDN* BH7 .... 60 B2
Barton Common La
  NMIL/BTOS BH25 .... 66 B2
Barton Common Rd
  NMIL/BTOS BH25 .... 66 B3
Barton Court Av
  NMIL/BTOS BH25 .... 65 H3
Barton Court Rd
  NMIL/BTOS BH25 .... 66 A1
Barton Cft *NMIL/BTOS* BH25 .... 66 A1
Barton Gn *NMIL/BTOS* BH25 .... 66 A4
Barton La *NMIL/BTOS* BH25 .... 65 H2
Bartonside Rd *NMIL/BTOS* BH25 .... 65 E2
Barton Wy *NMIL/BTOS* BH25 .... 65 G3
Barton Wood Rd
  NMIL/BTOS BH25 .... 65 G3
Bascott Cl *BWD* BH11 .... 57 E1
Bascott Rd *BWD* BH11 .... 56 D1
Bashley Cross Rd
  CHCH/BSGR BH23 .... 46 B2
Bashley Dr *NMIL/BTOS* BH25 .... 47 F1
Bassett Rd *BKME/WDN* BH12 .... 55 H4
Batchelor Crs *BWD* BH11 .... 37 H4
Batchelor Rd *BWD* BH11 .... 37 H4
Batcombe Cl *BWD* BH11 .... 37 G4
Bath Hill Rbt *BMTH* BH1 .... 3 K4
Bath Rd *BMTH* BH1 .... 3 K4
  LYMN SO41 .... 51 F4
Batten Cl *CHCH/BSGR* BH23 .... 62 B2
Baverstock Rd
  BKME/WDN BH12 .... 57 F2
Bay Cl *UPTN* BH16 .... 52 D4
Bay Hog La *PLE* BH15 .... 72 B3
Bays Rd *LYMN* SO41 .... 50 C4
Bay Tree Wy *CHCH/BSGR* BH23 .... 63 H1
Beach Av *NMIL/BTOS* BH25 .... 65 H3
Beach Rd *CCLF* BH13 .... 75 E5
  UPTN BH16 .... 52 C4
Beacon Cl *LYMN* SO41 .... 68 B1
Beacon Dr *CHCH/BSGR* BH23 .... 64 B3
Beacon Gdns *BDST* BH18 .... 34 C4
Beacon Park Crs *UPTN* BH16 .... 52 C2
Beacon Park Rd *UPTN* BH16 .... 52 C2
Beacon Rd *BDST* BH18 .... 34 B4
  UPTN BH16 .... 52 D3
  WCLF BH2 .... 3 F5
Beaconsfield Rd
  BKME/WDN BH12 .... 56 B5
  CHCH/BSGR BH23 .... 61 H3
Beacon Wy *BDST* BH18 .... 34 C4
Beamish Rd *CFDH* BH17 .... 55 F2
Bear Cross Av *BWD* BH11 .... 37 G1
Beatty Cl *RGWD* BH24 .... 9 E3
Beatty Rd *MOOR/WNTN* BH9 .... 58 D1
Beauchamps Gdns *LTDN* BH7 .... 60 A2
Beaucroft La *WIMB* BH21 .... 17 E3
Beaucroft Rd *WIMB* BH21 .... 16 D3
Beaufort Cl *CHCH/BSGR* BH23 .... 63 F3
Beaufort Rd *SBNE* BH6 .... 60 C5
Beaufoys Av *FERN* BH22 .... 19 C2
Beaufoys Cl *FERN* BH22 .... 19 C2
Beaulieu Av *CHCH/BSGR* BH23 .... 61 G3
Beaulieu Rd *CHCH/BSGR* BH23 .... 61 G3
  WBNE BH4 .... 75 F4
Beaumont Rd *CCLF* BH13 .... 85 H1
Beccles Cl *PLE* BH15 .... 71 H3
Becher Rd *PSTN* BH14 .... 74 C1
Beckhampton Rd *PLE* BH15 .... 71 G2
Beckley Copse
  CHCH/BSGR BH23 .... 45 G5
Becton La *NMIL/BTOS* BH25 .... 66 B3
Becton Md *NMIL/BTOS* BH25 .... 66 B3
Bedale Wy *PLE* BH15 .... 55 F5
Bedford Crs *LTDN* BH7 .... 60 C3
Bedford Rd North
  BKME/WDN BH12 .... 37 E5
Bedford Rd South
  BKME/WDN BH12 .... 37 E5
Beech Av *CHCH/BSGR* BH23 .... 60 D2
  SBNE BH6 .... 78 C1
Beech Cl *BDST* BH18 .... 34 B3
  LYMN SO41 .... 68 B2
  VWD BH31 .... 4 A3
Beech Ct *WIMB* BH21 .... 17 E5
Beechcroft La *RGWD* BH24 .... 8 D3
The Beeches *LTDN* BH7 .... 60 A2
Beechey Rd *CHAR* BH8 .... 58 D5
Beech La *RGWD* BH24 .... 11 G4
Beechwood Av *BOSC* BH5 .... 77 H1
  NMIL/BTOS BH25 .... 46 C3
Beech Wood Cl *BDST* BH18 .... 35 E4
Beechwood Gdns *BOSC* BH5 .... 78 A1
Beechwood Rd *FERN* BH22 .... 20 B1
Belben Cl *BKME/WDN* BH12 .... 37 E5
Belben Rd *BKME/WDN* BH12 .... 37 E5
Belfield Rd *SBNE* BH6 .... 79 G1

Belgrave Rd *CCLF* BH13 .... 75 E3
Belle Vue Cl *SBNE* BH6 .... 78 D1
Belle Vue Crs *SBNE* BH6 .... 79 F1
Belle Vue Gv *FERN* BH22 .... 10 A4
Belle Vue Rd *PSTN* BH14 .... 74 A2
  SBNE BH6 .... 78 D2
Belle Vue Wk *FERN* BH22 .... 28 A2
Bellflower Cl
  CHCH/BSGR BH23 .... 63 F2
Bell Heather Cl *UPTN* BH16 .... 52 D2
Belmont Av *CHAR* BH8 .... 40 A5
Belmont Cl *VWD* BH31 .... 4 C3
Belmont Rd *NMIL/BTOS* BH25 .... 47 C3
  PSTN BH14 .... 55 H5
Belmore La *LYMN* SO41 .... 51 E4
Belmore Rd *LYMN* SO41 .... 50 D4
Belvedere Rd *CHCH/BSGR* BH23 .... 61 G3
  TWDS BH3 .... 57 H1
Bemister Rd *MOOR/WNTN* BH9 .... 58 C2
Benbow Crs *BWD* BH11 .... 56 C1
Benbridge Av *BWD* BH11 .... 37 H2
Bendigo Rd *CHCH/BSGR* BH23 .... 61 E2
Benellen Av *WBNE* BH4 .... 2 B1
Benellen Gdns *WBNE* BH4 .... 2 B1
Benellen Rd *WBNE* BH4 .... 57 G5
Bengal Rd *MOOR/WNTN* BH9 .... 58 A1
Benjamin Rd *PLE* BH15 .... 71 G3
Benmoor Rd *CFDH* BH17 .... 54 A2
Benmore Cl *NMIL/BTOS* BH25 .... 47 G5
Benmore Rd *MOOR/WNTN* BH9 .... 58 C1
Bennett Rd *CHAR* BH8 .... 59 E4
Bennion Rd *NBNE* BH10 .... 38 C4
Benridge Cl *BDST* BH18 .... 35 E4
Benson Cl *CHCH/BSGR* BH23 .... 33 F3
Bentley Rd *MOOR/WNTN* BH9 .... 39 F4
Bere Cl *CFDH* BH17 .... 35 H5
Beresford Cl *BKME/WDN* BH12 .... 56 B4
Beresford Gdns
  CHCH/BSGR BH23 .... 62 C4
Beresford Rd *BKME/WDN* BH12 .... 56 B4
  LYMN SO41 .... 50 C3
  SBNE BH6 .... 78 B1
Berkeley Av *BKME/WDN* BH12 .... 56 A2
Berkeley Cl *TWDS* BH3 .... 4 A1
Berkeley Rd *TWDS* BH3 .... 58 A3
Berkley Av *FERN* BH22 .... 27 E5
Bernards Rd *CHCH/BSGR* BH23 .... 61 E2
Berrans Av *BWD* BH11 .... 38 B1
Berryfield Rd *LYMN* SO41 .... 48 C5
Bertram Rd *NMIL/BTOS* BH25 .... 47 G3
Berwick Rd *TWDS* BH3 .... 58 A4
Bessborough Rd *CCLF* BH13 .... 85 G1
Beswick Av *NBNE* BH10 .... 38 D5
Bethia Cl *BMTH* BH1 .... 59 F4
Bethia Rd *BMTH* BH1 .... 59 F4
Betsy Cl *CHCH/BSGR* BH23 .... 33 F3
Betsy La *CHCH/BSGR* BH23 .... 33 F3
Bettiscombe Cl *CFDH* BH17 .... 35 H5
Beverley Gdns *NBNE* BH10 .... 38 C4
Bexington Cl *BWD* BH11 .... 37 G4
Bickerley Gdns *RGWD* BH24 .... 8 B5
Bickerley Rd *RGWD* BH24 .... 8 B5
Bicton Rd *BWD* BH11 .... 38 B4
Bindon Cl *BKME/WDN* BH12 .... 56 C3
Bingham Av *PSTN* BH14 .... 85 F1
Bingham Cl *CHCH/BSGR* BH23 .... 62 C3
Bingham Dr *LYMN* SO41 .... 51 E4
Bingham Rd *CHCH/BSGR* BH23 .... 62 C3
  MOOR/WNTN BH9 .... 58 C2
  VWD BH31 .... 4 C4
Binnie Rd *BKME/WDN* BH12 .... 56 C5
Birch Av *CHCH/BSGR* BH23 .... 43 E4
  FERN BH22 .... 28 B3
  NMIL/BTOS BH25 .... 46 B1
Birch Cl *PSTN* BH14 .... 74 C2
  RGWD BH24 .... 11 F3
  WIMB BH21 .... 34 B1
Birchdale Rd *WIMB* BH21 .... 16 D4
Birch Dr *CHAR* BH8 .... 41 E5
Birch Rd *RGWD* BH24 .... 12 B2
Birchwood Cl
  CHCH/BSGR BH23 .... 64 A1
Birchwood Rd *PSTN* BH14 .... 74 C2
  UPTN BH16 .... 52 D4
Bird's Hill Rd *PLE* BH15 .... 73 E1
Birkdale Cl *WIMB* BH21 .... 35 E2
Birkdale Rd *WIMB* BH21 .... 35 E2
Bishop Cl *BKME/WDN* BH12 .... 57 G3
Bishop Rd *RGWD* BH24 .... 8 C4
Bishop Rd *MOOR/WNTN* BH9 .... 58 C2
Bishops Cl *LTDN* BH7 .... 59 H4
Bitterne Wy *LYMN* SO41 .... 50 D5
  VWD BH31 .... 4 C3
Blackberry La *CHCH/BSGR* BH23 .... 62 D4
Blackbird Cl *CFDH* BH17 .... 53 G2
Blackbird Wy *CHCH/BSGR* BH23 .... 33 G4
Blackburn Rd *BKME/WDN* BH12 .... 55 H4
Blackbush Rd *LYMN* SO41 .... 67 H4

Blackfield La *FERN* DI22 .... 10 A3
Blackfield Rd *CHAR* BH8 .... 40 B4
Black Hl *VWD* BH31 .... 4 C2
Blacksmith Cl *WIMB* BH21 .... 34 B2
Blackthorn Cl *LYMN* SO41 .... 50 B5
Blackthorn Wy *VWD* BH31 .... 4 D3
Blackwater Dr *WIMB* BH21 .... 24 D5
Blair Av *PSTN* BH14 .... 74 A1
Blair Cl *NMIL/BTOS* BH25 .... 46 C4
Blakedene Rd *PSTN* BH14 .... 73 H4
Blake Hill Av *PSTN* BH14 .... 74 A4
Blake Hill Crs *PSTN* BH14 .... 74 A4
Blandford Cl *PLE* BH15 .... 71 H3
Blandford Rd *PLE* BH15 .... 72 A4
  UPTN BH16 .... 53 E3
Blandford Rd North *UPTN* BH16 .. 52 D2
Blaney Wy *WIMB* BH21 .... 34 A1
Blenheim Crs *LYMN* SO41 .... 48 A3
Blenheim Dr *CHCH/BSGR* BH23 .... 63 F3
Blind La *WIMB* BH21 .... 16 B3
Bloomfield Av
  MOOR/WNTN BH9 .... 39 F5
Bloxworth Rd *BKME/WDN* BH12 .. 56 D2
Bluebell Cl *CHCH/BSGR* BH23 .... 63 F2
Bluebell La *CFDH* BH17 .... 53 C1
Blyth Cl *CHCH/BSGR* BH23 .... 41 H3
Blythe Rd *WIMB* BH21 .... 34 B1
Blythswood Ct
  NMIL/BTOS BH25 .... 65 H3
Bob Hann Cl *BKME/WDN* BH12 .. 56 C5
Bockhampton Rd
  CHCH/BSGR BH23 .... 43 G2
Bodley Rd *CCLF* BH13 .... 85 H1
Bodorgan Rd *WCLF* BH2 .... 3 C2
Bodowen Cl *CHCH/BSGR* BH23 .. 43 F5
Bodowen Rd *CHCH/BSGR* BH23... 43 F5
Bognor Rd *BDST* BH18 .... 34 D3
Boldre Cl *BKME/WDN* BH12 .... 56 C3
  NMIL/BTOS BH25 .... 65 F2
Boleyn Crs *MOOR/WNTN* BH9 .... 40 A3
Bolton Crs *FERN* BH22 .... 20 C3
Bolton Rd *SBNE* BH6 .... 79 E2
Bond Rd *PLE* BH15 .... 55 F5
Bonham Rd *TWDS* BH3 .... 58 B3
Bonington Cl
  CHCH/BSGR BH23 .... 22 C2
Border Dr *UPTN* BH16 .... 53 E5
Border Rd *UPTN* BH16 .... 53 E5
Boreham Rd *SBNE* BH6 .... 60 D5
Borley Rd *CFDH* BH17 .... 54 A2
Borthwick Rd *BMTH* BH1 .... 59 C5
Boscombe Cliff Rd *BOSC* BH5 .... 77 G2
Boscombe Grove Rd *BMTH* BH1 .. 59 F5
Boscombe Overcliff Dr
  BOSC BH5 .... 77 H2
Boscombe Spa Rd *BOSC* BH5 .... 77 F1
Bosley Cl *CHCH/BSGR* BH23 .... 42 A5
Bosley Wy *CHCH/BSGR* BH23 .... 42 A5
Bosworth Ms
  MOOR/WNTN BH9 .... 39 H3
Boulnois Av *PSTN* BH14 .... 74 C2
Boundary Dr *WIMB* BH21 .... 16 D3
Boundary La *RGWD* BH24 .... 11 F5
Boundary Rd *MOOR/WNTN* BH9 .. 57 H2
  NBNE BH10 .... 57 H1
Bourne Av *WCLF* BH2 .... 2 E3
Bourne Cl *WBNE* BH4 .... 2 C3
Bourne Ct *WIMB* BH21 .... 16 D4
Bournemouth International
  Centre Rbt *WCLF* BH2 .... 2 E5
Bournemouth Rd *PSTN* BH14 .... 74 A1
Bournemouth Road Castle Hl
  PSTN BH14 .... 73 H1
Bourne Valley Rd
  BKME/WDN BH12 .... 57 E5
  BKME/WDN BH12 .... 57 E5
Bournewood Dr *WBNE* BH4 .... 2 A1
Bourton Gdns *LTDN* BH7 .... 60 B2
Bouverie Cl *NMIL/BTOS* BH25 .... 65 H1
Boveridge Gdns
  MOOR/WNTN BH9 .... 39 H3
Bovington Cl *CFDH* BH17 .... 55 F1
Bowden Rd *BKME/WDN* BH12 .... 37 E5
Bower Rd *CHAR* BH8 .... 59 F2
Bowland Ri *NMIL/BTOS* BH25 .... 47 G5
Box Cl *CFDH* BH17 .... 54 B3
Boyd Rd *BKME/WDN* BH12 .... 56 B5
Brabazon Dr *CHCH/BSGR* BH23 .. 63 F3
Brabazon Rd *WIMB* BH21 .... 25 F3
Brabourne Av *FERN* BH22 .... 19 G5
Bracken Cl *RGWD* BH24 .... 11 G4
Brackendale Rd *CHAR* BH8 .... 59 E2
Bracken Gln *PLE* BH15 .... 73 E1
Brackenhill *CCLF* BH13 .... 75 E4
Brackenhill Rd *WIMB* BH21 .... 17 G2
Bracken Rd *FERN* BH22 .... 19 F2
  SBNE BH6 .... 78 C1
Brackens Wy *LYMN* SO41 .... 51 F5

Bracken Wy *CHCH/BSGR* BH23 .... 64 D1
Brackley Cl *CHCH/BSGR* BH23 .... 30 A4
Bradburne Rd *WCLF* BH2 .... 2 E2
Bradford Rd *MOOR/WNTN* BH9 .... 40 A3
Bradpole Rd *CHAR* BH8 .... 59 G1
Bradstock Cl *BKME/WDN* BH12 .... 56 D2
Braemar Av *SBNE* BH6 .... 79 G1
Braemar Cl *SBNE* BH6 .... 79 G1
Braemar Dr *CHCH/BSGR* BH23 .... 64 B1
Braeside Rd *FERN* BH22 .... 10 A3
  RGWD BH24 .... 11 G2
Braidley Rd *WCLF* BH2 .... 3 G2
Brailswood Rd *PLE* BH15 .... 72 D1
Braishfield Gdns *CHAR* BH8 .... 40 B5
Bramble La *CHCH/BSGR* BH23 .... 64 D1
Bramble Wk *LYMN* SO41 .... 50 C3
Bramble Wy *CHCH/BSGR* BH23 .. 33 F3
Bramley Cl *LYMN* SO41 .... 51 E5
Bramley Rd *FERN* BH22 .... 19 H5
  NBNE BH10 .... 38 C2
Brampton Cl *PLE* BH15 .... 54 D4
Brampton Rd *PLE* BH15 .... 54 D4
Bramshaw Gdns *CHAR* BH8 .... 40 B5
Bramshaw Wy *NMIL/BTOS* BH25... 65 F2
Branders Cl *SBNE* BH6 .... 79 G1
Branders La *SBNE* BH6 .... 61 G5
Branksea Av *PLE* BH15 .... 71 F4
Branksea Cl *PLE* BH15 .... 71 G4
Branksome Cl *NMIL/BTOS* BH25 .. 47 H4
Branksome Dene Rd *WBNE* BH4... 75 F3
Branksome Hill Rd *WBNE* BH4 .... 75 H1
Branksome Towers *CCLF* BH13 ... 75 F5
Branksome Wood Gdns
  WCLF BH2 .... 2 D1
Branksome Wood Rd
  WBNE BH4 .... 57 G5
Bransgore Gdns
  CHCH/BSGR BH23 .... 33 F3
Branwell Cl *CHCH/BSGR* BH23 .... 61 G3
Branwood Cl *LYMN* SO41 .... 68 C1
Brassey Cl *MOOR/WNTN* BH9 .... 58 C1
Brassey Rd *MOOR/WNTN* BH9 .... 58 B1
Breamore Cl *NMIL/BTOS* BH25 .. 46 C4
Brecon Cl *NBNE* BH10 .... 39 E1
  NMIL/BTOS BH25 .... 47 G5
Bredy Cl *NMIL/BTOS* BH25 .... 54 D1
Bremble Cl *BKME/WDN* BH12 .... 37 E5
Brendon Cl *CHAR* BH8 .... 40 C5
Briar Cl *CHCH/BSGR* BH23 .... 62 D4
  PLE BH15 .... 55 E5
Briarswood Rd *UPTN* BH16 .... 53 E3
Briar Wy *WIMB* BH21 .... 17 H4
Brickfield La *LYMN* SO41 .... 51 F2
Brickyard La *WIMB* BH21 .... 19 E5
Bridge Ap *PLE* BH15 .... 72 B4
Bridge Pl *NBNE* BH10 .... 27 H5
Bridge Rd *LYMN* SO41 .... 51 E5
Bridges Cl *FERN* BH22 .... 10 B3
The Bridges *RGWD* BH24 .... 8 A4
Bridge St *CHCH/BSGR* BH23 .... 62 A4
Bridgewater Rd
  BKME/WDN BH12 .... 56 B4
Bridle Cl *UPTN* BH16 .... 53 F3
Bridle Crs *LTDN* BH7 .... 60 C2
Bridle Wy *WIMB* BH21 .... 17 H3
Bridleways *VWD* BH31 .... 4 C2
Bridport Rd *BKME/WDN* BH12 .... 56 D2
  VWD BH31 .... 4 B2
Brierley Av *FERN* BH22 .... 28 A3
Brierley Cl *NBNE* BH10 .... 39 E2
Brierley Rd *NBNE* BH10 .... 39 E2
Brightlands Av *SBNE* BH6 .... 79 F1
Bright Rd *PLE* BH15 .... 54 D4
Brinsons Cl *CHCH/BSGR* BH23 .... 43 E4
Brisbane Rd *CHCH/BSGR* BH23 ... 61 E1
Britannia Rd *PSTN* BH14 .... 73 G2
Britannia Wy
  CHCH/BSGR BH23 .... 63 F3
Brixey Cl *BKME/WDN* BH12 .... 56 A3
Brixey Rd *BKME/WDN* BH12 .... 56 A3
Broad Av *CHAR* BH8 .... 59 F2
Broadfields Cl *LYMN* SO41 .... 68 B5
Broadhurst Av *NBNE* BH10 .... 39 E3
Broadlands Av *SBNE* BH6 .... 79 F1
Broadlands Cl *CHAR* BH8 .... 40 B4
  CHCH/BSGR BH23 .... 45 H5
Broadlands Rd *BROC* SO42 .... 14 C2
Broad La *LYMN* SO41 .... 51 F4
Broadly Cl *LYMN* SO41 .... 50 B5
Broadmayne Rd
  BKME/WDN BH12 .... 56 D3
Broadmoor Rd *WIMB* BH21 .... 34 A1
Broadshard La *RGWD* BH24 .... 8 C2
Broadstone Wy *CFDH* BH17 .... 54 B2
Broadwater Av *PSTN* BH14 .... 73 H5
Broadway *SBNE* BH6 .... 79 G1
Broadway La *CHAR* BH8 .... 40 A4
The Broadway *NBNE* BH10 .... 38 D1

Brockenhurst Rd
  MOOR/WNTN BH9 .... 39 H5
Brockhills La NMIL/BTOS BH25 .... 47 G2
Brockley Rd NBNE BH10 .... 38 D3
Brocks Pine RGWD BH24 .... 11 H3
Bronte Av CHCH/BSGR BH23 .... 61 G1
Brook Av North
  NMIL/BTOS BH25 .... 47 F3
Brook Av NMIL/BTOS BH25 .... 47 F2
Brook Cl WIMB BH21 .... 38 C3
Brookdale Cl WIMB BH21 .... 35 E3
Brook Dr VWD BH31 .... 4 D4
Brookland Cl LYMN SO41 .... 50 C4 🔲
Brook La CHCH/BSGR BH23 .... 33 E5
  WIMB BH21 .... 34 A1
Brookley Rd BROC SO42 .... 14 D3
Brooklyn Ct NMIL/BTOS BH25 .. 46 D4 🔲
Brook Rd BKME/WDN BH12 .... 56 A5
  LYMN SO41 .... 51 F5
  NBNE BH10 .... 38 C3
  WIMB BH21 .... 17 E5
Brooks Cl RGWD BH24 .... 8 D5
Brookside Cl CHCH/BSGR BH23 .. 33 E3 🔲
Brookside Rd BROC SO42 .... 14 D2
  CHCH/BSGR BH23 .... 33 E4
  WIMB BH21 .... 17 E5
Brookside Wy CHCH/BSGR BH23.. 64 A1
Brook Wy CHCH/BSGR BH23 .... 63 G3
Broomfield La LYMN SO41 .... 51 E3
Broom Rd BKME/WDN BH12 .... 56 A1
Broughton Av NBNE BH10 .... 39 E3
Broughton Dr NBNE BH10 .... 39 E4 🔲
Brownen Rd MOOR/WNTN BH9.. 58 D2
Browning Av BOSC BH5 .... 77 H1
Browning Rd
  BKME/WDN BH12 .... 56 B4 🔲
Brownings Cl LYMN SO41 .... 50 A3
Brownsea Av WIMB BH21 .... 34 B1
Brownsea Cl NMIL/BTOS BH25 ... 46 C4
Brownsea Rd CCLF BH13 .... 85 E5
Brownsea View Av PSTN BH14 .... 73 H4
Brudenell Av CCLF BH13 .... 85 F1
Brudenell Rd CCLF BH13 .... 85 F1
Brune Wy FERN BH22 .... 27 H1 🔲
Brunstead Pl BKME/WDN BH12... 75 F1
Brunstead Rd BKME/WDN BH12 .. 75 F1
Brunswick Pl LYMN SO41 .... 51 E3
Bryanstone Rd TWDS BH3 .... 58 A3
Bryant Rd BKME/WDN BH12 .... 57 E2
Bryon Rd WIMB BH21 .... 16 C3
Bryony Cl BDST BH18 .... 34 D4
Bub La CHCH/BSGR BH23 .... 62 C4
Buccaneers Cl
  CHCH/BSGR BH23 .... 62 C4 🔲
Buccleuch Rd CCLF BH13 .... 75 E4
Bucehayes Cl
  CHCH/BSGR BH23 .... 64 C2
Buchanan Av LTDN BH7 .... 59 G4
Buckingham Rd
  BKME/WDN BH12 .... 56 B3
Buckland Dene LYMN SO41 .... 50 D2
Buckland Rd CHCH/BSGR BH23 .. 45 E3
Buckland Rd BKME/WDN BH12 ... 56 A5
Buckland Ter BKME/WDN BH12... 56 A5
The Bucklers LYMN SO41 .... 67 G5
Bucklers Wy CHAR BH8 .... 40 B4
Buckstone Cl LYMN SO41 .... 68 C1
Buckthorn Cl WIMB BH21 .... 34 D5 🔲
Bugdens La VWD BH31 .... 4 B2
Bullfinch Cl CFDH BH17 .... 53 H1
Bunting Rd FERN BH22 .... 19 F1
Burbridge Cl CFDH BH17 .... 55 E2 🔲
Burcombe Rd NBNE BH10 .... 38 C4
Burdock Cl CHCH/BSGR BH23.... 63 F1
Bure Cl CHCH/BSGR BH23 .... 63 F4
Bure Haven Dr
  CHCH/BSGR BH23 .... 63 E4
Bure Homage Gdns
  CHCH/BSGR BH23 .... 63 F4 🔲
Bure Homage La
  CHCH/BSGR BH23 .... 63 E4
Bure La CHCH/BSGR BH23........... 63 F5
Bure Pk CHCH/BSGR BH23 .... 63 F4
Bure Rd CHCH/BSGR BH23 .... 63 F4
Burford Cl CHCH/BSGR BH23 ..... 60 D1
Burford La BROC SO42 .... 15 E4
Burgess Cl BWD BH11 .... 37 H3
Burleigh Rd SBNE BH6 .... 60 D4
Burley Cl NMIL/BTOS BH25 .... 4 A3
  VWD BH31 .... 4 A3
Burley Rd BKME/WDN BH12........ 56 A4
  CHCH/BSGR BH23 .... 33 G3
Burnaby Rd WBNE BH4 .... 2 A7
Burnbake Rd VWD BH31 .... 4 D4
Burnbrae Rd FERN BH22 .... 27 H3
Burn Cl VWD BH31 .... 4 D4
Burnett Av CHCH/BSGR BH23 ..... 61 E3
Burnett Rd CHCH/BSGR BH23 .... 61 F3

Burngate Rd PLE BH15 .... 71 G3
Burnham Dr CHAR BH8 .... 59 E3
Burnham Rd CHCH/BSGR BH23 .. 43 E5
Burnleigh Gdns
  NMIL/BTOS BH25 .... 47 G3 🔲
Burnside CHCH/BSGR BH23 ..... 63 H2 🔲
Burns Rd SBNE BH6 .... 60 D3
Burnt House La
  CHCH/BSGR BH23 .... 33 F3
Burrard Gv LYMN SO41 .... 51 F5
Burtley Rd SBNE BH6 .... 79 E2
Burton Cl CHCH/BSGR BH23 ... 62 A1 🔲
  RGWD BH24 .... 11 F1
Burtoncroft CHCH/BSGR BH23 ... 43 E4
Burton Hall Pl
  CHCH/BSGR BH23 .... 43 F4 🔲
Burton Rd CCLF BH13 .... 75 E2
  CHCH/BSGR BH23 .... 62 C3
Burt's Hl WIMB BH21 .... 16 C3
Bury Rd CCLF BH13 .... 74 D3 🔲
Bushell Rd PLE BH15 .... 54 C3
Bushey Rd CHAR BH8 .... 59 E1
Bushmead Dr RGWD BH24 .... 11 G1
Bute Dr CHCH/BSGR BH23 .... 64 D3
Butlers La CHCH/BSGR BH23 .... 9 E2
Buttercup Dr CHCH/BSGR BH23 . 63 F1
The Buttery CHCH/BSGR BH23 ... 62 B3
Butts Lawn BROC SO42 .... 14 D2
Butts Paddock BROC SO42 .... 14 D2
Byron Cl BOSC BH5 .... 77 H1
  NMIL/BTOS BH25 .... 65 G2

C

Cabot La CFDH BH17 .... 54 A2
Cabot Wy NMIL/BTOS BH25 .... 46 D4
Cadhay Cl NMIL/BTOS BH25 .... 46 C4
Cadnam Wy CHAR BH8 .... 40 B4
Cadogan Rd RGWD BH24 .... 8 C4
Caesar's Wy WIMB BH21 .... 34 C3
Caird Av NMIL/BTOS BH25 .... 66 C1
Cairns Cl CHCH/BSGR BH23........ 61 F2
Caister Cl FERN BH22 .... 19 G3
Calder Rd CFDH BH17 .... 55 F2
Caledonian Cl
  CHCH/BSGR BH23 .... 63 F3 🔲
Caledon Rd PSTN BH14 .... 74 B2
Calkin Cl CHCH/BSGR BH23 .... 61 G1
Calluna Rd WIMB BH21 .... 16 C5
Calmore Cl CHAR BH8 .... 40 B4 🔲
Calvin Rd MOOR/WNTN BH9....... 58 B2
Cambridge Gdns
  CHCH/BSGR BH23 .... 42 B5
Cambridge Rd WCLF BH2 .... 2 D3
Camden Cl MOOR/WNTN BH9 .. 58 D1 🔲
Camellia Gdns NMIL/BTOS BH25.. 47 E5
Cameron Rd CHCH/BSGR BH23 .. 62 B3 🔲
Cammel Rd FERN BH22 .... 27 H2
Campbell Rd BMTH BH1 .... 59 G5
  CHCH/BSGR BH23 .... 43 E4
Campion Cl LYMN SO41 .... 51 E2 🔲
Campion Gv CHCH/BSGR BH23 .. 62 C4
Campion Wy LYMN SO41 .... 51 E2
Canberra Rd CHCH/BSGR BH23 .. 61 E1
Canford Av BWD BH11 .... 56 D1
Canford Bottom WIMB BH21...... 18 A3
Canford Cliffs Av PSTN BH14 ...... 74 B3
Canford Cliffs Rd CCLF BH13 ...... 74 C3
Canford Crs CCLF BH13 .... 85 C1
Canford Heath Rd CFDH BH17.... 36 C5
Canford Rd BWD BH11 .... 57 E1
  PLE BH15 .... 72 D1
Canford View Dr WIMB BH21 .... 17 H3 🔲
Canford Wy BKME/WDN BH12.... 37 E5
Cannon Cl BDST BH18 .... 53 H1
Cannon Hill Gdns WIMB BH21 .. 17 H2 🔲
Cannon Hill Rd WIMB BH21 .... 17 G2
Cannon St LYMN SO41 .... 51 E3
Canterbury Cl FERN BH22 .... 10 B5 🔲
Canute Dr CHCH/BSGR BH23 ..... 33 H3
Capesthorne CHCH/BSGR BH23 . 63 F5
Capstone Pl CHAR BH8 .... 59 F4
Capstone Rd CHAR BH8 .... 59 E4
Captain's Rw LYMN SO41 .... 51 F5
Carbery Av SBNE BH6 .... 78 D1
Carbery Gdns SBNE BH6 .... 61 E5
Cardigan Rd CCLF BH13 .... 74 D1 🔲
Cardigan Rd MOOR/WNTN BH9 . 58 B2
Carey Rd MOOR/WNTN BH9 .... 58 B2
Careys Cottages BROC SO42 ...... 14 D2
Careys Rd CHAR BH8 .... 40 B3
Carisbrooke Ct
  NMIL/BTOS BH25 .... 46 D4
Carisbrooke Crs PLE BH15 .... 71 G2 🔲
Carisbrooke Wy
  CHCH/BSGR BH23 .... 64 A1

Carlton Av NMIL/BTOS BH25 ...... 65 I-5
Carlton Gv PSTN BH14 .... 56 B5
Carlton Rd BMTH BH1 .... 77 E1
Carlyle Rd SBNE BH6 .... 60 D4
Carnarvon Rd BOSC BH5 .... 77 G1 🔲
Carnegie Cl BKME/WDN BH12 ... 56 B5
Caroline Av CHCH/BSGR BH23 ... 62 C5
Caroline Rd BWD BH11 .... 38 A4
Carpenter Cl LYMN SO41 .... 50 D2 🔲
Carrbridge Cl TWDS BH3 .... 57 H3
Carrbridge Rd TWDS BH3 .... 57 H3
Carrick Wy NMIL/BTOS BH25 ..... 47 G5
Carrington Cl LYMN SO41 .... 82 C1
Carrington La LYMN SO41 .... 68 C5
Carroll Av FERN BH22 .... 19 H4
Carroll Cl BKME/WDN BH12 .... 57 E4
Carsworth Wy CFDH BH17 ...... 36 C5 🔲
Carters Av PLE BH15 .... 71 F1
Carter's La PLE BH15 .... 72 C3 🔲
Cartref Cl VWD BH31 .... 4 B2
Cartwright Cl NBNE BH10 .... 38 C3 🔲
Carvers La RGWD BH24 .... 8 C4
Carysfort Rd BMTH BH1 .... 77 F1
Cashmoor Cl BKME/WDN BH12 . 56 D3 🔲
Caslake Cl NMIL/BTOS BH25 ...... 65 H1
Cassel Av WBNE BH4 .... 75 F4
Castle Av CHCH/BSGR BH23 .... 60 D2
Castle Cl LYMN SO41 .... 82 C2
Castledene Crs PSTN BH14.......... 73 G3
Castle Gate Cl CHAR BH8 .... 40 A5
Castle La East LTDN BH7 .... 60 B2
Castle La West
  MOOR/WNTN BH9 .... 39 G3 🔲
Castlemain Av SBNE BH6 .... 60 C5
Castleman Trailway CFDH BH17 .. 53 G2
Castleman Wy RGWD BH24 .... 8 C5
Castlemews RGWD BH24 .... 12 C1
Castle Rd MOOR/WNTN BH9....... 58 B1
Castle St CHCH/BSGR BH23........ 61 H4
  PLE BH15 .... 72 C4
Castleton Av NBNE BH10 .... 38 D1
Castlewood RGWD BH24 .... 12 D1
Catalina Cl CHCH/BSGR BH23 .... 63 E4
Catalina Dr PLE BH15 .... 73 E4
Caton Cl BKME/WDN BH12 .... 57 F2
Cattistock Rd CHAR BH8 .... 59 G1
Cavan Crs CFDH BH17 .... 54 B1
Cavendish Pl BMTH BH1 .... 58 C5
Cavendish Rd WCLF BH2 .... 58 B5
Caversham Cl PLE BH15 .... 71 G2
Cawdor Rd TWDS BH3 .... 57 H3
Caxton Cl CHCH/BSGR BH23 ...... 62 D3
Cecil Av CHAR BH8 .... 59 G1
Cecil Cl WIMB BH21 .... 34 C1
Cecil Hl MOOR/WNTN BH9 ...... 58 D2 🔲
  BOSC BH5 .... 77 G1
Cedar Av CHCH/BSGR BH23 .... 60 D2
  NBNE BH10 .... 38 D1
  RGWD BH24 .... 11 G3 🔲
Cedar Cl UPTN BH16 .... 52 D2
Cedar Dr LYMN SO41 .... 68 B2 🔲
  CHAR BH8 .... 17 H4
Cedar Pl CHCH/BSGR BH23 .... 33 F3
The Cedars WBNE BH4 .... 2 B1
Cedar Wy FERN BH22 .... 19 G1
Celandine Cl CHCH/BSGR BH23 . 63 F2
Cellars Farm Rd SBNE BH6 .... 79 C2
Cemetery Av PLE BH15 .... 55 F4
Cemetery Rd WIMB BH21 .... 16 B4
Centenary Wy BMTH BH1 .... 59 G5
Central Av BKME/WDN BH12 .... 56 C4 🔲
Central Dr WCLF BH2 .... 3 F2
Centre La LYMN SO41 .... 68 C1
Centre Pl RGWD BH24 .... 8 B4 🔲
Cerne Cl MOOR/WNTN BH9 .... 39 H3 🔲
Chaddesley Gln CCLF BH13 .... 85 F2
Chaddesley Wood Rd
  CCLF BH13 .... 85 G3 🔲
Chaffey Cl RGWD BH24 .... 9 E5
Chaffinch Cl CFDH BH17 .... 34 D5 🔲
  NMIL/BTOS BH25 .... 46 D5
Chalbury Cl CFDH BH17 .... 36 C5
Chaldecott Gdns NBNE BH10 .... 38 C3
Chaldon Rd CFDH BH17 .... 36 B5
Chalfont Av CHCH/BSGR BH23 .. 41 H4
Champion Cl LYMN SO41 .... 51 F5
Chander Cl FERN BH22 .... 20 A5
Chandlers Cl LTDN BH7 .... 60 B2 🔲
Chandos Av BKME/WDN BH12.... 57 E2
Chant Cl CHCH/BSGR BH23 ..... 62 B3 🔲
Chantry Cl CHCH/BSGR BH23 .... 64 B1
Chapel Cl WIMB BH21 .... 34 A1
Chapel La CHCH/BSGR BH23 ...... 29 E1
  CHCH/BSGR BH23 .... 63 G3
  PLE BH15 .... 72 C3 🔲
  WIMB BH21 .... 16 B4
  WIMB BH21 .... 34 A2

Chapel Rd RGWD BH24 .... 12 D4
Chapel Rd PSTN BH14 .... 73 G1
Charborough Rd BDST BH18 ...... 35 F4
Charing Cl RGWD BH24 .... 8 C5 🔲
Charles Crs NMIL/BTOS BH25 .... 47 F2
Charles Gdns BOSC BH5 .... 58 C5
Charles Rd CHCH/BSGR BH23 ... 62 D2 🔲
  PLE BH15 .... 72 D2
Charlotte Cl BKME/WDN BH12.... 57 G3
  CHCH/BSGR BH23 .... 63 E4
Charlton Cl LYMN SO41 .... 48 B4 🔲
  MOOR/WNTN BH9 .... 40 A3
Charminster Av
  MOOR/WNTN BH9 .... 58 D1
Charminster Cl
  MOOR/WNTN BH9 .... 39 H5 🔲
Charminster Pl CHAR BH8 .... 40 A5 🔲
Charminster Rd CHAR BH8 .... 58 C4
Charmouth Gv PSTN BH14 .... 73 G1
Charnock Cl LYMN SO41 .... 48 B4
Charnwood Av
  MOOR/WNTN BH9 .... 39 H4 🔲
Charnwood Cl FERN BH22 .... 10 A4 🔲
Charter Rd BWD BH11 .... 37 F1
Chaseside LTDN BH7 .... 60 A2
The Chase RGWD BH24 .... 12 D1
  VWD BH31 .... 4 D2
Chatsworth Rd CHAR BH8 .... 58 D4
  PSTN BH14 .... 55 H5
Chatsworth Wy
  NMIL/BTOS BH25 .... 46 C4
Chaucer Cl WIMB BH21 .... 16 C3
Chaucer Dr LYMN SO41 .... 68 B5
Chaucer Rd CCLF BH13 .... 74 D5 🔲
Cheam Rd BDST BH18 .... 34 D3
Cheddington Rd
  MOOR/WNTN BH9 .... 39 G3
Chedington Cl CFDH BH17 .... 36 A5
Chelmsford Rd UPTN BH16 .... 52 D3
Cheltenham Rd
  BKME/WDN BH12 .... 56 A5
Chene Rd WIMB BH21 .... 16 D5
Cherford Rd BWD BH11 .... 38 B5
Cherita Ct PLE BH15 .... 55 F4
Cheriton Av LTDN BH7 .... 60 C1
Cheriton Wy WIMB BH21 .... 16 C3
Cherrett Cl BWD BH11 .... 37 H3 🔲
Cherries Dr MOOR/WNTN BH9 .. 39 E5
Cherry Cl PSTN BH14 .... 73 H1
Cherry Gv FERN BH22 .... 19 G3
Cherry Hill Gv UPTN BH16 .... 52 D4
Cherry Tree Cl LYMN SO41 ...... 68 B2 🔲
  RGWD BH24 .... 11 F3
Cherry Tree Dr
  NMIL/BTOS BH25 .... 46 C2 🔲
Cheshire Dr CHAR BH8 .... 41 E5
Chesildene Av CHAR BH8 .... 40 B5
Chesildene Dr CHAR BH8 .... 40 B4
Chessel Av BOSC BH5 .... 77 H1
Chesterfield Cl CCLF BH13 .... 74 D5
Chester Rd CCLF BH13 .... 75 E3
Chestnut Av CHCH/BSGR BH23 . 60 D1
  NMIL/BTOS BH25 .... 66 A2
  SBNE BH6 .... 78 C1
Chestnut Gv WIMB BH21 .... 18 C3
Chestnut Rd BROC SO42 .... 15 E3
Chestnut Wy CHCH/BSGR BH23.. 43 E4
Chetnole Cl CFDH BH17 .... 55 F1
Chetwode Wy CFDH BH17 .... 35 F5
Cheviot Wy VWD BH31 .... 4 D1
Chewton Common Rd
  CHCH/BSGR BH23 .... 64 C1
Chewton Farm Rd
  CHCH/BSGR BH23 .... 65 E1
Chewton Ldg CHCH/BSGR BH23 .. 64 D1
Chewton Wy CHCH/BSGR BH23.. 64 D1
Cheyne Gdns WBNE BH4 .... 2 B5
Chichester Rd RGWD BH24 .... 9 E3
Chichester Wk WIMB BH21 .... 25 E3
Chickerell Cl
  MOOR/WNTN BH9 .... 39 H4 🔲
Chideock Cl BKME/WDN BH12 .. 56 C4 🔲
Chigwell Rd CHAR BH8 .... 59 E1
Chilcombe Rd SBNE BH6 .... 60 B5 🔲
Chilfrome Cl CFDH BH17 .... 54 C1
Chiltern Cl NMIL/BTOS BH25...... 65 H1
  WBNE BH4 .... 57 F5
Chiltern Dr NMIL/BTOS BH25 ..... 65 G2
  VWD BH31 .... 4 B2
Chine Crs WCLF BH2 .... 2 D5
Chine Crescent Rd WBNE BH4 ...... 2 D5
Chine Wk FERN BH22 .... 28 A3
Chisels La CHCH/BSGR BH23..... 44 B1
Chiswell Rd CFDH BH17 .... 54 D1
Chorley Cl PLE BH15 .... 54 C4
Christchurch Bay Rd
  NMIL/BTOS BH25 .... 65 H3
Christchurch By-pass

CHCH/BSGR BH23 .... 67 C2
Christchurch Rd *BMTH* BH1 ...... 77 E2
  BOSC BH5 .... 60 A5
  CHCH/BSGR BH23 .... 41 F1
  FERN BH22 .... 27 F2
  LYMN SO41 .... 67 F3
  NMIL/BTOS BH25 .... 65 G2
  RGWD BH24 .... 8 B4
Christopher Crs *PLE* BH15 ...... 54 C4
Churchfield *VWD* BH31 .... 4 A2
Churchfield Crs *PLE* BH15 ...... 73 E1
Churchfield Rd *PLE* BH15 .... 73 E2
Church HI *LYMN* SO41 .... 68 C5
  VWD BH31 .... 4 A2
Churchill Crs *BKME/WDN* BH12 .. 56 A4
Churchill Gdns
  BKME/WDN BH12 .... 56 A5
Churchill Rd *BKME/WDN* BH12 .. 56 A4
  BMTH BH1 .... 59 F5
  WIMB BH21 .... 24 D1
Church La *BROC* SO42 .... 15 E4
  CHCH/BSGR BH23 .... 61 H4
  FERN BH22 .... 28 B5
  LYMN SO41 .... 51 E4
  NMIL/BTOS BH25 .... 65 H1
Church Md *LYMN* SO41 .... 51 E5
Churchmoor Rd *WIMB* BH21 .... 17 C4
Church Rd *FERN* BH22 .... 19 C4
  PSTN BH14 .... 73 C1
  SBNE BH6 .... 79 F2
Church St *CHCH/BSGR* BH23.... 61 H4
  PLE BH15 .... 72 B4
  WIMB BH21 .... 16 B5
Cinnamon La *PLE* BH15 .... 72 B4
The Circle *MOOR/WNTN* BH9 .. 39 G3
Clare Lodge Cl
  CHCH/BSGR BH23 .... 33 E4
Claremont Av
  MOOR/WNTN BH9 .... 39 H5
Claremont Rd
  MOOR/WNTN BH9 .... 39 H5
Clarence Park Rd *LTDN* BH7 .... 60 A4
Clarence Rd *PSTN* BH14 .... 73 C1
Clarendon Cl *BDST* BH18 .... 34 C5
Clarendon Pk *LYMN* SO41 ...... 50 D5
Clarendon Rd *BDST* BH18 .... 34 C4
  CHCH/BSGR BH23 .... 61 G3
  WBNE BH4 .... 2 C5
Clark's Cl *RGWD* BH24 .... 8 C4
Clausen Wy *LYMN* SO41 .... 69 G1
Clayford Av *FERN* BH22 .... 19 F2
Clayford Cl *CFDH* BH17 .... 35 H5
Claylake Dr *VWD* BH31 .... 4 C3
Cleeves Cl *BKME/WDN* BH12 ... 37 F5
Clematis Cl *CHCH/BSGR* BH23 .. 63 G2
Cleveland Cl *NMIL/BTOS* BH25 .. 65 F1
Cleveland Gdns *BMTH* BH1 ...... 59 F5
Cleveland Rd *BMTH* BH1 .... 59 F5
Cliff Crs *NMIL/BTOS* BH25 ...... 65 G4
Cliff Dr *CCLF* BH13 .... 85 H1
  CHCH/BSGR BH23 .... 63 G4
Cliffe Rd *NMIL/BTOS* BH25 ..... 65 G3
Clifford Rd *MOOR/WNTN* BH9 ... 58 C1
Cliff Rd *LYMN* SO41 .... 67 G5
Clifton Gdns *FERN* BH22 .... 19 G2
Clifton Rd *PSTN* BH14 .... 74 B3
  SBNE BH6 .... 78 D2
Clingan Rd *SBNE* BH6 .... 60 D4
Clinton Cl *CHCH/BSGR* BH23 ... 45 H5
Clinton Rd *LYMN* SO41 .... 51 E2
Cliveden Cl *FERN* BH22 .... 19 G2
Clive Rd *CHCH/BSGR* BH23 ...... 45 E5
  MOOR/WNTN BH9 .... 58 B1
The Cloisters *RGWD* BH24 .... 9 E5
The Close *BDST* BH18 .... 34 C4
  NMIL/BTOS BH25 .... 65 H4
  RGWD BH24 .... 8 B4
  RGWD BH24 .... 12 A2
  RGWD BH24 .... 12 D2
Clough's Rd *RGWD* BH24.......... 8 D4
Clover Cl *CHCH/BSGR* BH23 ..... 63 F2
Clover Ct *NMIL/BTOS* BH25 ..... 47 H3
Clover Dr *CFDH* BH17 .... 53 H1
The Clovers *BKME/WDN* BH12 .. 57 E2
Clowes Av *SBNE* BH6 .... 79 H2
Clyde Rd *CFDH* BH17 .... 35 F5
Coastguard Wy
  CHCH/BSGR BH23 .... 80 D1
Cobbs La *PLE* BH15 .... 55 E4
Cobb's Rd *WIMB* BH21 .... 17 E3
Cobham Rd *MOOR/WNTN* BH9 ... 39 G4
  WIMB BH21 .... 18 D2
Cobham Wy *WIMB* BH21 .... 25 E3
Cockerell Cl *WIMB* BH21 .... 25 F3
Cogdeane Rd *CFDH* BH17 .... 35 H5
Colborne Av *WIMB* BH21 .... 17 H4
Colborne Cl *LYMN* SO41 .... 51 E2
  PLE BH15 .... 72 D4

Colbourne Cl *CHCH/BSGR* BH23.. 55 E4
Colehill Crs *MOOR/WNTN* BH9 .. 39 H4
Colehill La *WIMB* BH21 .... 17 E2
Coleman Rd *BWD* BH11 .... 38 A4
Colemere Gdns
  CHCH/BSGR BH23 .... 64 B1
Colemore Rd *LTDN* BH7 .... 60 C5
Coleridge Gn
  CHCH/BSGR BH23 .... 62 D2
Coles Av *PLE* BH15 .... 71 G3
Coles Gdns *PLE* BH15 .... 71 G3
Colin Cl *WIMB* BH21 .... 34 B2
College Rd *BOSC* BH5 .... 78 A1
  RGWD BH24 .... 8 C4
Collingbourne Av *SBNE* BH6 ..... 60 D4
Collins La *RGWD* BH24 .... 8 C4
Collwood Cl *PLE* BH15 .... 54 C3
Collyers Rd *BROC* SO42 .... 14 B4
Colonnade Rd *BOSC* BH5 .... 60 A5
Colt Cl *WIMB* BH21 .... 17 H3
Columbian Wy *NBNE* BH10 ...... 38 C5
Columbia Rd *NBNE* BH10 .... 38 B5
Columbia Trees La *NBNE* BH10 .. 57 G1
Columbine Cl
  CHCH/BSGR BH23 .... 63 F1
Colville Cl *BOSC* BH5 .... 60 A5
Colville Rd *BOSC* BH5 .... 60 A5
Comber Rd *MOOR/WNTN* BH9 ... 39 F4
Comet Wy *CHCH/BSGR* BH23 .... 63 E4
Comley Rd *MOOR/WNTN* BH9 ... 39 F5
Commercial Rd *PLE* BH15 .... 73 F1
  WCLF BH22 .... 2 E4
Compton Av *PSTN* BH14 .... 74 B3
Compton Beeches
  RGWD BH24 .... 12 A1
Compton Cl *VWD* BH31 .... 4 B2
Compton Crs *FERN* BH22 .... 10 C5
Compton Dr *PSTN* BH14 .... 74 A3
Compton Gdns *PSTN* BH14........ 74 A3
Compton Rd *NMIL/BTOS* BH25 ... 47 E5
Coneygar La *FERN* BH22 .... 27 E1
Conference Pl *LYMN* SO41 .... 51 F5
Conifer Av *LTDN* BH7 .... 73 H3
Conifer Cl *CHCH/BSGR* BH23 .... 41 H4
  FERN BH22 .... 28 B3
  RGWD BH24 .... 11 F2
Conifer Crs *LYMN* SO41 .... 50 B4
Coniston Av *BWD* BH11 .... 37 G2
Coniston Cl *VWD* BH31 .... 4 A3
Coniston Rd *RGWD* BH24 .... 8 D5
Connaught Cl *NMIL/BTOS* BH25 .. 65 G2
Connaught Crs
  BKME/WDN BH12 .... 56 C4
Connaught Rd *SBNE* BH6 .... 60 B5
Connell Rd *PLE* BH15 .... 54 C5
Consort Cl *BKME/WDN* BH12 .... 56 A5
Constitution Hill Rd *PSTN* BH14 .. 73 F1
Conway Cl *NMIL/BTOS* BH25 .... 47 H4
Conways Dr *PSTN* BH14 .... 73 G1
Cook Cl *RGWD* BH24................. 9 E3
Cooke Rd *BKME/WDN* BH12 ..... 56 D4
Cook Rw *WIMB* BH21 .... 16 B5
Coombe Av *NBNE* BH10 .... 39 E5
Coombe Gdns *NBNE* BH10 .... 38 D5
Cooper Dean Dr *CHAR* BH8 ...... 59 H1
Coopers La *VWD* BH31 .... 4 B1
Copeland Dr *PSTN* BH14 .... 73 H3
Copper Beech Cl
  BKME/WDN BH12 .... 75 E1
Copper Beech Gdns *NBNE* BH10.. 38 D5
Coppice Av *FERN* BH22 .... 19 F3
Coppice Cl *NMIL/BTOS* BH25 .... 47 H3
  RGWD BH24 .... 11 H2
The Coppice *BROC* SO42 .... 14 C5
  CHCH/BSGR BH23 .... 63 F4
Coppice Vw *NBNE* BH10 .... 39 E4
Copse Av *NMIL/BTOS* BH25 ..... 47 H5
Copse Cl *PLE* BH15 .... 73 F2
Copse Rd *NMIL/BTOS* BH25 ..... 47 H5
  VWD BH31 .... 4 B2
Copse Wy *CHCH/BSGR* BH23 .... 64 A2
Copsewood Av *CHAR* BH8 .... 59 G1
Copythorne Cl *CHAR* BH8 .... 40 B5
Corbar Rd *CHCH/BSGR* BH23 .... 61 E2
Corbiere Av *BKME/WDN* BH12 ... 56 B1
Corbin Av *FERN* BH22 .... 20 C3
Corbin Rd *LYMN* SO41 .... 50 B5
Corfe Lodge Rd *WIMB* BH21 ..... 34 A3
Corfe View Rd *PSTN* BH14 .... 73 H2
  WIMB BH21 .... 34 A2
Corfe Wy *BDST* BH18 .... 34 C5
Corhampton Rd *SBNE* BH6........ 60 C4
Cornelia Crs *BKME/WDN* BH12 .. 57 E4
Cornflower Dr
  CHCH/BSGR BH23 .... 63 G1
Cornford Wy *CHCH/BSGR* BH23 .. 63 H2
Cornish Gdns *NBNE* BH10 .... 57 H1
Coronation Av

  MOOR/WNTN BH9................ 39 F5
  UPTN BH16 .... 52 D3
Coronation Rd *VWD* BH31 .... 4 A1
Corscombe Cl *CFDH* BH17 .... 36 A5
Cotes Av *PSTN* BH14 .... 55 G5
Cotlands Rd *BMTH* BH1 .... 76 D1
Cotswold Cl *VWD* BH31 .... 4 B3
Cottage Gdns *BKME/WDN* BH12 .. 56 A5
Cottage Ms *RGWD* BH24 .... 8 B4
Cottagers La *LYMN* SO41 .... 48 C4
Cotton Cl *BDST* BH18 .... 34 D2
Countess Cl *WIMB* BH21 .... 25 E3
Countess Gdns *LTDN* BH7 .... 59 H2
Court Cl *CHCH/BSGR* BH23 ...... 62 C3
  LYMN SO41 .... 50 D5
Courtenay Dr *WIMB* BH21 .... 16 C3
Courtenay Pl *LYMN* SO41 .... 51 E5
Courtenay Rd *PSTN* BH14 .... 73 H1
Courthill Rd *PSTN* BH14 .... 74 A1
Court Rd *MOOR/WNTN* BH9 ...... 58 D1
Covena Rd *SBNE* BH6 .... 60 D4
Coventry Cl *WIMB* BH21 .... 34 A3
Coventry Crs *CFDH* BH17 .... 54 A1
Cove Rd *NBNE* BH10 .... 38 C5
Cowdrey Gdns *CHAR* BH8 .... 40 D5
Cowdrys Fld *WIMB* BH21 .... 16 B3
Cowell Dr *LTDN* BH7 .... 60 D4
Cowgrove Rd *WIMB* BH21 .... 16 A4
Cowley Rd *LYMN* SO41 .... 50 C3
Cowleys Rd *CHCH/BSGR* BH23 ... 45 E5
Cowper Av *NMIL/BTOS* BH25 .... 66 A1
Cowper Rd *MOOR/WNTN* BH9 ... 39 F5
Cowpitts La *RGWD* BH24........... 9 F1
Cowslip Rd *WIMB* BH21 .... 34 C5
Cox Av *MOOR/WNTN* BH9 .... 39 H4
Cox Cl *MOOR/WNTN* BH9 .... 39 H3
Coxstone La *RGWD* BH24 .... 8 C5
Coy Pond Rd *BKME/WDN* BH12 .. 57 E5
Crabton Close Rd *BOSC* BH5 .... 59 H5
Crabtree Cl *CHCH/BSGR* BH23 ... 43 E5
Craigmoor Av *CHAR* BH8 .... 59 C1
Craigmoor Cl *CHAR* BH8 .... 59 C1
Craigmoor Wy *CHAR* BH8 .... 40 C5
Craigside Rd *RGWD* BH24 .... 11 F2
Craigwood Dr *FERN* BH22 .... 20 A5
Cranborne Crs
  BKME/WDN BH12 .... 56 C2
Cranborne Rd *WCLF* BH2 .... 3 F5
  WIMB BH21 .... 16 C1
Cranbrook Rd *BKME/WDN* BH12.. 55 H4
Crane Cl *VWD* BH31 .... 4 A1
Crane Dr *VWD* BH31 .... 4 A2
Cranemoor Av
  CHCH/BSGR BH23 .... 45 E5
Cranemoor Cl *CHCH/BSGR* BH23 .. 45 E5
Cranemoor Gdns
  CHCH/BSGR BH23 .... 45 F5
Cranes Ms *PLE* BH15 .... 72 D2
Cranfield Av *WIMB* BH21 .... 16 D4
Cranleigh Cl *SBNE* BH6 .... 61 E5
Cranleigh Gdns *SBNE* BH6 .... 61 E5
Cranleigh Rd *SBNE* BH6 .... 60 D4
Cranmer Rd *MOOR/WNTN* BH9 .. 58 B2
Crantock Gv *CHAR* BH8 .... 40 D5
Cranwell Cl *BWD* BH11 .... 37 G3
  CHCH/BSGR BH23 .... 33 F3
Crawshaw Rd *PSTN* BH14......... 73 H3
Creasey Rd *BWD* BH11 .... 38 A2
Creech Rd *BKME/WDN* BH12 ..... 56 A5
Creekmoor La *CFDH* BH17 .... 53 H1
Crescent Dr *NMIL/BTOS* BH25 ... 45 H1
Crescent Rd *PSTN* BH14 .... 55 H5
  VWD BH31 .... 4 C2
  WCLF BH22 .... 2 E3
  WIMB BH21 .... 16 C3
The Crescent *BMTH* BH1.......... 77 G1
  NMIL/BTOS BH25 .... 47 G1
Crescent Wk *FERN* BH22 .... 28 A2
Cresta Gdns *FERN* BH22 .... 28 A2
Crest Rd *BKME/WDN* BH12 .... 56 A4
Cribb Cl *CFDH* BH17 .... 55 H1
Crichel Mount Rd *PSTN* BH14 ... 74 A5
Crichel Rd *MOOR/WNTN* BH9 .... 58 C2
Cricket Cl *CHCH/BSGR* BH23 .... 62 D5
Crimea Rd *MOOR/WNTN* BH9 .... 58 B3
Cringle Av *SBNE* BH6 .... 79 C1
Crispin Cl *CHCH/BSGR* BH23 ..... 64 B2
Crockford Cl *NMIL/BTOS* BH25... 47 H3
Crofton Cl *CHCH/BSGR* BH23 .... 61 E2
Croft Rd *BKME/WDN* BH12 .... 55 H4
  CHCH/BSGR BH23 .... 28 A3
  CHCH/BSGR BH23 .... 62 D3
  MOOR/WNTN BH9 .... 39 F5
  RGWD BH24 .... 9 E2
Cromer Gdns
  BKME/WDN BH12 .... 56 D5
Cromer Rd *BKME/WDN* BH12 .... 56 D5
  CHAR BH8 .... 59 F3

Cromwell Pl *BOSC* BH5 .... 60 B5
Cromwell Rd *BKME/WDN* BH12 ... 56 B5
  BOSC BH5 .... 60 B5
Crosby Rd *WBNE* BH4 .... 75 G4
Crossmead Av *NMIL/BTOS* BH25.. 47 E5
Cross Wy *CHCH/BSGR* BH23 ..... 60 D1
Crossways *LYMN* SO41 .... 68 B1
The Crossways *UPTN* BH16 ...... 53 E3
Crow Arch La *RGWD* BH24 .... 8 D5
Crow La *RGWD* BH24 .... 9 E5
Crown Cl *BKME/WDN* BH12 .... 56 A5
Crown Md *WIMB* BH21 .... 16 C4
Crusader Rd *WIMB* BH21 .... 37 F3
Cucklington Gdns
  MOOR/WNTN BH9 .... 39 H4
Cuckoo Hill Wy
  CHCH/BSGR BH23 .... 33 G3
Cuckoo Rd *BKME/WDN* BH12..... 55 G2
Cudnell Av *BWD* BH11 .... 37 H1
Cul-de-sac *NMIL/BTOS* BH25 .... 65 E2
Culford Cl *CHAR* BH8 .... 40 D5
Cull Cl *BKME/WDN* BH12 .... 57 G2
Culliford Crs *CFDH* BH17 .... 36 A5
Cull La *NMIL/BTOS* BH25 .... 47 F2
Cullwood La *NMIL/BTOS* BH25 ... 47 G2
Culverhayes Pl *WIMB* BH21 ...... 16 B3
Culverhayes Rd *WIMB* BH21 ..... 16 B3
Culverley Cl *BROC* SO42 .... 14 D3
Culver Rd *NMIL/BTOS* BH25 ...... 46 D5
Cumnor Rd *BMTH* BH1 .... 3 J3
Cunningham Cl *BWD* BH11 .... 38 A4
  CHCH/BSGR BH23 .... 63 E4
  RGWD BH24 .... 9 E3
Cunningham Crs *BWD* BH11 ..... 38 A4
Cunningham Pl *BWD* BH11 .... 38 A4
Curlew Cl *FERN* BH22 .... 19 F2
Curlew Rd *CHAR* BH8 .... 40 B5
  CHCH/BSGR BH23 .... 63 E4
The Curlews *VWD* BH31 .... 4 C3
Curlieu Rd *PLE* BH15 .... 55 E4
Curtis Rd *BKME/WDN* BH12 ...... 56 A5
Curzon Pl *LYMN* SO41 .... 50 D5
Curzon Rd *CHAR* BH8 .... 59 F4
  PSTN BH14 .... 73 G2
Curzon Wy *CHCH/BSGR* BH23 ... 63 H2
Cuthburga Rd *WIMB* BH21 .... 16 C4
Cuthbury Cl *WIMB* BH21 .... 16 A4
Cuthbury Gdns *WIMB* BH21 ...... 16 A4
Cutler Cl *BKME/WDN* BH12 .... 57 G3
  NMIL/BTOS BH25 .... 47 G4
Cutlers Pl *WIMB* BH21 .... 17 G4
Cynthia Cl *BKME/WDN* BH12 ..... 55 H3
Cynthia Rd *BKME/WDN* BH12 .... 55 H3
Cyril Rd *CHAR* BH8 .... 59 E4

D

Dacombe Cl *UPTN* BH16 .... 53 E3
Dacombe Dr *UPTN* BH16 .... 53 E3
Dairy Cl *CHCH/BSGR* BH23 .... 62 B3
Dale Cl *PLE* BH15 .... 55 F4
Dale Rd *PLE* BH15 .... 55 F4
Dales Cl *WIMB* BH21 .... 18 A3
Dales Dr *WIMB* BH21 .... 17 H6
Dales La *CHCH/BSGR* BH23 ...... 29 G5
Dale Valley Rd *PLE* BH15 .... 55 E3
Dalewood Av *BWD* BH11 .... 37 G2
Dalkeith Rd *CCLF* BH13 .... 34 B3
  WIMB BH21 .... 34 B3
Dalling Rd *BKME/WDN* BH12 ..... 57 E5
Dalmeny Rd *SBNE* BH6 .... 79 E3
Damerham Rd *CHAR* BH8 .... 40 B4
Danecourt Cl *PSTN* BH14 .... 73 F1
Danecourt Rd *PSTN* BH14 .... 73 F1
Danecrest Rd *LYMN* SO41 .... 48 B4
Dane Dr *FERN* BH22 .... 28 A1
Dane Rd *LYMN* SO41 .... 67 G4
Danesbury Av *SBNE* BH6 .... 79 F1
Danes Cl *NMIL/BTOS* BH25 ...... 66 A3
Danestream Cl *LYMN* SO41 ...... 82 B1
Daneswood Rd
  NMIL/BTOS BH25 .... 47 G4
Daniell's Cl *LYMN* SO41 .... 51 E5
Daniell's Wk *LYMN* SO41 .... 51 E5
Dansie Cl *PSTN* BH14 .... 73 H1
Darby's Cl *PLE* BH15 .... 54 D3
Darby's La *PLE* BH15 .... 54 D3
Dark La *CHCH/BSGR* BH23 .... 45 G5
Darley Rd *FERN* BH22 .... 27 G4
Darracott Rd *BOSC* BH5 .... 78 A4
Darwin Av *CHCH/BSGR* BH23 .... 61 E5
Davenport Cl *UPTN* BH16 .... 53 E3
David's La *RGWD* BH24 .... 12 C5
David Wy *PLE* BH15 .... 71 F4
Davis Fld *NMIL/BTOS* BH25 ...... 46 D4
Davis Rd *PSTN* BH14 .... 56 C4

Dawkins Rd PLE BH15 ...... 71 F2
Dawlish Wy NMIL/BTOS BH25..... 47 E5
Dawn Cl NBNE BH10 .... 38 C5
Daws Av BWD BH11 .... 38 B5
Daylesford Cl PSTN BH14 .... 73 G3
Day's Ct WIMB BH21 .... 16 D5
Deacon Gdns BWD BH11 .... 38 A2
Deacon Rd BWD BH11 .... 38 A2
Dean Cl PLE BH15 .... 71 G2
Dean Park Crs BMTH BH1 ...... 3 G2
  WCLF BH2 .... 3 H2
Dean Park Rd BMTH BH1 .... 3 H1
  WCLF BH2 .... 3 H1
Deans Ct LYMN SO41 .... 68 B5
Deans Court La WIMB BH21 ..... 16 B5
Deanscroft Rd NBNE BH10 .... 39 E3
Deans Gv WIMB BH21 .... 16 C4
Deansleigh Rd LTDN DH7 .... 60 D1
Dean's Rd BOSC BH5 .... 60 B5
The Deans BMTH BH1 .... 3 H1
Dean Swift Crs PSTN BH14 .... 74 A5
Dear Hay La PLE BH15 .... 72 C3
Decies Rd PSTN BH14 .... 55 H5
De Courtenai Cl BWD BH11 .... 37 G2
Deepdene La BWD BH11 .... 37 G2
Deerleap Wy NMIL/BTOS BH25 ..... 47 F1
Deer Park Cl NMIL/BTOS BH25 .. 46 D5
Dee Wy PLE BH15... 72 B3
De Haviland Cl WIMB BH21 .... 25 F2
De Havilland Wy
  CHCH/BSGR BH23 .... 63 E5
Delamere Rd NBNE BH10 .... 39 E4
De La Warr Rd LYMN SO41 .... 82 A1
Delft Ms CHCH/BSGR BH23 .... 62 B3
Delhi Cl PSTN BH14 .... 74 B2
Delhi Rd NBNE BH10 .... 39 E5
Delilah Rd PLE BH15 .... 71 F3
De Lisle Rd TWDS BH3 .... 58 B3
Dell Cl BDST BH18.... 34 C3
The Dell NMIL/BTOS BH25.... 66 C1
Delph Rd WIMB BH21 .... 24 D4
Delta Cl CHCH/BSGR BH23 .... 63 E5
De Mauley Rd CCLF BH13 .... 74 C5
De Montfort Rd WIMB BH21 .... 24 D3
De Mowbray Wy LYMN SO41 .... 50 D5
Denby Rd PLE BH15.... 72 D1
Dene Cl RGWD BH24 .... 8 D5
Deneside Copse LYMN SO41.... 69 F1
Deneside Gdns LYMN SO41.... 50 B5
Deneve Av CFDH BH17 .... 54 C1
Dene Wk FERN BH22 .... 28 A3
Denewood Rd WBNE BH4 .... 75 F3
Denham Cl CFDH BH17 .... 36 A4
Denham Dr CHCH/BSGR BH23 .... 64 B1
Denholm Cl RGWD BH24 .... 9 F2
Denison Rd CFDH BH17 .... 54 C1
Denmark La PLE BH15 .... 72 D2
Denmark Rd MOOR/WNTN BH9... 58 D1
  PLE BH15 .... 72 D2
Denmead NMIL/BTOS BH25 .... 47 H3
Denmead Rd SBNE BH6 .... 60 D3
Dennis Rd WIMB BH21 .... 34 B2
Dennistoun Av
  CHCH/BSGR BH23 .... 62 D3
Derby Rd BMTH BH1 .... 77 E1
De Redvers Rd PSTN BH14 .... 74 A4
Dereham Wy BKME/WDN BH12.. 56 D4
Derritt La CHCH/BSGR BH23.... 32 A5
Derrybrian Gdns
  NMIL/BTOS BH25 .... 47 E5
Derwent Cl FERN BH22 .... 20 C1
  MOOR/WNTN BH9 .... 39 G5
Derwent Rd NMIL/BTOS BH25 .... 47 F2
Derwentwater Rd WIMB BH21 .... 24 D2
Deverel Cl CHCH/BSGR BH23 .... 61 G2
Devon Rd CHCH/BSGR BH23.... 61 G2
  PLE BH15 .... 55 E5
Dewlish Cl CFDH BH17 .... 36 C5
Dial Cl CHCH/BSGR BH23 .... 33 G2
Dibden Cl CHAR BH8 .... 40 B4
Dilly La NMIL/BTOS BH25 .... 66 A3
Dingle Rd BOSC BH5 .... 78 B1
Dingley Rd PLE BH15 .... 54 D4
Dinham Rd NMIL/BTOS BH25 .... 47 H3
Disraeli Rd CHCH/BSGR BH23.... 44 A2
Ditchbury LYMN SO41 .... 50 D1
Dodge Copse Wy NMIL/BTOS BH25.. 46 D2
Dogdean WIMB BH21 .... 16 C1
Dogwood Rd WIMB BH21.... 34 C3
Dolbery Rd North
  BKME/WDN BH12 .... 37 F5
Dolbery Rd South
  BKME/WDN BH12 .... 56 A1
Dolphin Av NBNE BH10 .... 39 E2
Dolphin Pl NMIL/BTOS BH25 .... 66 A3
Dominion Rd BWD BH11.... 37 H5
Donnelly Rd SBNE BH6 .... 61 F5

Donnington Dr
  CHCH/BSGR BH23 .... 63 F3
Donoughmore Rd BMTH BH1 .... 77 F1
Dorchester Gdns PLE BH15 .... 55 E5
Dorchester Rd PLE BH15 .... 55 E4
  UPTN BH16 .... 52 C5
Dornie Rd CCLF BH13.... 85 F1
Dorset Av FERN BH22 .... 19 H5
Dorset Lake Av PSTN BH14.... 73 H5
Dorset Rd CHCH/BSGR BH23 .... 62 D2
  WBNE BH4 .... 57 C5
Dorset Wy BKME/WDN BH12 .... 55 G2
  PLE BH15 .... 54 D3
Douglas Av CHCH/BSGR BH23 .... 61 F4
Douglas Cl UPTN BH16 .... 53 E3
Douglas Gdns BKME/WDN BH12 .. 56 C5
Douglas Ms SBNE BH6 .... 60 C5
Douglas Rd BKME/WDN BH12 .... 56 C5
  SBNE BH6 .... 79 E2
Doulton Gdns PSTN BH14 .... 73 H3
Doussie Cl UPTN BH16 .... 52 C2
Dover Cl CCLF BH13 .... 75 E2
Dover Rd CCLF BH13 .... 75 E2
Doveshill Crs NBNE BH10 .... 38 A4
Doveshill Gdns NBNE BH10 .... 38 A4
Dowlands Cl NBNE BH10 .... 38 D3
Dowlands Rd NBNE BH10 .... 38 C3
Downey Cl BWD BH11 .... 37 H5
Downton Cl CHAR BH8 .... 40 A4
Downton La LYMN SO41 .... 67 F4
Doyne Rd PSTN BH14 .... 74 C1
Dragon La RGWD BH24 .... 23 G1
Dragoon Wy CHCH/BSGR BH23 .... 61 F3
Drake Cl CHCH/BSGR BH23 .... 62 D4
  NMIL/BTOS BH25.... 46 D4
  RGWD BH24 .... 9 F2
Drake Rd PLE BH15 .... 72 C4
Draper Rd BWD BH11 .... 38 A3
  CHCH/BSGR BH23 .... 62 C3
Draycott Rd NBNE BH10 .... 38 D5
Dreswick Cl CHCH/BSGR BH23 .... 41 H3
Drew Cl BKME/WDN BH12 .... 57 G3
The Drive PSTN BH14 .... 56 B5
Droxford Rd LTDN BH7 .... 60 B4
Druids Cl FERN BH22 .... 27 H2
Druitt Rd CHCH/BSGR BH23 .... 62 D3
Drummond Rd BMTH BH1 .... 77 F1
Drury Rd WBNE BH4 .... 75 F3
Dryden Cl RGWD BH24 .... 11 G1
Dryden Pl LYMN SO41 .... 68 B5
Ducking Stool La
  CHCH/BSGR BH23 .... 61 H4
Duck Island La RGWD BH24 .... 8 C5
Duck La BWD BH11 .... 37 H3
Dudley Av LYMN SO41 .... 48 B5
Dudley Gdns NBNE BH10 .... 38 D2
Dudley Rd NBNE BH10 .... 38 D2
Dudmoor Farm Rd
  CHCH/BSGR BH23 .... 42 B4
Dudmoor La CHCH/BSGR BH23 .... 42 B3
Dudsbury Av FERN BH22 .... 19 H5
Dudsbury Crs FERN BH22 .... 19 H5
Dudsbury Gdns FERN BH22 .... 28 A4
Dudsbury Rd FERN BH22 .... 27 H3
Dugdell Cl FERN BH22 .... 20 B3
Dukes Dr BWD BH11 .... 37 G2
Dukesfield CHCH/BSGR BH23 .... 41 H5
Dulsie Rd TWDS BH3 .... 57 G3
Dunbar Crs CHCH/BSGR BH23 .... 45 E5
Dunbar Rd TWDS BH3 .... 58 A4
Duncan Rd NMIL/BTOS BH25 .... 47 H3
Duncliff Rd SBNE BH6 .... 79 G1
Duncombe Dr RGWD BH24.... 7 F1
Dundas Rd CFDH BH17 .... 55 E2
Dunedin Cl FERN BH22 .... 27 F1
Dunedin Dr FERN BH22 .... 27 F1
Dunedin Gdns FERN BH22 .... 27 F1
Dunedin Gv FERN BH22 .... 63 G3
Dunford Cl NMIL/BTOS BH25 .... 65 G2
Dunford Rd BKME/WDN BH12 .... 56 B5
Dunkeld Rd TWDS BH3 .... 57 H4
Dunlin Cl CHCH/BSGR BH23 .... 63 F5
Dunnock Cl FERN BH22 .... 19 F1
Dunstans La PSTN BH14 .... 55 F4
Dunyeats Rd BDST BH18 .... 35 F3
Durdells Av BWD BH11 .... 38 A2
Durdells Gdns BWD BH11 .... 38 A2
Durland Cl NMIL/BTOS BH25 .... 66 A1
Durley Chine Rd WCLF BH2 .... 2 D4
Durley Chine Rd South
  WCLF BH2 .... 2 D6
Durley Gdns WCLF BH2 .... 2 D5
Durley Rd WCLF BH2 .... 2 E5
Durley Rd South WCLF BH2 .... 2 E5
Durley Rbt WCLF BH2 .... 2 D5
Durlston Crs CHCH/BSGR BH23 .... 41 H3
Durlston Rd PSTN BH14 .... 74 A3
Durrant Rd PSTN BH14 .... 74 A2

  WCLF BH2 .... 3 F2
Durrington Pl LTDN BH7 .... 60 B4
Durrington Rd LTDN BH7 .... 60 B3
Durweston Cl CHAR BH8 .... 40 A4

E

Eagle Rd BKME/WDN BH12 .... 75 E1
Earle Rd WBNE BH4 .... 2 A7
Earlham Dr PSTN BH14 .... 74 A1
Earlsdon Wy CHCH/BSGR BH23 .... 64 B2
East Av NMIL/BTOS BH25 .... 65 E3
  TWDS BH3 .... 57 C4
East Bank Rd BROC SO42 .... 15 E4
East Borough WIMB BH21 .... 16 B4
East Cliff Wy CHCH/BSGR BH23 .... 63 G3
East Cl NMIL/BTOS BH25.... 65 E3
Eastcott Cl LTDN BH7 .... 60 A2
Eastern Rd LYMN SO41 .... 50 D3
Eastern Wy LYMN SO41 .... 82 D1
Easter Rd MOOR/WNTN BH9 .... 39 G5
Eastfield Ct RGWD BH24 .... 9 E4
Eastfield La RGWD BH24 .... 9 E3
East Hl LYMN SO41 .... 51 E3
East Howe La NBNE BH10 .... 38 C3
Eastlake Av BKME/WDN BH12 .... 55 H4
Eastlands NMIL/BTOS BH25 .... 66 B1
East La LYMN SO41 .... 68 C1
East Overcliff Dr BMTH BH1.... 3 K5
East Quay Rd PLE BH15 .... 72 C4
East St PLE BH15 .... 72 C3
  WIMB BH21 .... 16 B5
East View Rd RGWD BH24 .... 8 D4
East Wy CHAR BH8 .... 58 D1
  WIMB BH21 .... 34 B2
Eastwood Av FERN BH22 .... 20 A3
Eastworth Rd VWD BH31 .... 4 A1
Eaton Rd CCLF BH13 .... 75 E3
Ebor Cl FERN BH22 .... 28 A2
Ebor Rd BKME/WDN BH12 .... 56 B4
Eccles Rd PLE BH15 .... 72 A3
Eden Gv WIMB BH21 .... 24 D1
Edgarton Rd CFDH BH17 .... 35 H4
Edgehill Rd MOOR/WNTN BH9.... 58 A2
Edgemoor Rd FERN BH22 .... 10 D5
Edifred Rd MOOR/WNTN BH9 .... 39 G3
Edmunds Cl NMIL/BTOS BH25 .... 66 A1
Edward Rd BWD BH11 .... 38 B4
  CHCH/BSGR BH23 .... 62 D2
  PSTN BH14 .... 56 A5
Edwina Cl RGWD BH24 .... 9 E2
Edwina Dr CFDH BH17.... 35 F5
Efford Wy LYMN SO41 .... 50 B5
Egdon Ct UPTN BH16 .... 52 D3
Egdon Dr WIMB BH21 .... 25 E4
Egerton Gdns BMTH BH1 .... 59 F4
Egerton Rd CHAR BH8 .... 59 F4
Egmont Cl RGWD BH24 .... 12 C4
Egmont Dr RGWD BH24 .... 12 C4
Egmont Gdns RGWD BH24 .... 12 C4
Egmont Rd UPTN BH16 .... 70 D1
Elderberry La CHCH/BSGR BH23 .. 62 D4
Eldon Av NMIL/BTOS BH25 .... 65 G2
Eldon Cl NMIL/BTOS BH25.... 65 G2
Eldon Pl WBNE BH4 .... 75 F2
Eldon Rd MOOR/WNTN BH9 .... 58 A1
Eleanor Dr BWD BH11 .... 37 F2
Eleanor Gdns
  CHCH/BSGR BH23 .... 61 E2
Elfin Dr FERN BH22 .... 19 G2
Elgar Rd NBNE BH10 .... 38 D3
Elgin Rd PSTN BH14 .... 73 H3
  WBNE BH4 .... 57 H5
Elise Cl LTDN BH7 .... 60 B2
Elizabeth Av CHCH/BSGR BH23 .... 61 F2
Elizabeth Crs LYMN SO41 .... 48 C5
Elizabeth Rd PLE BH15 .... 72 D2
  WIMB BH21 .... 16 C4
Elkhams Cl LYMN SO41 .... 68 B1
Ellery Gv LYMN SO41 .... 51 E2
Ellesfield Dr FERN BH22 .... 27 H1
Ellingham Rd NMIL/BTOS BH25 .... 65 F2
Elliott Rd BWD BH11 .... 37 G4
Elm Av CHCH/BSGR BH23 .... 61 E1
  LYMN SO41 .... 69 G1
  NMIL/BTOS BH25.... 47 E5
Elmers Wy CHCH/BSGR BH23.... 33 F3
Elmes Rd MOOR/WNTN BH9.... 39 E5
Elm Gdns WBNE BH4 .... 57 G5
Elmgate Dr LTDN BH7 .... 59 H3
Elmhurst Rd BWD BH11 .... 38 A2
  FERN BH22 .... 10 B5
Elmhurst Wy FERN BH22 .... 10 B5
Elmore Dr RGWD BH24 .... 6 C5
Elms Av PSTN BH14 .... 73 G4
Elms Cl PSTN BH14 .... 73 G4

Elmstead Rd CCLF BH13 .... 74 D5
Elms Wy SBNE BH6 .... 79 E1
Elm Tree Wk FERN BH22 .... 28 A4
Elmwood Wy CHCH/BSGR BH23 .. 64 D2
Elphinstone Rd CHCH/BSGR BH23 64 D2
Eltham Cl LTDN BH7 .... 60 B2
Elvin Cl LYMN SO41 .... 48 B3
Embankment Wy RGWD BH24 .... 8 B3
Emberley Cl FERN BH22 .... 20 C2
Emerson Cl PLE BH15 .... 72 C3
Emerson Rd PLE BH15 .... 72 C3
Emily Cl CHCH/BSGR BH23 .... 61 G1
Emsworth Rd LYMN SO41 .... 51 E3
Encombe Cl BKME/WDN BH12 .... 56 D2
Endfield Cl CHCH/BSGR BH23 .... 61 F1
Endfield Rd CHCH/BSGR BH23 .. 61 F2
  MOOR/WNTN BH9 .... 39 G5
Enfield Av PLE BH15 .... 55 F4
Enfield Crs PLE BH15 .... 55 E4
Enfield Rd PLE BH15 .... 55 E4
Englands Wy BWD BH11 .... 37 F3
Ensbury Av NBNE BH10 .... 57 H1
Ensbury Cl NBNE BH10 .... 57 H1
Ensbury Park Rd
  MOOR/WNTN BH9 .... 39 G5
Erica Dr WIMB BH21 .... 34 B1
Ericksen Rd NBNE BH10 .... 38 C4
Erpingham Rd
  BKME/WDN BH12 .... 57 E5
Esmonde Wy CFDH BH17 .... 55 F2
Esplanade CCLF BH13 .... 85 H1
  PLE BH15 .... 72 C5
Essex Av CHCH/BSGR BH23 .... 42 B5
Ethelbert Rd WIMB BH21 .... 16 D5
Eton Gdns WBNE BH4 .... 2 A1
Ettrick Rd CCLF BH13.... 75 E4
Eucalyptus Av RGWD BH24 .... 12 A4
Euston Gv RGWD BH24 .... 8 D5
Evans Cl BWD BH11 .... 56 D1
  RGWD BH24 .... 8 C5
Evelyn Rd MOOR/WNTN BH9 .... 58 C5
Evening Gld FERN BH22 .... 28 A1
Everest Rd CHCH/BSGR BH23 .... 62 C2
Everglades Cl FERN BH22 .... 19 H2
Evergreens RGWD BH24 .... 11 G1
Evering Av BKME/WDN BH12 .... 56 A1
Evering Gdns BKME/WDN BH12 .. 56 A1
Everlea Cl LYMN SO41 .... 68 B1
Everon Gdns NMIL/BTOS BH25 .. 66 B1
Evershot Rd CHAR BH8 .... 59 G1
Everton Rd LYMN SO41 .... 48 B3
Evesham Cl LTDN BH7 .... 60 A2
Exbury Dr BWD BH11 .... 37 H2
Excelsior Rd PSTN BH14 .... 74 A3
Exeter Crs WCLF BH2 .... 3 C5
Exeter Park Rd WCLF BH2 .... 3 C5
Exeter Rd WCLF BH2 .... 3 C4
Exton Rd SBNE BH6 .... 60 D3

F

Factory Rd UPTN BH16 .... 53 F4
Fairfield CHCH/BSGR BH23 .... 61 H3
Fairfield Cl LYMN SO41 .... 51 E4
  WIMB BH21 .... 17 E4
Fairfield Rd NMIL/BTOS BH25 .... 65 G3
  WIMB BH21 .... 16 D5
Fairlea Rd LYMN SO41 .... 51 E3
Fairlie RGWD BH24 .... 9 E2
Fairlie Pk RGWD BH24 .... 8 D2
Fairmile Rd CHCH/BSGR BH23 .... 61 G1
Fairview Crs WIMB BH21 .... 35 E2
Fairview Dr WIMB BH21 .... 35 E2
Fairview Rd WIMB BH21 .... 35 E2
Fairway Dr CHCH/BSGR BH23 .... 61 F4
Fairway Rd PSTN BH14 .... 74 A5
Fairways FERN BH22 .... 20 B3
The Fairway NMIL/BTOS BH25 .... 66 B3
Fairwood Rd VWD BH31 .... 5 E3
Falcon Dr CHCH/BSGR BH23.... 63 F5
Falconer Dr PLE BH15 .... 71 G1
Fancy Rd BKME/WDN BH12 .... 55 H2
Farcroft Rd PSTN BH14.... 55 H5
Farm Cl RGWD BH24 .... 8 C3
Farmdene Cl
  CHCH/BSGR BH23 .... 63 H2
Farmers Wk LYMN SO41 .... 68 B2
  WIMB BH21 .... 16 B3
Farm La CHCH/BSGR BH23 .... 63 E5
Farm La North NMIL/BTOS BH25.. 66 A4
Farm La South NMIL/BTOS BH25.. 66 A3
Farnham Rd BKME/WDN BH12 .... 57 E3
Farnleys Md LYMN SO41 .... 51 E5
Farriers Cl WIMB BH21 .... 17 H3
Farwell Cl CHCH/BSGR BH23 .... 43 E4
Farwell Rd BKME/WDN BH12.... 37 E5

Fatherstfield *DRUL* SO42 .... **14** D3
Fawcett Rd *NMIL/BTOS* BH25 .... **46** D5
Fawley Gn *CHAR* BH8 .... **40** B4
Fawn Gdns *NMIL/BTOS* BH25 ..... **46** D3
Felton Crs *CHCH/BSGR* BH23 ..... **64** B2
Felton Rd *PSTN* BH14 .... **55** F5
Fenleigh Cl *NMIL/BTOS* BH25 .... **66** B2
Fennel Gdns *LYMN* SO41 .... **50** C5
Fenton Rd *SBNE* BH6 .... **60** C4
Fern Barrow *BKME/WDN* BH12 ... **57** F2
Fern Cl *CHCH/BSGR* BH23 .... **43** E5
Ferncroft Gdns *NBNE* BH10 .... **38** D2
Ferncroft Rd *NBNE* BH10 .... **38** D2
Ferndale Rd *NMIL/BTOS* BH25 ... **47** F3
FerndownStour & Forest Trail
  WIMB **18** A2
Fernglade *NMIL/BTOS* BH25....... **47** E4
Fernheath Cl *BWD* BH11 .... **38** A5
Fernheath Rd *BWD* BH11 .... **38** A4
Fernhill Cl *CFDH* BH17 .... **36** C5
Fernhill La *NMIL/BTOS* BH25 ..... **47** E3
Fernhill Rd *NMIL/BTOS* BH25 .... **47** E3
Fernlea Av *CHAR* BH22 .... **19** H5
Fernlea Rd *FERN* BH22 .... **19** H5
  RGWD BH24 .... **11** G2
Fernlea Gdns *FERN* BH22 .... **19** H5
Fernside Av *PSTN* BH14 .... **74** C4
Fernside Rd *FERN* BH22 .... **10** A4
  MOOR/WNTN BH9 .... **57** H2
  PLE BH15 .... **73** E1
Fernway Cl *WIMB* BH21 .... **17** H5
Fernwood Cl *RGWD* BH24 .... **12** B1
Ferris Av *CHAR* BH8 .... **40** A5
Ferris Cl *CHAR* BH8 .... **40** A5
Ferris Pl *CHAR* BH8 .... **40** B5
Ferry Rd *PLE* BH15 .... **72** B4
  SBNE BH6 .... **79** F2
Ferry Wy *CCLF* BH13 .... **84** D5
Feversham Av *CHAR* BH8 .... **59** H3
Fibbards Rd *BROC* SO42 .... **14** D3
Field Pl *NMIL/BTOS* BH25 .... **65** E2
Field Wk *LYMN* SO41 .... **50** C5
Field Wy *CHCH/BSGR* BH23....... **63** H1
Fieldway *RGWD* BH24 .... **8** D3
Filton Rd *LYMN* SO41 .... **50** C5
Finchfield Av *BWD* BH11 .... **37** H1
Fir Av *NMIL/BTOS* BH25 .... **47** F5
Firbank Rd *MOOR/WNTN* BH9 ... **58** D2
Fir Cl *FERN* BH22 .... **10** A3
Firmain Rd *BKME/WDN* BH12 ... **56** B1
Firmount Cl *LYMN* SO41 .... **50** C5
Firs Glen Rd *FERN* BH22 .... **10** A4
  MOOR/WNTN BH9 .... **57** H2
  VWD BH31 .... **4** B3
Firshill *CHCH/BSGR* BH23 .... **64** A1
Firside Rd *WIMB* BH21................ **34** A3
Firs La *PSTN* BH14 .... **73** H5
The Firs *BMTH* BH1 .... **3** K2
First Marine Av
  NMIL/BTOS BH25 .... **65** H3
Fir Tree Cl *RGWD* BH24 .... **11** F4
Firtree Crs *LYMN* SO41 .... **48** B4
Fir Tree La *CHCH/BSGR* BH23 ... **63** H1
Fir Vale Rd *BMTH* BH1 .... **3** H5
Fisherman's Av *SBNE* BH6 .... **78** B1
Fishermans Rd *PLE* BH15 .... **72** C4
Fitzharris Av *MOOR/WNTN* BH9 .. **58** C3
Fitzmaurice Rd
  CHCH/BSGR BH23 .... **61** E2
Fitzpain Cl *FERN* BH22............... **27** H2
Fitzpain Rd *FERN* BH22 .... **27** H2
Fitzwilliam Cl *BWD* BH11 .... **37** G2
Fitzworth Av *UPTN* BH16 .... **71** E1
Flaghead Chine Rd *CCLF* BH13 ... **85** G1
Flaghead Rd *CCLF* BH13 .... **85** G1
Flambard Av *CHCH/BSGR* BH23 .. **61** F1
Flambard Rd *PSTN* BH14 .... **74** A4
Flazen Cl *BWD* BH11 .... **37** F4
Fleets La *PLE* BH15 .... **54** C4
Fletcher Cl *NBNE* BH10 .... **38** D4
Fletcher Rd *NBNE* BH10 .... **38** D4
Flexford La *LYMN* SO41 .... **49** E1
Floral Farm *WIMB* BH21 .... **25** C2
Florence Rd *BOSC* BH5 .... **77** G1
  PSTN BH14 .... **74** B4
Floriston Gdns *NMIL/BTOS* BH25.. **47** H4
Flushards *LYMN* SO41 .... **51** H1
Folly Farm La *RGWD* BH24 .... **7** C5
Fontmell Rd *BDST* BH18 .... **35** G5
Footners La *CHCH/BSGR* BH23 .. **43** E5
Ford Cl *FERN* BH22 .... **20** B2
Ford La *FERN* BH22 .... **20** C2
Forest Cl *CHCH/BSGR* BH23 ..... **63** H1
  VWD BH31 .... **4** D1
Forest Court Hills *RGWD* BH24 .. **9** F5
Forest Edge Cl *RGWD* BH24 ..... **11** F1

Forest Edge Dr *RGWD* BH24....... **11** F1
Forest Gate Gdns *LYMN* SO41 ... **69** H1
Forest Glade Cl *BROC* SO42 ...... **14** B3
Forest Hall *BROC* SO42 .... **15** E3
Forestlake Av *RGWD* BH24 .... **9** F5
Forest La *RGWD* BH24 .... **9** G5
  VWD **4** A1
Forest Oak Dr *NMIL/BTOS* BH25 .. **47** F3
Forest Park Rd *BROC* SO42 .... **14** C2
Forest Pines *NMIL/BTOS* BH25 .. **47** E3
Forest Ri *CHCH/BSGR* BH23 ..... **44** D5
Forest Rd *CCLF* BH13 .... **75** E3
  FERN BH22 .... **10** B3
Forestside Gdns *RGWD* BH24..... **9** E2
The Forestside *VWD* BH31 .... **5** F3
Forest Vw *BROC* SO42 .... **14** B3
  NMIL/BTOS BH25...................... **46** B2
Forest View Cl
  MOOR/WNTN BH9 .... **39** G5
Forest View Dr *WIMB* BH21 .... **19** E3
Forest View Rd
  MOOR/WNTN BH9 .... **39** G4
Forest Wy *CHCH/BSGR* BH23 .... **63** H1
  LYMN SO41 .... **68** B1
  WIMB BH21 .... **19** E4
Forsyth Gdns *NBNE* BH10 .... **57** G1
Fortescue Rd *BKME/WDN* BH12 .. **56** B3
  TWDS BH3 .... **58** C4
Forward Dr *LYMN* SO41 .... **50** C5
Fountain Wy *CHCH/BSGR* BH23 .. **61** H4
Four Wells Rd *WIMB* BH21 .... **17** C2
Foxbury Rd *RGWD* BH24 .... **11** H5
Foxcote Gdns
  NMIL/BTOS BH25 .... **46** D4
Foxcroft Dr *WIMB* BH21 .... **17** H4
Foxes Cl *VWD* BH31 .... **4** B3
Fox Fld *LYMN* SO41 .... **68** B1
Foxglove Cl *CHCH/BSGR* BH23 .. **63** C2
Foxglove Pl *NMIL/BTOS* BH25 ... **47** H3
Foxgloves *UPTN* BH16 .... **52** D3
Foxhills *VWD* BH31 .... **4** D2
Foxholes Rd *PLE* BH15 .... **55** F4
  SBNE BH6 .... **79** F1
Fox La *WIMB* BH21 .... **18** A4
Fox Pond La *LYMN* SO41 .... **50** C5
Foxwood Av *CHCH/BSGR* BH23 .. **62** D5
Frampton Cl *NMIL/BTOS* BH25 .. **47** G2
Frampton Pl *RGWD* BH24 .... **8** C4
Frampton Rd *MOOR/WNTN* BH9 .. **58** C2
Frances Rd *BMTH* BH1 .... **77** E1
Francis Av *BWD* BH11 .... **37** F4
Francis Rd *BKME/WDN* BH12 .... **56** C5
Frankland Crs *PSTN* BH14.......... **74** C2
Franklin Rd *MOOR/WNTN* BH9 .. **39** G4
  NMIL/BTOS BH25...................... **47** G3
Franklyn Cl *UPTN* BH16 .... **52** D3
Frankston Rd *SBNE* BH6 .... **78** C1
Fraser Rd *BKME/WDN* BH12 ...... **56** D1
Freda Rd *CHCH/BSGR* BH23 ...... **61** F4
Frederica Rd *MOOR/WNTN* BH9 .. **58** A2
Freemans Cl *WIMB* BH21 .... **17** H3
Freemans La *WIMB* BH21 .... **17** H4
French Rd *CFDH* BH17 .... **54** B1
French's Farm Rd *UPTN* BH16 ... **52** C3
Frensham Cl *NBNE* BH10 .... **39** E4
Freshwater Dr *PLE* BH15 .... **71** F2
  PLE BH15 .... **71** F2
Freshwater Rd
  CHCH/BSGR BH23 .... **63** C4
Friars Rd *CHCH/BSGR* BH23 ..... **63** F4
Friars Wk *NMIL/BTOS* BH25 ...... **66** A2
Fritham Gdns *CHAR* BH8 .... **40** B4
Frobisher Av *BKME/WDN* BH12 .. **56** D1
Frobisher Cl *CHCH/BSGR* BH23 .. **62** D4
  RGWD BH24 .... **9** E2
Fromond Cl *LYMN* SO41 .... **51** E2
Frost Rd *BWD* BH11 .... **37** H4
Froud Wy *WIMB* BH21 .... **34** A3
Fryer Cl *BWD* BH11 .... **38** B2
Fryer's Copse *WIMB* BH21 .... **18** A3
Frys La *LYMN* SO41 .... **68** B1
Fullerton Rd *LYMN* SO41 .... **50** C3
Fulmar Rd *CHCH/BSGR* BH23 ... **63** E5
Fulwood Av *BWD* BH11................ **37** G2
The Furlong *RGWD* BH24 .... **8** B4
Furnell Rd *PLE* BH15 .... **72** D4
Furzebrook Cl *CFDH* BH17 .... **36** A5
Furze Cft *NMIL/BTOS* BH25 .... **66** A1
Furzehill *WIMB* BH21 .... **16** C1
Furze Hill Dr *PSTN* BH14 .... **74** A4
Furzey Rd *UPTN* BH16 .... **52** D4

G

Gainsborough Av
  NMIL/BTOS BH25...................... **47** F2

Gainsborough Rd *LTDN* BH7 ...... **59** H5
  RGWD BH24 .... **11** G1
Gallop Wy *BKME/WDN* BH12 ..... **57** G3
Galloway Rd *PLE* BH15 .... **71** F1
Gallows Dr *FERN* BH22 .... **27** H3
Galton Av *CHCH/BSGR* BH23 .... **61** F4
Garden Cl *NMIL/BTOS* BH25 ...... **66** A1
Garden-lane *RGWD* BH24 .... **11** G3
Gardens Crs *PSTN* BH14 .... **73** H5
Gardens Rd *PLE* BH15 .... **73** H5
Garden Wk *FERN* BH22 .... **20** A2
Gardner Rd *CHCH/BSGR* BH23 .. **61** E2
  RGWD BH24 .... **8** D5
Garfield Av *BMTH* BH1 .... **59** F5
Garland Rd *PLE* BH15 .... **72** D1
Garrow Dr *LYMN* SO41 .... **51** E2
Garsdale Cl *BWD* BH11 .... **38** A1
Garth Cl *RGWD* BH24 .... **11** F2
Garth Rd *MOOR/WNTN* BH9 ..... **58** C1
Gaydon Ri *BWD* BH11 .... **37** G3
Geneva Av *SBNE* BH6 .... **60** D5
Genoa Cl *LYMN* SO41 .... **69** C1
George Rd *LYMN* SO41 .... **68** A5
Georgian Cl *RGWD* BH24 .... **8** C3
Georgian Wy *NBNE* BH10 .... **39** F3
Georgina Cl *BKME/WDN* BH12 .. **57** G2
Gerald Rd *TWDS* BH3 .... **58** C4
Germaine Cl *CHCH/BSGR* BH23 .. **64** B2
Gervis Crs *PSTN* BH14 .... **73** G1
Gervis Pl *BMTH* BH1 .... **3** C4
Gervis Rd *BMTH* BH1 .... **3** K4
Gibson Rd *CFDH* BH17 .... **55** E3
Giddylake *WIMB* BH21 .... **16** C3
Gilbert Cl *LYMN* SO41 .... **50** D5
Gilbert Rd *CHAR* BH8 .... **59** F4
Gillam Rd *NBNE* BH10 .... **38** D2
Gillett Rd *BKME/WDN* BH12 ...... **57** G3
Gillingham Cl
  MOOR/WNTN BH9 .... **40** A3
Gillingham Rd *LYMN* SO41 .... **82** B1
Gladdis Rd *BWD* BH11 .... **37** H3
Gladelands Cl *BDST* BH18 .... **34** C3
Gladelands Wy *BDST* BH18 .... **34** C3
The Glade *RGWD* BH24 .... **11** G1
Gladstone Cl *CHCH/BSGR* BH23 .. **62** B4
Gladstone Rd *BKME/WDN* BH12 .. **56** A5
  LTDN BH7 .... **59** H5
Gladstone Rd East *LTDN* BH7 ... **59** H5
Gladstone Rd West *BMTH* BH1 .. **59** C5
Glamis Av *NBNE* BH10 .... **39** E2
Gleadowe Av *CHCH/BSGR* BH23 .. **61** H4
Glebefields *LYMN* SO41 .... **68** B5
Glenair Av *PSTN* BH14 .... **73** G2
Glenair Rd *PSTN* BH14 .... **73** G2
Glenavon *NMIL/BTOS* BH25 ...... **47** F5
Glenavon Rd *CHCH/BSGR* BH23 .. **64** B1
Glen Cl *NMIL/BTOS* BH25 .... **65** F2
Glencoe Rd *BKME/WDN* BH12 ... **56** B5
  LTDN BH7 .... **59** H3
Glendale Av *FERN* BH22 .... **19** H3
Glendale Cl *CHCH/BSGR* BH23 .. **41** H4
  WIMB BH21 .... **16** C4
Glendale Rd *SBNE* BH6 .... **79** C1
Glendon Av *NBNE* BH10 .... **38** C1
Glendrive *NMIL/BTOS* BH25 ...... **65** C2
Gleneagles Av *PSTN* BH14 .... **74** B3
Gleneagles Cl *FERN* BH22 .... **20** B3
Glenferness Av *TWDS* BH3 .... **57** H4
Glen Fern Rd *BMTH* BH1 .... **3** J3
Glengariff Rd *PSTN* BH14 .... **74** A3
Glengarry *NMIL/BTOS* BH25 ...... **47** G5
Glengarry Wy *CHCH/BSGR* BH23 .. **63** C4
Glenives Cl *RGWD* BH24 .... **11** H2
Glenme Adows Dr *BWD* BH11 .... **38** B2
Glenmoor Cl *NBNE* BH10 .... **57** H1
Glenmoor Rd *FERN* BH22 .... **27** H1
  MOOR/WNTN BH9 .... **57** H1
Glenmount Dr *PSTN* BH14 .... **55** H5
Glen Rd *BOSC* BH5 .... **77** G1
  PSTN BH14 .... **73** H1
Glenroyd Gdns *SBNE* BH6 .... **78** B1
Glenside *NMIL/BTOS* BH25 .... **64** D3
Glen Spey *NMIL/BTOS* BH25 ..... **47** H5
The Glen *CCLF* BH13 .... **74** C5
Glenville Cl *CHCH/BSGR* BH23.... **45** H5
Glenville Gdns *NBNE* BH10 .... **38** C5
Glenville Rd *CHCH/BSGR* BH23 .. **45** H5
  NBNE BH10 .... **38** C5
Glenwood Cl *FERN* BH22 .... **10** A4
Glenwood La *FERN* BH22 .... **10** A4
Glenwood Rd *FERN* BH22 .... **10** A4
  VWD BH31 .... **4** A3
Glenwood Wy *FERN* BH22 .... **10** A4
Glissons *FERN* BH22 .... **27** H2
Gloucester Rd *BKME/WDN* BH12 .. **56** C5
  LTDN BH7 .... **59** H5
Glynville Cl *WIMB* BH21 .... **17** C2
Glynville Rd *WIMB* BH21 .... **17** C2

Goathorn Cl *UPTN* BH16 .... **71** F1
Godmanston Cl *CFDH* BH17 ...... **55** G1
Godshill Cl *CHAR* BH8 .... **40** B4
Golden Crs *LYMN* SO41 .... **68** B1
Goldenleas Dr *BWD* BH11 .... **37** F3
Goldfinch Cl *NMIL/BTOS* BH25 .. **46** D5
Goldfinch Rd *CFDH* BH17 .... **53** G2
Gold Mead Cl *LYMN* SO41 .... **51** E5
Golf Links Rd *BDST* BH18 .... **35** F2
  FERN BH22 .... **20** A4
Goliath Rd *PLE* BH15 .... **71** F3
Good Rd *BKME/WDN* BH12 .... **56** A3
Gordon Mt *CHCH/BSGR* BH23 .. **64** D1
Gordon Rd *BKME/WDN* BH12 .... **57** E5
  BMTH BH1 .... **77** F1
  CHCH/BSGR BH23 .... **64** C2
  LYMN SO41 .... **50** C4
  WIMB BH21 .... **17** E5
Gordon Rd South
  BKME/WDN BH12 .... **75** E1
Gordon Wy *CHCH/BSGR* BH23 .. **62** A1
Gore Rd *NMIL/BTOS* BH25......... **46** C5
Gorey Rd *BKME/WDN* BH12 ...... **56** B1
Gorleston Rd *BKME/WDN* BH12 .. **56** D5
Gorley Rd *RGWD* BH24 .... **9** E3
Gorsecliff Rd *NBNE* BH10 .... **57** H1
Gorse Cl *NMIL/BTOS* BH25 .... **47** H3
  RGWD BH24 .... **11** F2
Gorsefield Rd *NMIL/BTOS* BH25.. **47** F2
Gorse Hill Cl *PLE* BH15 .... **55** E5
Gorse Hill Crs *PLE* BH15 .... **55** E5
Gorse Hill Rd *PLE* BH15 .... **55** E5
Gorseland Ct *FERN* BH22 .... **28** A1
Gorse La *UPTN* BH16 .... **53** E3
Gorse Rd *WIMB* BH21 .... **34** A2
Gort Rd *BWD* BH11 .... **38** B4
  CFDH BH17 .... **54** A1
Gosling Cl *CFDH* BH17 .... **55** F3
Gosport St *LYMN* SO41 .... **51** F3
Gough Crs *CFDH* BH17 .... **35** F5
Grafton Cl *CHCH/BSGR* BH23 ... **62** B4
  TWDS BH3 .... **58** C3
Grafton Gdns *LYMN* SO41 .... **69** C1
Grafton Rd *TWDS* BH3 .... **58** C4
Grammar School La *WIMB* BH21.. **16** B5
Granby Rd *MOOR/WNTN* BH9 ... **39** G3
Grand Av *SBNE* BH6 .... **78** C1
Grange Cl *LYMN* SO41 .... **68** C2
Grange Gdns
  BKME/WDN BH12 .... **56** C3
Grange Rd *BDST* BH18 .... **35** E3
  CHCH/BSGR BH23 .... **63** F3
  RGWD BH24 .... **11** F4
  SBNE BH6 .... **78** D2
The Grange *LYMN* SO41............. **68** C2
Grantham Rd *BMTH* BH1 .... **59** C5
Grantley Rd *BOSC* BH5 .... **77** H1
Grant's Av *BMTH* BH1 .... **59** F4
Grants Cl *BMTH* BH1 .... **59** F4
Granville Rd *BOSC* BH5 .... **60** A5
  PSTN BH14 .... **55** H5
Grasmere Cl *CHCH/BSGR* BH23 .. **41** H4
Grasmere Gdns
  NMIL/BTOS BH25...................... **47** F2
Grasmere Rd *BOSC* BH5 .... **78** A1
  CCLF BH13 .... **84** D5
Gravel Hl *WIMB* BH21 .... **24** D3
Gravel La *RGWD* BH24 .... **8** C3
Gray Cl *CFDH* BH17 .... **55** F2
Graycot Cl *NBNE* BH10 .... **38** C2
Grebe Cl *CFDH* BH17 .... **53** G2
  CHCH/BSGR BH23 .... **63** E4
  LYMN SO41 .... **82** C1
Greenacre *NMIL/BTOS* BH25 ..... **66** A2
Greenacre Cl *UPTN* BH16 .... **53** E4
Greenacres Cl *NBNE* BH10 .... **28** A5
Green Acres Cl *RGWD* BH24 ..... **12** D1
Greenbanks Cl *LYMN* SO41 ...... **68** B5
Green Bottom *WIMB* BH21 .... **17** C2
Green Cl *PLE* BH15 .... **72** D4
Greenclose La *WIMB* BH21 .... **16** D5
Greenfield Gdns
  NMIL/BTOS BH25...................... **66** B2
Greenfield Rd *PLE* BH15 .... **55** E4
Greenfinch Cl *CFDH* BH17 .... **53** H1
Greenfinch Wk *RGWD* BH24 .... **9** E5
Greenhayes *BDST* BH18 .... **35** C5
Greenhays Ri *WIMB* BH21 .... **16** C4
Greenhill Cl *WIMB* BH21 .... **16** D3
Greenhill La *WIMB* BH21 .... **16** D3
Greenhill Rd *WIMB* BH21 .... **16** D3
Green La *FERN* BH22 .... **27** E3
  NBNE BH10 .... **38** C4
  NMIL/BTOS BH25...................... **66** B3
  RGWD BH24 .... **8** C4
  RGWD BH24 .... **13** H1

Greenmead Av *LYMN* SO41 .... 68 B1
Green Rd *MOOR/WNTN* BH9 .... 58 C2
  PLE BH15 .... 72 C3
Greensleeves Av *BDST* BH18 .... 35 F1
Greensome Dr *FERN* BH22 .... 20 B3
Greenway Cl *LYMN* SO41 .... 50 C3
Greenway Crs *UPTN* BH16 .... 52 C5
Greenways *CHCH/BSGR* BH23 ...... 64 A2
  LYMN SO41 .... 68 A3
Greenways Av *CHAR* BH8 .... 40 A4
Greenways Rd *BROC* SO42 .... 15 E3
Greenwood Av *FERN* BH22 .... 19 H3
  PSTN BH14 .... 74 A5
Greenwood Copse
  RGWD BH24 .... 12 A2
Greenwood Rd
  MOOR/WNTN BH9 .... 58 A1
Greenwoods *NMIL/BTOS* BH25 ... 66 B1
Greenwood Wy *RGWD* BH24 .... 11 H2
Grenfell Rd *MOOR/WNTN* BH9 .... 39 F4
Grenville Cl *RGWD* BH24 .... 9 E2
Grenville Rd *WIMB* BH21 .... 16 D5
Gresham Rd *MOOR/WNTN* BH9 ... 58 C1
Greystoke Av *BWD* BH11 .... 37 H1
Griffiths Gdns *BWD* BH11 .... 38 B2
Grigg La *BROC* SO42 .... 15 E3
Grosvenor Cl *RGWD* BH24 .... 11 F1
Grosvenor Gdns *BMTH* BH1 .... 77 C1
Grosvenor Rd *WBNE* BH4 .... 2 A4
Groveley Rd *CHCH/BSGR* BH23 ... 62 C4
  WBNE BH4 .... 75 F3
Grovely Av *BOSC* BH5 .... 77 H1
Grove Pastures *LYMN* SO41 .... 51 H4
Grove Pl *LYMN* SO41 .... 51 H4
Grove Rd *BKME/WDN* BH12 .... 55 H4
  BMTH BH1 .... 3 K4
  LYMN SO41 .... 51 H4
  NMIL/BTOS BH25 .... 45 H4
  WIMB BH21 .... 16 C5
Grove Rd East *CHCH/BSGR* BH23.. 61 G2
Grove Rd West
  CHCH/BSGR BH23 .... 61 F2
The Grove *CHCH/BSGR* BH23 ...... 61 E1
  FERN BH22 .... 19 G5
  MOOR/WNTN BH9 .... 58 C3
  VWD BH31 .... 4 C3
Grower Gdns *BWD* BH11 .... 38 A3
Guernsey Rd *BKME/WDN* BH12 ... 56 B1
Guest Av *BKME/WDN* BH12 .... 56 B1
Guest Cl *BKME/WDN* BH12 .... 57 E4
Guest Rd *UPTN* BH16 .... 52 D3
Guildhill Rd *SBNE* BH6 .... 79 E1
Gulliver Cl *PSTN* BH14 .... 74 A5
Gunville Crs *MOOR/WNTN* BH9 ... 39 H4
Gurjun Cl *UPTN* BH16 .... 52 C2
Gurney Rd *WIMB* BH21 .... 34 C1
Gussage Rd *BKME/WDN* BH12 .... 56 C2
Gwenlyn Rd *UPTN* BH16 .... 53 E4
Gwynne Rd *BKME/WDN* BH12 ...... 56 C5
Gypsy La *RGWD* BH24 .... 8 D3

Haarlem Ms *CHCH/BSGR* BH23 .... 62 B3
Hadden Rd *CHAR* BH8 .... 59 F2
Hadley Wy *BDST* BH18 .... 34 C4
Hadow Rd *BWD* BH11 .... 38 C4
Hadrian Cl *FERN* BH22 .... 27 H2
Haglane Copse *LYMN* SO41 .... 50 B5
Hahnemann Rd *WCLF* BH2 .... 2 E5
Haig Av *PSTN* BH14 .... 74 C4
Hainault Dr *VWD* BH31 .... 4 C2
Halking Rd *CHCH/BSGR* BH23 ..... 62 F5
Hale Av *NMIL/BTOS* BH25 .... 47 F5
Hale Gdns *NMIL/BTOS* BH25 .... 47 F5
Halewood Wy *CHCH/BSGR* BH23.. 61 G2
Halifax Wy *CHCH/BSGR* BH23 ...... 63 F3
Hall Rd *BWD* BH11 .... 37 H4
Halstock Crs *CFDH* BH17 .... 35 H5
Halter Pth *PLE* BH15 .... 71 G2
Halter Ri *WIMB* BH21 .... 18 A3
Halton Cl *CHCH/BSGR* BH23 .... 33 F4
Hambledon Gdns *SBNE* BH6 .... 60 C4
Hambledon Rd *LTDN* BH7 .... 60 B3
  SBNE BH6 .... 60 C4
Hamble Rd *PLE* BH15 .... 55 F5
Hamilton Cl *BMTH* BH1 .... 59 F5
  CHCH/BSGR BH23 .... 80 D1
  PLE BH15 .... 71 G3
Hamilton Cl *LYMN* SO41 .... 82 A1
Hamilton Crs *PLE* BH15 .... 71 G3
Hamilton Rd *BMTH* BH1 .... 59 F5
  PLE BH15 .... 71 G3
  WIMB BH21 .... 34 C2
Ham La *WIMB* BH21 .... 18 A4
Hampden La *SBNE* BH6 .... 60 B5

Hampshire Cl *CHCH/BSGR* BH23 .. 42 B5
Hampshire Hatches La
  RGWD BH24 .... 13 C2
Hampton Dr *RGWD* BH24 .... 8 D2
Hanham Rd *WIMB* BH21 .... 16 C4
  WIMB BH21 .... 34 B2
Hankinson Rd
  MOOR/WNTN BH9 .... 58 C2
Hanlon Cl *BWD* BH11 .... 38 A3
Hannington Rd *LTDN* BH7 .... 60 A5
Harbeck Rd *CHAR* BH8 .... 40 A4
Harbour Cl *CCLF* BH13 .... 85 F2
Harbour Crs *CHCH/BSGR* BH23 ... 62 C5
Harbour Hill Crs *PLE* BH15 .... 55 F5
Harbour Hill Rd *PLE* BH15............. 55 E5
Harbour Rd *SBNE* BH6 .... 79 C2
Harbour View Cl *PSTN* BH14 .... 55 G5
Harbour View Rd *PSTN* BH14 ...... 55 G5
Harcombe Cl *CFDH* BH17 .... 36 A4
Harcourt Rd *BOSC* BH5 .... 60 A5
Hardy Cl *FERN* BH22 .... 10 B5
  NMIL/BTOS BH25 .... 46 D4
Hardy Crs *WIMB* BH21 .... 24 D1
Hardy Rd *FERN* BH22 .... 10 B5
  PSTN BH14 .... 74 B5
Hare La *NMIL/BTOS* BH25 .... 47 H4
Hares Gn *LTDN* BH7 .... 60 A2
Harewood Av *LTDN* BH7 .... 59 H3
Harewood Crs *LTDN* BH7 .... 59 H3
Harewood Gdns *LTDN* BH7 .... 59 H3
Harewood Gn *LYMN* SO41 .... 83 F1
Harewood Pl *LTDN* BH7 .... 60 B4
Harford Cl *LYMN* SO41 .... 69 F1
Harford Rd *BKME/WDN* BH12 ...... 56 A2
Harkwood Dr *PLE* BH15 .... 71 C1
Harland Rd *SBNE* BH6 .... 79 C1
Harness Cl *WIMB* BH21 .... 17 H3
Harpway La *CHCH/BSGR* BH23 .... 43 E1
Harrier Dr *WIMB* BH21 .... 24 D2
Harriers Cl *CHCH/BSGR* BH23 ..... 63 H2
Harrison Av *BMTH* BH1 .... 59 F4
Harrison Cl *CHCH/BSGR* BH23 .... 43 E4
Harrison Wy *FERN* BH22 .... 10 A3
Harrow Cl *CHCH/BSGR* BH23 ...... 33 F5
Harrow Rd *CHCH/BSGR* BH23 ..... 33 E5
Harry Barrow Cl *RGWD* BH24 .... 8 C5
Hart Cl *NMIL/BTOS* BH25 .... 46 D3
Harting Rd *SBNE* BH6 .... 60 D3
Hartsbourne Dr *LTDN* BH7 .... 60 B2
Harts Wy *LYMN* SO41 .... 68 B1
Harvester Wy *LYMN* SO41 .... 50 D1
Harvey Rd *BOSC* BH5 .... 60 A5
  WIMB BH21 .... 25 F3
Haskells Rd *BKME/WDN* BH12 .... 55 H3
Haslemere Av *CHCH/BSGR* BH23.. 64 A2
Haslemere Pl *CHCH/BSGR* BH23.. 64 C2
Hasler Rd *CFDH* BH17 .... 35 G5
Haslop Rd *WIMB* BH21 .... 17 F2
Hastings Rd *CFDH* BH17 .... 35 F5
  CHAR BH8 .... 40 D5
Hatch Pond Rd *CFDH* BH17 .... 54 C2
Hatfield Ct *NMIL/BTOS* BH25 ...... 46 C4
Hatfield Gdns *LTDN* BH7 .... 60 B2
Hathaway Rd *SBNE* BH6 .... 78 D1
Hatherden Av *PSTN* BH14 .... 55 F5
Havelock Rd *BKME/WDN* BH12 ... 57 E3
Havelock Wy *CHCH/BSGR* BH23 .. 44 D5
Haven Gdns *NMIL/BTOS* BH25 .... 47 F5
Haven Rd *CCLF* BH13 .... 85 C2
  WIMB BH21 .... 34 A1
Haverstock Rd
  MOOR/WNTN BH9 .... 39 H5
Haviland Rd *BMTH* BH1 .... 59 H5
  WIMB BH21 .... 19 E2
Haviland Rd East *LTDN* BH7 .... 59 H5
Haviland Rd West *LTDN* BH7 .... 59 H5
Hawden Rd *BWD* BH11 .... 57 E1
Hawkchurch Gdns *CFDH* BH17 ... 36 A5
Hawk Cl *WIMB* BH21 .... 17 C2
Hawker Cl *WIMB* BH21 .... 25 F3
Hawkins Cl *RGWD* BH24 .... 9 E2
Hawkins Rd *BKME/WDN* BH12 .... 56 D1
Hawkwood Rd *BOSC* BH5 .... 77 C1
Haworth Cl *CHCH/BSGR* BH23 .... 61 G1
Hawthorn Cl *NMIL/BTOS* BH25 ... 47 C3
Hawthorn Dr *CFDH* BH17 .... 53 H1
Hawthorn Rd *CHCH/BSGR* BH23 .. 43 G5
  MOOR/WNTN BH9 .... 58 B2
The Hawthorns
  CHCH/BSGR BH23 .... 62 D4
Haydon Rd *CCLF* BH13 .... 75 F4
Hayes Av *LTDN* BH7 .... 59 G4
Hayes Cl *WIMB* BH21 .... 17 G5
Hayes La *WIMB* BH21 .... 17 H5
Hayeswood Rd *WIMB* BH21 .... 17 H5
Haymoor Rd *PLE* BH15 .... 55 F5
Haynes Av *PLE* BH15 .... 72 D1
Haysoms Cl *NMIL/BTOS* BH25 .... 66 B3

Hayward Crs *VWD* BH31 .... 4 A3
Haywards Farm Cl *VWD* BH31 ...... 4 A3
Hazel Cl *CHCH/BSGR* BH23 .... 63 G1
Hazel Dr *FERN* BH22 .... 19 H1
Hazell Av *NBNE* BH10 .... 38 B5
Hazel Rd *LYMN* SO41 .... 50 A3
Hazelton Cl *LTDN* BH7 .... 60 A2
Hazelwood Av
  NMIL/BTOS BH25 .... 46 C3
Hazelwood Dr *VWD* BH31 .... 4 D4
Hazlebury Rd *CFDH* BH17 .... 54 B3
Hazlemere Dr *RGWD* BH24 .... 11 G3
Heads Farm Cl *NBNE* BH10 .... 39 E2
Headsell Av *NBNE* BH10 .... 39 E3
Headswell Crs *NBNE* BH10 .... 39 E3
Headswell Gdns *NBNE* BH10 .... 39 E3
Heanor Cl *NBNE* BH10 .... 38 C5
Heath Av *PLE* BH15 .... 54 D4
Heathcote Rd *BMTH* BH1 .... 77 H1
  BOSC BH5 .... 77 H1
Heatherbank Rd *CCLF* BH13 .... 75 E2
  WBNE BH4 .... 2 A3
Heatherbrae La *UPTN* BH16 .... 52 D4
Heather Cl *CHAR* BH8 .... 40 B3
  CHCH/BSGR BH23 .... 64 C1
  LYMN SO41 .... 48 C4
  RGWD BH24 .... 11 G3
  WIMB BH21 .... 34 C1
Heatherdell *UPTN* BH16 .... 52 D4
Heatherdown Rd *FERN* BH22 ...... 10 C5
Heatherdown Wy *FERN* BH22 ...... 10 C5
Heather Dr *FERN* BH22 .... 19 H2
Heatherlands Ri
  BKME/WDN BH12 .... 56 B5
Heatherlea Rd *SBNE* BH6 .... 78 D1
Heather Rd *NBNE* BH10 .... 38 D4
Heather View Rd
  BKME/WDN BH12 .... 56 D3
Heather Wy *FERN* BH22 .... 19 H2
Heath Farm Cl *FERN* BH22 .... 27 G1
Heath Farm Rd *FERN* BH22 .... 27 G1
Heath Farm Wy *FERN* BH22 .... 27 G1
Heathfield Av *BKME/WDN* BH12 .. 57 E2
Heathfield Rd *FERN* BH22 .... 10 C5
Heathfield Wy *FERN* BH22 .... 10 B5
Heathlands Av *FERN* BH22 .... 27 H2
Heathlands Cl
  CHCH/BSGR BH23 .... 43 E4
  VWD BH31 .... 4 C2
Heath Rd *CHCH/BSGR* BH23 .... 64 D1
  LYMN SO41 .... 48 B4
  RGWD BH24 .... 11 F2
Heath Rd West
  CHCH/BSGR BH23 .... 21 H5
Heathwood Av
  NMIL/BTOS BH25 .... 65 G2
Heathwood Rd
  MOOR/WNTN BH9 .... 58 A2
Heathy Cl *NMIL/BTOS* BH25 .... 65 H2
Heaton Rd *NBNE* BH10 .... 38 B5
Heavytree Rd *PSTN* BH14 .... 73 H1
Heckford La *PLE* BH15 .... 72 D1
Heckford Rd *PLE* BH15 .... 72 D1
  WIMB BH21 .... 34 A2
Hedgerley *NMIL/BTOS* BH25 .... 66 B2
Heights Ap *UPTN* BH16 .... 53 E3
Heights Rd *UPTN* BH16 .... 53 E2
Helyar Rd *CHAR* BH8 .... 40 C5
Henbury Cl *CFDH* BH17 .... 36 C5
  WIMB BH21 .... 34 B1
Henbury Ri *WIMB* BH21 .... 34 B1
Henbury View Rd *WIMB* BH21 .... 34 B1
Hendford Rd *NBNE* BH10 .... 38 D5
Hengistbury Rd
  NMIL/BTOS BH25 .... 64 C5
  SBNE BH6 .... 79 F2
Hengist Rd *BMTH* BH1 .... 77 F1
Henley Gdns *LTDN* BH7 .... 60 A3
Henning's Park Rd *PLE* BH15 ..... 54 D5
Herbert Av *BKME/WDN* BH12 ..... 56 A2
Herberton Rd *SBNE* BH6 .... 60 C5
Herbert Rd *NMIL/BTOS* BH25 .... 47 H4
  WBNE BH4 .... 75 F3
Hercules Rd *PLE* BH15 .... 71 F2
Hermitage Rd *PSTN* BH14 .... 55 G4
Herm Rd *BKME/WDN* BH12 .... 56 A1
Heron Court Rd
  MOOR/WNTN BH9 .... 58 C3
  TWDS BH3 .... 58 C3
Heron Dr *WIMB* BH21 .... 17 G2
Herstone Cl *CFDH* BH17 .... 55 F1
Hesketh Cl *RGWD* BH24 .... 12 A1
Heston Cl *CHCH/BSGR* BH23 ...... 41 H5
Hewitt Rd *PLE* BH15 .... 71 G1
Heysham Rd *BDST* BH18 .... 35 E4
Heytesbury Rd *SBNE* BH6 .... 60 D5

Hibberd Wy *NBNE* BH10 .... 57 H1
Hibbs Cl *UPTN* BH16 .... 53 E3
Hickes Cl *BWD* BH11 .... 37 H3
Hickory Cl *UPTN* BH16 .... 52 C2
Highbridge Rd *PSTN* BH14 .... 74 A2
Highbury Cl *NMIL/BTOS* BH25 .... 47 F4
Highcliffe Rd *CHCH/BSGR* BH23 .. 63 E2
Higher Blandford Rd
  BDST BH18 .... 35 E2
  WIMB BH21 .... 34 D1
Highfield Cl *LYMN* SO41 .... 50 D4
Highfield Av *LYMN* SO41 .... 50 C4
  RGWD BH24 .... 8 C3
Highfield Cl *WIMB* BH21 .... 34 C2
Highfield Dr *RGWD* BH24 .... 8 C2
Highfield Rd *LYMN* SO41 .... 50 C3
  MOOR/WNTN BH9 .... 39 E5
  RGWD BH24 .... 8 C3
  WIMB BH21 .... 34 C2
High Howe Cl *BWD* BH11 .... 37 G3
High Howe Gdns *BWD* BH11 .... 37 G3
High Howe La *BWD* BH11 .... 37 G3
Highland Av *CHCH/BSGR* BH23 ... 64 D1
Highland Rd *PSTN* BH14 .... 55 H5
  WIMB BH21 .... 16 D4
Highlands Crs *NBNE* BH10 .... 38 C3
Highlands Rd *NMIL/BTOS* BH25.. 66 A2
Highland View Cl *WIMB* BH21 ..... 16 D4
High Md *FERN* BH22 .... 27 E2
High Mead La *FERN* BH22 .... 27 E3
Highmoor Cl *WIMB* BH21 .... 34 B2
Highmoor Rd *BWD* BH11 .... 57 E1
  PSTN BH14 .... 74 A2
  WIMB BH21 .... 34 B2
High Oaks Gdns *BWD* BH11 .... 37 G3
High Park Rd *BDST* BH18 .... 34 C3
High Ridge Crs *NMIL/BTOS* BH25.. 47 G4
High St *CHCH/BSGR* BH23 .... 61 H4
  LYMN SO41 .... 51 H4
  LYMN SO41 .... 82 C1
  PLE BH15 .... 72 B4
  RGWD BH24 .... 6 C5
  RGWD BH24 .... 8 B4
  WIMB BH21 .... 16 B5
High St North *PLE* BH15 .... 72 D2
Hightown Gdns *RGWD* BH24 .... 8 D5
Hightown Hl *RGWD* BH24 .... 9 H4
Hightown Rd *RGWD* BH24 .... 9 H4
Hightrees Av *CHAR* BH8 .... 59 G1
High Trees Wk *FERN* BH22 .... 19 H2
Highview Cl *CHCH/BSGR* BH23 ... 42 A4
Highview Gdns
  BKME/WDN BH12 .... 56 A3
High Wy *BDST* BH18 .... 34 D4
Highwood La *RGWD* BH24 .... 9 E1
Highwood Rd *BROC* SO42 .... 14 D4
  PSTN BH14 .... 74 C1
Hilary Rd *CFDH* BH17 .... 54 C1
Hilda Rd *BKME/WDN* BH12 .... 56 C4
Hiley Rd *PLE* BH15 .... 54 C4
Hillary Rd *CHCH/BSGR* BH23 ...... 62 C2
Hillbourne Rd *CFDH* BH17 .... 35 E5
Hillbrow Rd *SBNE* BH6 .... 60 B4
Hill Cl *CHCH/BSGR* BH23 .... 33 E5
Hillcrest Av *FERN* BH22 .... 19 C5
Hillcrest Cl *MOOR/WNTN* BH9 ... 39 E4
Hillcrest Rd *BKME/WDN* BH12 ... 55 G5
  MOOR/WNTN BH9 .... 39 C4
  WIMB BH21 .... 34 A2
Hillditch *LYMN* SO41 .... 50 D1
Hill La *CHCH/BSGR* BH23 .... 33 E4
  CHCH/BSGR BH23 .... 43 H5
Hillman Rd *PSTN* BH14 .... 56 B5
Hillmeadow *VWD* BH31 .... 4 C4
Hill Rd *RGWD* BH24 .... 22 A3
Hillside Dr *CHCH/BSGR* BH23 .... 41 H3
Hillside Gdns *WIMB* BH21 .... 34 A3
Hillside Rd *BKME/WDN* BH12 ..... 56 D1
  LYMN SO41 .... 50 C4
  VWD BH31 .... 4 C1
  WIMB BH21 .... 34 A2
Hill St *PLE* BH15 .... 72 C3
Hilltop Cl *FERN* BH22 .... 19 F2
Hilltop Rd *FERN* BH22 .... 19 F2
  WIMB BH21 .... 34 A2
Hill View Rd *FERN* BH22 .... 19 G3
Hillview Rd *NBNE* BH10 .... 38 D4
Hill Wy *RGWD* BH24 .... 11 C1
Hiltom Rd *RGWD* BH24 .... 8 D4
Hilton Cl *PLE* BH15 .... 55 G4
Hilton Rd *NMIL/BTOS* BH25 .... 47 F3
Hinchliffe Cl *PLE* BH15 .... 71 H3
Hinchliffe Rd *PLE* BH15 .... 71 H3
Hinton Rd *BMTH* BH1 .... 3 H4
Hinton Wood Av
  CHCH/BSGR BH23 .... 64 A1
Hintonwood La
  CHCH/BSGR BH23 .... 45 E5

Hives Wy *LYMN* SO41 .... **50** D1 🔲
Hobart Rd *NMIL/BTOS* BH25....... **46** D5
Hobbs Pk *RGWD* BH24................ **11** H2
Hobbs Rd *BKME/WDN* BH12...... **56** A2
Hoburne Gdns
   CHCH/BSGR BH23 .... **63** G1
Hoburne La *CHCH/BSGR* BH23 .. **63** G1
Hodges CI *CFDH* BH17............... **55** E3
Hogue Av *NBNE* BH10 .... **38** D2
Holbury CI *CHAR* BH8................ **40** C4
Holcombe Rd *UPTN* BH16.......... **52** D4
Holdenhurst Av *LTDN* BH7 .... **60** C3
Holdenhurst Rd *CHAR* BH8........ **41** E4
   CHAR BH8.............................. **59** F4
Holes Bay Rd *PLE* BH15............. **72** B1
Holes CI *LYMN* SO41 .... **48** B3
Hollands Wood Dr
   NMIL/BTOS BH25................. **47** F2
Holland Wy *BDST* BH18............. **34** D2
Holloway Av *BWD* BH11........... **37** H2
Holly CI *RGWD* BH24................. **11** F2
   UPTN BH16............................ **52** C3
Holly Gdns *CHCH/BSGR* BH23... **62** B1
   LYMN SO41 .... **68** A5
Holly Green Ri *BWD* BH11 .... **37** G3 🔲
Holly Hedge La *CFDH* BH17 ...... **54** C2
Holly La *CHCH/BSGR* BH23 .... **46** A5
   NMIL/BTOS BH25................. **47** G3
Hollywood La *LYMN* SO41........ **50** D2
Holm CI *RGWD* BH24................. **9** E2
Holme Rd *CHCH/BSGR* BH25...... **64** D1
Holmfield Av *LTDN* BH7............ **60** C3
Holmhurst Av *CHCH/BSGR* BH23.. **64** B1
Holmsley CI *LYMN* SO41........... **50** B5
Holmwood Garth *RGWD* BH24... **9** F5
Holnest Rd *CFDH* BH17.............. **54** D1
Holt Rd *BKME/WDN* BH12........ **56** D4
Holworth CI *BWD* BH11 .... **37** G4 🔲
Holywell CI *CFDH* BH17 .... **35** H4
Home Farm Wy *VWD* BH31........ **4** A2
Home Rd *BWD* BH11 .... **37** F2
Homeside Rd *MOOR/WNTN* BH9 .. **39** C5
Homewood CI *NMIL/BTOS* BH25 ... **47** C4 🔲
Honeybourne Crs *SBNE* BH6 ..... **79** C1
Honeysuckle La *CFDH* BH17 ...... **53** H1
Honeysuckle Wy
   CHCH/BSGR BH23 .... **63** F2 🔲
Hood CI *NBNE* BH10................... **57** F1
Hood Crs *NBNE* BH10................ **57** F1
Hooke CI *CFDH* BH17................. **36** C5
Hop CI *UPTN* BH16..................... **52** B3 🔲
Hopkins CI *CHAR* BH8 .... **41** E5
Horace Rd *BOSC* BH5................. **77** C1
Hordle La *LYMN* SO41............... **67** F2
Horlock Rd *BROC* SO42 .... **15** E2 🔲
Hornbeam Wy *WIMB* BH21 ...... **16** D4
Horning Rd *BKME/WDN* BH12... **56** D5
Horsa CI *SBNE* BH6.................... **79** E1
Horsa Ct *SBNE* BH6 .... **79** E1
Horsa Rd *SBNE* BH6................... **79** E1
Horseshoe CI *WIMB* BH21......... **17** H3
Horsham Av *NBNE* BH10........... **38** C1
Horton CI *MOOR/WNTN* BH9 .... **40** A4
Horton Rd *RGWD* BH24............. **6** A5
Hosker Rd *BOSC* BH5................. **60** B5
Houlton Rd *PLE* BH15................ **73** E1
Hounds Wy *WIMB* BH21........... **17** H4
Hounslow CI *PLE* BH15.............. **71** G3
Howard CI *CHCH/BSGR* BH23.... **62** D4
Howard Rd *CHAR* BH8............... **59** E3
   VWD BH31 .... **4** B2
Howards Md *LYMN* SO41.......... **50** B5
Howe CI *CHCH/BSGR* BH23 .... **62** D5
   NMIL/BTOS BH25................. **46** D4
Howe La *VWD* BH31 .... **4** A3
Howeth CI *NBNE* BH10.............. **38** D4
Howeth Rd *NBNE* BH10............. **38** C4
Howlett CI *LYMN* SO41............. **50** C3
Howton CI *NBNE* BH10.............. **38** C2 🔲
Howton Rd *NBNE* BH10............. **38** C2
Hoxley Rd *NBNE* BH10.............. **38** D3
Hoyal Rd *PLE* BH15................... **71** F2
Hudson CI *BKME/WDN* BH12 .... **57** E3
   RGWD BH24............................ **9** E3 🔲
Hull Crs *BWD* BH11................... **37** F3
Hull Rd *BWD* BH11.................... **37** F3
Hull Wy *BWD* BH11................... **37** F3
Humber Rd *FERN* BH22............. **20** C3
Hungerfield CI
   CHCH/BSGR BH23 .... **33** E3
Hungerford Rd *CHAR* BH8 .... **40** B4 🔲
Hunter CI *CHCH/BSGR* BH23 ..... **63** E4
   WIMB BH21 .... **18** A3 🔲
Hunters CI *VWD* BH31 .... **5** E3
Huntfield Rd *MOOR/WNTN* BH9 . **39** H4
Huntingdon Dr *WIMB* BH21 ..... **25** E3
Huntingdon Gdns
   CHCH/BSGR BH23 .... **42** B5

Huntly Rd *TWDS* BH3................ **57** H4
Hunt Rd *CHCH/BSGR* BH23 ...... **62** D2
   PLE BH15................................ **73** E1
Huntvale Rd *MOOR/WNTN* BH9 .. **39** H4
The Hurdles *CHCH/BSGR* BH23 .. **61** E2 🔲
Hurn CI *RGWD* BH24.................. **7** H5
Hurn Court La *CHCH/BSGR* BH23.. **40** D1
Hurn La *RGWD* BH24................. **7** H5
Hurn Rd *CHCH/BSGR* BH23 .... **41** H3
   RGWD BH24............................ **22** C1
Hurn Wy *CHCH/BSGR* BH23 ...... **60** E1
Hursley CI *LTDN* BH7................. **60** C2 🔲
Hurstbourne Av
   CHCH/BSGR BH23 .... **64** A1
Hurst CI *CHCH/BSGR* BH23 .... **46** A5
Hurstdene Rd *CHAR* BH8........... **40** A5
Hurst HI *PSTN* BH14.................. **74** A5
Hurst Rd *LYMN* SO41................ **82** C2
   RGWD BH24............................ **8** C2
Hussar CI *CHCH/BSGR* BH23 ..... **61** F3 🔲
Hyacinth CI *CFDH* BH17............ **53** H1
Hyde Rd *NBNE* BH10................. **38** C2
The Hyde *NMIL/BTOS* BH25...... **46** C3 🔲
Hynesbury Rd *CHCH/BSGR* BH23.. **63** G4
Hythe Rd *PLE* BH15................... **55** G3

I

Ibbertson CI *CHAR* BH8 .... **40** D1
Ibbertson Rd *CHAR* BH8 .... **59** H1
Ibbertson Wy *CHAR* BH8........... **40** D5
Ibbett Rd *NBNE* BH10............... **38** C5
Ibsley CI *CHAR* BH8................... **59** E4
Iddesleigh Rd *TWDS* BH3.......... **58** B4
Iford Gdns *LTDN* BH7................ **60** C3
Iford La *SBNE* BH6.................... **61** E3
Iley La *LYMN* SO41................... **69** G3
Ilford CI *SBNE* BH6.................... **61** F4
Imber Dr *CHCH/BSGR* BH23 ...... **64** B2
Imbrecourt *CCLF* BH13.............. **85** G1
Inglesham Wy *PLE* BH15........... **71** G1 🔲
   PLE BH15................................ **71** G2 🔲
Inglewood Av *CHAR* BH8 .... **59** H1
Inglewood Dr *NMIL/BTOS* BH25.. **47** F5
Ingworth Rd *BKME/WDN* BH12.. **57** E5
Insley Crs *WIMB* BH21............... **34** C2
Inveravon *CHCH/BSGR* BH23 .... **80** D1
Inverclyde Rd *PSTN* BH14......... **74** A1
Inverleigh Rd *SBNE* BH6........... **60** C4
Ipswich Rd *WBNE* BH4.............. **75** F1
Iris Rd *MOOR/WNTN* BH9......... **58** B1
Irvine CI *CHCH/BSGR* BH23 .... **62** C2
Irving Rd *SBNE* BH6................... **60** D5
Isaacs CI *BKME/WDN* BH12....... **57** F3
Island View Av
   CHCH/BSGR BH23 .... **63** F4
Island View CI *LYMN* SO41 .... **82** C2
Island View Rd
   NMIL/BTOS BH25................. **65** F3
Ivamy PI *BWD* BH11.................. **37** H5
Ivor Rd *PLE* BH15...................... **72** A4
   WIMB BH21 .... **34** B3
Ivy CI *RGWD* BH24 .... **11** F2
Ivy Rd *WIMB* BH21.................... **24** D4
Iwerne CI *MOOR/WNTN* BH9 .... **39** H3 🔲

J

Jackson Rd *BKME/WDN* BH12 .... **56** A4
Jacobean CI *CHCH/BSGR* BH23... **64** D1
Jacobs Rd *PLE* BH15.................. **71** G3
Jacqueline Rd *BKME/WDN* BH12.. **55** H3
Jameson Rd *MOOR/WNTN* BH9 .. **58** A1
James Rd *BKME/WDN* BH12....... **57** E5
Jasmine Ct *WIMB* BH21 .... **51** E3 🔲
Jaundrells CI *NMIL/BTOS* BH25 ... **47** G4
Jay's Ct *CHCH/BSGR* BH23 .... **64** D2 🔲
Jefferson Av *CHAR* BH8............. **59** F4
Jellicoe CI *PSTN* BH14............... **55** F5
Jellicoe Dr *CHCH/BSGR* BH23 ... **62** D4
Jennings Rd *PSTN* BH14............ **74** A3
Jephcote Rd *BWD* BH11............ **37** H3
Jersey CI *BKME/WDN* BH12....... **56** A1
Jersey Rd *BKME/WDN* BH12...... **56** B1
Jesmond Av *CHCH/BSGR* BH23 .. **64** B2
Jessopp CI *NBNE* BH10.............. **39** F3
Jessopp Rd *WIMB* BH21............ **17** H3
Jewell Rd *CHAR* BH8 .... **59** H1
Jimmy Brown Av *WIMB* BH21 ... **10** A1
Johnson Rd *WIMB* BH21............ **19** E2
Johnstone Rd
   CHCH/BSGR BH23 .... **62** C4 🔲
Johnston Rd *PLE* BH15.............. **54** D3
Jolliffe Av *PLE* BH15.................. **72** D1

Jolliffe Rd *PLE* BH15................. **72** D1
Jonathan CI *LYMN* SO41 .... **51** E2
Jopps Cnr *CHCH/BSGR* BH23 .... **43** E3
Joshua CI *PLE* BH15 .... **71** G3 🔲
Jowitt Dr *NMIL/BTOS* BH25...... **46** D5
Joyce Dickson CI *RGWD* BH24 ... **9** E3
Jubilee CI *RGWD* BH24.............. **9** E3
Jubilee Crs *PSTN* BH14.............. **56** B5 🔲
Jubilee Gdns *NBNE* BH10.......... **38** D5
Jubilee Rd *PSTN* BH14............... **56** B5
   WIMB BH21 .... **34** C1
Julia CI *CHCH/BSGR* BH23 .... **64** B2
Julian's Rd *WIMB* BH21............ **16** A5
Julyan Av *BKME/WDN* BH12...... **57** E2
Jumpers Av *CHCH/BSGR* BH23 .. **61** F2
Jumpers Rd *CHCH/BSGR* BH23... **61** F2
Junction Rd *MOOR/WNTN* BH9 .. **58** B2 🔲
   UPTN BH16............................ **71** F1
Juniper CI *FERN* BH22............... **19** G1
   LYMN SO41 .... **50** B5
Justin Gdns *NBNE* BH10............ **39** E3

K

Kamptee Copse
   NMIL/BTOS BH25................. **47** F1 🔲
Kangaw PI *PLE* BH15................. **71** F3 🔲
Katherine Chance CI
   CHCH/BSGR BH23 .... **43** E4 🔲
Katterns CI *CHCH/BSGR* BH23 ... **42** A5
Keats Av *LYMN* SO41................. **68** B5
Keeble CI *NBNE* BH10................ **38** D1
Keeble Crs *NBNE* BH10.............. **38** D1
Keeble Rd *NBNE* BH10............... **38** D1
Keepers La *WIMB* BH21............. **18** C4
Keighley Av *BDST* BH18............. **34** D5
Keith Rd *TWDS* BH3.................. **57** G4
Kellaway Rd *CFDH* BH17........... **55** F2
Kelly CI *CFDH* BH17.................. **55** F2
Kelsall Gdns *NMIL/BTOS* BH25 .. **47** E4
Kemp Rd *MOOR/WNTN* BH9 ..... **58** B2
Kenilworth CI *NMIL/BTOS* BH25.. **47** E4
Kennard Ct *NMIL/BTOS* BH25.... **46** D5
Kennard Rd *NMIL/BTOS* BH25.... **46** D3
Kennart Rd *CFDH* BH17............ **54** A3
Ken Rd *SBNE* BH6...................... **79** E1
Kensington Dr *WCLF* BH2.......... **2** A3
Kensington Pk *LYMN* SO41....... **82** A1
Kent Rd *BKME/WDN* BH12........ **56** D4
Kenyon CI *PLE* BH15.................. **55** E3
Kenyon Rd *PLE* BH15................. **55** E3
Keppel CI *RGWD* BH24.............. **8** D4
Kerley Rd *WCLF* BH2................. **3** F5
Kerry CI *LYMN* SO41................. **50** C4
Kestrel CI *FERN* BH22............... **19** F2
   UPTN BH16............................ **52** D2
Kestrel Ct *RGWD* BH24............. **8** C3
Kestrel Dr *CHCH/BSGR* BH23 .... **64** D4
Keswick Rd *BOSC* BH5.............. **77** H1
   NMIL/BTOS BH25................. **47** G2
Keswick Wy *VWD* BH31............ **4** A3
Keyes CI *BKME/WDN* BH12....... **56** D4
   CHCH/BSGR BH23 .... **62** D4
Keyhaven Rd *LYMN* SO41......... **82** C1
Keysworth Av *NMIL/BTOS* BH25 .. **65** H3
Keysworth Rd *UPTN* BH16........ **71** E1
Khyber Rd *BKME/WDN* BH12.... **56** A4
Kilmarnock Rd
   MOOR/WNTN BH9 .... **58** B1 🔲
Kilmington Wy
   CHCH/BSGR BH23 .... **64** B2
Kiln CI *WIMB* BH21................... **34** A3
Kimberley CI
   CHCH/BSGR BH23 .... **61** F2 🔲
Kimberley Rd *PSTN* BH14.......... **73** F2 🔲
   SBNE BH6.............................. **60** C4
Kimber Rd *BWD* BH11 .... **37** H4 🔲
Kimmeridge Av
   BKME/WDN BH12................ **56** A2
King CI *RGWD* BH24.................. **11** H2
Kingcup CI *BDST* BH18.............. **34** C5
King Edward Av
   MOOR/WNTN BH9 .... **39** F5
Kingfisher CI *FERN* BH22.......... **10** B4
   SBNE BH6.............................. **61** E4 🔲
The Kingfishers *VWD* BH31 ...... **4** C3
Kingfisher Wy *CHCH/BSGR* BH23.. **63** E5
   RGWD BH24............................ **8** D2
King George Av
   MOOR/WNTN BH9 .... **39** F5
King John Av *BWD* BH11........... **37** F5
Kingland Rd *PLE* BH15.............. **72** D3
King Richard Dr *BWD* BH11 ...... **37** F2
Kings Arms La *RGWD* BH24 ...... **8** B4
Kings Arms Rw *RGWD* BH24 ..... **8** B4 🔲
King's Av *CHCH/BSGR* BH23 ..... **61** F4

   PSTN BH14............................. **74** B3
Kingsbere Av *NBNE* BH10......... **38** B5
Kingsbere Rd *PLE* BH15............ **55** E5 🔲
Kingsbridge Rd *PSTN* BH14 ...... **74** A2
Kingsbury's La *RGWD* BH24...... **8** B5
Kings Crs *LYMN* SO41 .... **50** D3
   PSTN BH14............................. **74** C3
Kingsfield *LYMN* SO41.............. **51** G5 🔲
   RGWD BH24............................ **8** C4 🔲
Kingsley Av *SBNE* BH6.............. **79** G1 🔲
Kingsley CI *SBNE* BH6............... **79** G1
Kingsmill Rd *CFDH* BH17.......... **55** E3
King's Park Dr *LTDN* BH7.......... **59** G4
King's Park Rd *BMTH* BH1......... **59** G4
Kings Rd *LYMN* SO41................ **50** D3
   NMIL/BTOS BH25................. **47** G3
   TWDS BH3 .... **58** C3
King's Saltern Rd *LYMN* SO41 ... **51** G5
Kingston Pk *LYMN* SO41 .... **50** C5 🔲
Kingston Rd *PLE* BH15.............. **72** D1
King St *WIMB* BH21................... **16** B5
Kingsway *FERN* BH22................ **19** F1
Kingsway CI *CHCH/BSGR* BH23 .. **61** F1
Kingswell CI *NBNE* BH10........... **38** D5 🔲
Kingswell Gdns *NBNE* BH10...... **38** B5
Kingswell Gv *NBNE* BH10.......... **38** B5
Kingswell Rd *NBNE* BH10.......... **38** C5
Kinross Rd *TWDS* BH3.............. **58** A4
Kinsbourne Av *NBNE* BH10....... **38** D5
Kinson Av *PLE* BH15.................. **55** C4
Kinson Gv *NBNE* BH10.............. **38** C1
Kinson Park Rd *NBNE* BH10...... **38** C1
Kinson Rd *NBNE* BH10.............. **57** E1
Kipling Rd *PSTN* BH14.............. **55** H5
Kirby CI *PLE* BH15..................... **55** F4
Kirby Wy *SBNE* BH6.................. **78** D1
Kirkham Av *CHCH/BSGR* BH23 .. **43** E4 🔲
Kirkway *BDST* BH18.................. **35** F3
Kitchener Crs *CFDH* BH17......... **35** F5
Kitscroft Rd *NBNE* BH10........... **38** C2
Kittiwake CI *SBNE* BH6............. **60** D4 🔲
Kitwalls La *LYMN* SO41............ **68** B5
Kivernell Rd *LYMN* SO41.......... **82** A1
Kiwi CI *PLE* BH15...................... **73** E2
Knapp CI *CHCH/BSGR* BH23 ..... **61** G2
Knapp Mill Av *CHCH/BSGR* BH23 .. **61** G2
Knighton Heath CI *BWD* BH11 .. **37** G2
Knighton La *BWD* BH11............ **26** B5
Knighton Pk *NMIL/BTOS* BH25 .. **65** G2
Knights Rd *BWD* BH11.............. **37** F2
Knightwood CI
   CHCH/BSGR BH23 .... **64** A2 🔲
Knobcrook Rd *WIMB* BH21........ **16** B3
Knole Gdns *BMTH* BH1.............. **77** F1
Knole Rd *BMTH* BH1.................. **59** F5
Knoll Gdns *RGWD* BH24........... **11** H2
Knowland Dr *LYMN* SO41......... **68** B5
Knowle Rd *BROC* SO42 .... **14** C2
Knowles CI *CHCH/BSGR* BH23 .. **62** C3
Knowlton Gdns
   MOOR/WNTN BH9 .... **39** H4 🔲
Knowlton Rd *CFDH* BH17.......... **36** B5
Knyveton Rd *BMTH* BH1........... **77** E1
Kyrchil La *WIMB* BH21.............. **17** E3
Kyrchil Wy *WIMB* BH21............ **17** F2

L

Labrador Dr *PLE* BH15............... **72** D4 🔲
Laburnum Cl *FERN* BH22........... **19** F3
   VWD BH31 .... **5** E3
Laburnum Dr *LYMN* SO41......... **68** C2 🔲
Lacey Crs *PSTN* BH14................ **55** G4
Lacy CI *WIMB* BH21.................. **16** D5
Lacy Dr *WIMB* BH21.................. **16** C5
Ladysmith CI *CHCH/BSGR* BH23 .. **62** C3
Lagado CI *PSTN* BH14................ **74** A5
Lagland St *PLE* BH15................. **72** C4
Lagoon Rd *PSTN* BH14.............. **73** H4
Laidlaw CI *BKME/WDN* BH12.... **57** F2
Lake Av *PLE* BH15..................... **71** F4
Lake Crs *PLE* BH15.................... **71** G2
Lake Dr *PLE* BH15..................... **71** G3
Lake Grove Rd *NMIL/BTOS* BH25.. **47** E3
Lake Rd *BWD* BH11................... **38** B*
   PLE BH15................................ **71** G3
   VWD BH31 .... **4** C3
Lakeside *RGWD* BH24 .... **9** E5
Lakeside Rd *CCLF* BH13............ **75** E4
Lakeview Dr *RGWD* BH24......... **9** E5
Lakewood Rd *CHCH/BSGR* BH23 .. **64** B3
Lambs CI *CFDH* BH17................ **54** C1
Lampton Gdns
   MOOR/WNTN BH9 .... **58** B1 🔲
Lancaster CI *BDST* BH18........... **34** D2

CHCH/BSGR BH23 ...... 63 F3
Lancaster Dr BDST BH18 ...... 34 C2
VWD BH31 ...... 4 A2
Lancaster Rd WIMB BH21 ...... 19 E1
Lancer Cl CHCH/BSGR BH23 ...... 61 F3
Lander Cl PLE BH15 ...... 72 D4
Landford Gdns CHAR BH8 ...... 40 B5
Landford Wy CHAR BH8 ...... 40 B5
The Landsdown Rbt BMTH BH1 ... 3 K3
Landseer Rd CCLF BH13 ...... 75 E2
WBNE BH4 ...... 2 A3
The Lanes NMIL/BTOS BH25 ...... 47 E2
Langdon Rd PSTN BH14 ...... 74 A1
Langley Cha RGWD BH24 ...... 12 A1
Langley Rd CHCH/BSGR BH23 ...... 64 A1
PSTN BH14 ...... 74 D1
Langsdale Av BKME/WDN BH12 ... 57 B2
Langton Cl NMIL/BTOS BH25 ...... 66 B2
Langton Rd BH7 ...... 59 H5
Lansdowne Gdns BMTH BH1 ...... 3 K1
Lansdowne Rd BMTH BH1 ...... 3 K2
BMTH BH1 ...... 58 C5
Lapwing Rd WIMB BH21 ...... 17 C2
Lara Cl CHAR BH8 ...... 40 B4
Larch Cl CFDH BH17 ...... 53 C5
LYMN SO41 ...... 48 B4
RGWD BH24 ...... 12 A2
Larch Wy FERN BH22 ...... 19 C2
Larksdale Av BKME/WDN BH12 ... 57 B2
Larks Cl FERN BH22 ...... 19 F2
Larksfield Av MOOR/WNTN BH9 .. 39 H4
Larkshill Cl NMIL/BTOS BH25 ...... 47 F3
Larks Ri FERN BH22 ...... 19 C5
Lascelles Rd LTDN BH7 ...... 60 B4
Latch Farm Av
CHCH/BSGR BH23 ...... 61 G2
Latimer Rd MOOR/WNTN BH9 .... 58 A2
Latimers Cl CHCH/BSGR BH23 .... 64 B1
Laundry La LYMN SO41 ...... 82 C1
Laurel Cl CHCH/BSGR BH23 ...... 63 H1
LYMN SO41 ...... 48 A3
RGWD BH24 ...... 11 G3
WIMB BH21 ...... 34 B1
Laurel Dr BDST BH18 ...... 35 F3
Laurel Gdns BDST BH18 ...... 35 G3
Laurel La RGWD BH24 ...... 11 G3
The Laurels FERN BH22 ...... 19 G2
Lavender Cl VWD BH31 ...... 5 E3
Lavender Rd CHAR BH8 ...... 40 B3
LYMN SO41 ...... 48 A4
Lavender Wy BDST BH18 ...... 34 B4
Lavinia Rd BKME/WDN BH12 ...... 56 B4
Lawford Rd MOOR/WNTN BH9 .... 39 G4
Lawn Cl LYMN SO41 ...... 82 C1
Lawn Rd LYMN SO41 ...... 82 C1
LYMN SO41 ...... 82 C1
Lawns Cl WIMB BH21 ...... 18 A3
Lawns Rd WIMB BH21 ...... 17 H5
The Lawns CHCH/BSGR BH23 ..... 64 D2
Lawn Vw CHCH/BSGR BH23 ...... 64 B2
Lawrence Cl CHAR BH8 ...... 59 E4
Lawrence Dr PSTN BH14 ...... 72 C2
Lawrence Rd RGWD BH24 ...... 9 E1
Lawson Rd BKME/WDN BH12 ..... 55 H4
Layard Dr WIMB BH21 ...... 24 D3
Layton Rd BKME/WDN BH12 ..... 56 B5
Leamington Rd
MOOR/WNTN BH9 ...... 58 C3
Leaphill Rd LTDN BH7 ...... 60 A4
Learoyd Rd CFDH BH17 ...... 54 D3
The Lea VWD BH31 ...... 4 B1
Lea Wy BWD BH11 ...... 37 G1
Lechlade Gdns LTDN BH7 ...... 60 A2
Ledbury Rd CHCH/BSGR BH23 .... 62 D5
Ledgard Cl PSTN BH14 ...... 73 H1
Leedam Rd NBNE BH10 ...... 38 D3
Lee Lands LYMN SO41 ...... 69 H5
Lees Cl CHCH/BSGR BH23 ...... 41 H3
Leeson Dr FERN BH22 ...... 19 F1
Leeson Rd LTDN BH7 ...... 59 G3
Legg La WIMB BH21 ...... 16 D5
Legion Cl PLE BH15 ...... 71 G3
Legion Rd PLE BH15 ...... 71 G3
Leicester Rd CCLF BH13 ...... 75 E3
Leigham Vale Rd SBNE BH6 ...... 78 D1
Leigh Common WIMB BH21 ...... 17 E4
Leigh Gdns WIMB BH21 ...... 16 D5
Leigh La WIMB BH21 ...... 17 F4
Leigh Pk LYMN SO41 ...... 50 C3
Leigh Rd NMIL/BTOS BH25 ...... 47 E4
WIMB BH21 ...... 16 C5
Lentham Cl CFDH BH17 ...... 53 H1
Lentune Wy LYMN SO41 ...... 50 D5
Le Patourel Cl CHCH/BSGR BH23.. 62 B3
Leslie Rd MOOR/WNTN BH9 ...... 58 A2
PSTN BH14 ...... 73 G2
Leven Av WBNE BH4 ...... 57 H5
Leven Cl WBNE BH4 ...... 2 C1

Levet's La PLE BH15 ...... 72 B3
Lewens Cl WIMB BH21 ...... 16 C5
Lewesdon Dr BDST BH18 ...... 34 D3
Leybourne Av NBNE BH10 ...... 38 D2
Leybourne Cl NBNE BH10 ...... 38 C2
Leydene Av CHAR BH8 ...... 59 H1
Leydene Cl CHAR BH8 ...... 59 H1
Leyland Rd BKME/WDN BH12 ..... 37 G5
Leyside CHCH/BSGR BH23 ...... 62 D4
Library Rd BKME/WDN BH12 ...... 56 C5
FERN BH22 ...... 19 H4
MOOR/WNTN BH9 ...... 58 B1
Lilac Cl RGWD BH24 ...... 8 D3
Lilliput Rd PSTN BH14 ...... 74 A5
Lime Cl PLE BH15 ...... 55 F4
Lime Gv LYMN SO41 ...... 68 B2
Limitcd Rd MOOR/WNTN BH9 ..... 58 C1
Lin Brook Dr RGWD BH24 ...... 9 E1
Lincoln Av BMTH BH1 ...... 59 F4
CHCH/BSGR BH23 ...... 42 B5
Lincoln Rd BKME/WDN BH12 ..... 56 B3
Lindbergh Rd WIMB BH21 ...... 19 E1
Linden Cl FERN BH22 ...... 27 H3
Linden Gdns RGWD BH24 ...... 8 B3
Linden Rd BKME/WDN BH12 ...... 56 A4
FERN BH22 ...... 27 H3
MOOR/WNTN BH9 ...... 39 C4
The Lindens CHCH/BSGR BH23.... 43 F4
Linden Wy LYMN SO41 ...... 50 C3
Lindsay Rd CCLF BH13 ...... 75 E1
Lineside CHCH/BSGR BH23 ...... 62 A2
Linford Cl NMIL/BTOS BH25 ...... 47 E3
Linford Rd RGWD BH24 ...... 9 F2
Lingdale Rd SBNE BH6 ...... 60 D4
Ling Rd BKME/WDN BH12 ...... 55 H1
Lingwood Av CHCH/BSGR BH23 .. 62 D4
Linhorns La NMIL/BTOS BH25 ..... 47 E1
Link Ri WIMB BH21 ...... 34 C1
Link Rd RGWD BH24 ...... 9 E2
Links Dr CHCH/BSGR BH23 ...... 60 D1
Linkside Av CHAR BH8 ...... 59 C2
Links Rd PSTN BH14 ...... 74 B3
Links View Av PSTN BH14 ...... 74 C4
Linmead Dr BWD BH11 ...... 38 A1
Linnet Cl RGWD BH24 ...... 9 E5
Linnet Ct NMIL/BTOS BH25 ...... 46 D4
Linnet Rd CFDH BH17 ...... 53 C2
Linthorpe Rd PLE BH15 ...... 73 F1
Linwood Rd MOOR/WNTN BH9 .. 58 D3
Lionheart Cl BWD BH11 ...... 37 F2
Lions Hill Wy RGWD BH24 ...... 11 E1
Lions La RGWD BH24 ...... 11 F2
Lions Wd RGWD BH24 ...... 11 G2
Lisle Cl LYMN SO41 ...... 50 D4
Lisle Court Rd LYMN SO41 ...... 51 H4
Litchford Rd NMIL/BTOS BH25 .... 47 C5
Little Barrs Dr NMIL/BTOS BH25 .. 47 F3
Littlecroft Av MOOR/WNTN BH9 .. 39 H4
Little Croft Rd
BKME/WDN BH12 ...... 55 H4
Little Dene Copse LYMN SO41 .... 50 B5
Littledown Av LTDN BH7 ...... 59 G3
Littledown Dr LTDN BH7 ...... 59 C3
Little Forest Rd WBNE BH4 ...... 57 H5
Little Lonnen WIMB BH21 ...... 17 F1
Littlemead Cl CFDH BH17 ...... 54 A3
Littlemoor Av BWD BH11 ...... 37 F3
Livingstone Rd
BKME/WDN BH12 ...... 56 A4
BOSC BH5 ...... 78 B1
CHCH/BSGR BH23 ...... 62 B3
WIMB BH21 ...... 17 E5
Llewellin Cl UPTN BH16 ...... 53 C2
Loch Rd PSTN BH14 ...... 56 C5
Lockerley Cl LYMN SO41 ...... 51 C5
Locksley Dr FERN BH22 ...... 27 C1
Lockyers Dr FERN BH22 ...... 20 B3
Loders Cl CFDH BH17 ...... 35 C4
Lodge Cl PSTN BH14 ...... 74 C1
Lodge Ct PSTN BH14 ...... 74 C1
Lodge Rd CHCH/BSGR BH23 ...... 61 E2
LYMN SO41 ...... 50 B4
Loewy Crs BKME/WDN BH12 ..... 37 F5
Lombard Av SBNE BH6 ...... 60 D5
Lombardy Cl VWD BH31 ...... 4 D3
London La CHCH/BSGR BH23 ..... 31 F2
Lone Pine Dr FERN BH22 ...... 28 A1
Lone Pine Wy FERN BH22 ...... 28 B2
Longbarrow Cl CHAR BH8 ...... 60 A1
Longespee Rd WIMB BH22 ...... 25 E4
Longfield Dr BWD BH11 ...... 38 A1
FERN BH22 ...... 28 A4
Longfield Rd LYMN SO41 ...... 48 D5
Longfleet Dr WIMB BH21 ...... 25 C5
Longfleet Rd PLE BH15 ...... 73 E1
Long La RGWD BH24 ...... 13 H2
WIMB BH21 ...... 16 D2
Longleat Gdns NMIL/BTOS BH25 .. 46 C4

Longmeadow La CFDH BH17 ...... 53 G1
Long Rd NBNE BH10 ...... 38 C3
Lonnen Rd WIMB BH21 ...... 17 G1
Lonnen Wood Cl WIMB BH21 .... 17 G1
Lonsdale Rd TWDS BH3 ...... 58 B3
Loraine Av CHCH/BSGR BH23 ..... 65 E2
Lord Cl CFDH BH17 ...... 55 F3
Lorne Park Rd BMTH BH1 ...... 3 J3
Lower Ashley Rd
NMIL/BTOS BH25 ...... 47 H4
Lower Blandford Rd
BDST BH18 ...... 35 E3
Lower Buckland Rd LYMN SO41 .. 50 D2
Lower Golf Links Rd BDST BH18 .. 35 F2
Lower Pennington La
LYMN SO41 ...... 69 H1
Lowther Rd CHAR BH8 ...... 58 C4
Lucas Rd BKME/WDN BH12 ...... 56 A4
Lucerne Av SBNE BH6 ...... 60 D5
Lucerne Rd LYMN SO41 ...... 82 B1
Luckham Cl MOOR/WNTN BH9 ... 39 H5
Luckham Pl MOOR/WNTN BH9 ... 39 H5
Luckham Rd MOOR/WNTN BH9... 39 H5
Luckham Rd East
MOOR/WNTN BH9 ...... 39 H5
Lulworth Av PLE BH15 ...... 71 G4
Lulworth Cl PLE BH15 ...... 71 G4
Lulworth Crs PLE BH15 ...... 71 G4
Lumby Dr RGWD BH24 ...... 8 D3
Lumby Drive Pk RGWD BH24 ..... 8 D3
Luscombe Rd PSTN BH14 ...... 74 A3
Luther Rd MOOR/WNTN BH9 ..... 58 B2
Lych Gate Ct RGWD BH24 ...... 9 E5
Lydford Gdns BWD BH11 ...... 38 A5
Lydford Rd BWD BH11 ...... 38 A5
Lydgate LYMN SO41 ...... 67 G5
Lydlinch Cl FERN BH22 ...... 27 H3
Lydwell Cl BWD BH11 ...... 37 H2
Lyell Rd BKME/WDN BH12 ...... 56 A4
Lyme Crs CHCH/BSGR BH23 ...... 64 B2
Lymefields LYMN SO41 ...... 68 C4
Lymington Rd CHCH/BSGR BH23.. 63 H3
LYMN SO41 ...... 68 C3
NMIL/BTOS BH25 ...... 66 A1
Lymington Road Shelley Hl
CHCH/BSGR BH23 ...... 63 G3
Lymore La LYMN SO41 ...... 68 C2
Lymore Va LYMN SO41 ...... 68 C2
Lyndale Cl LYMN SO41 ...... 68 C5
Lyndhurst Rd BROC SO42 ...... 15 C2
CHCH/BSGR BH23 ...... 43 H3
CHCH/BSGR BH23 ...... 63 F1
Lynes La RGWD BH24 ...... 8 B4
Lynn Rd CFDH BH17 ...... 55 F2
Lynric Cl NMIL/BTOS BH25 ...... 65 H3
Lynton Crs CHCH/BSGR BH23 .... 41 H4
Lynwood Cl FERN BH22 ...... 19 H2
Lynwood Dr WIMB BH21 ...... 25 F3
Lyon Av NMIL/BTOS BH25 ...... 47 F4
Lyon Rd BKME/WDN BH12 ...... 37 G5
Lysander Cl CHCH/BSGR BH23 ... 63 F3
Lystra Rd MOOR/WNTN BH9 ..... 39 C4
Lytchett Dr BDST BH18 ...... 35 E4
Lytchett Wy UPTN BH16 ...... 52 D4
Lylteltane Rd LYMN SO41 ...... 50 D5
Lytham Rd BDST BH18 ...... 35 E4
Lytton Rd BMTH BH1 ...... 59 E5

M

Mabey Av NBNE BH10 ...... 38 D5
Macandrew Rd CCLF BH13 ...... 85 H1
Macaulay Rd BDST BH18 ...... 35 E3
Maclaren Rd MOOR/WNTN BH9... 39 F4
Maclean Rd BWD BH11 ...... 37 H4
Madeira Rd BMTH BH1 ...... 3 J2
PSTN BH14 ...... 56 B5
Madeline Crs BKME/WDN BH12... 55 H3
Madison Av BMTH BH1 ...... 59 F4
Magdalen La CHCH/BSGR BH23 .. 61 G4
Magna Cl BWD BH11 ...... 37 H1
Magna Gdns BWD BH11 ...... 37 H1
Magna Rd WIMB BH21 ...... 25 H4
Magnolia Cl SBNE BH6 ...... 61 G5
VWD BH31 ...... 5 E4
Magpie Cl CHAR BH8 ...... 40 A4
Magpie Gv NMIL/BTOS BH25 ..... 46 D5
Mag's Barrow FERN BH22 ...... 10 C5
Maidment Cl BWD BH11 ...... 37 G3
Main Rd LYMN SO41 ...... 51 G1
Malan Cl CFDH BH17 ...... 55 G1
Malcomb Cl SBNE BH6 ...... 79 G2
Mallard Cl CHCH/BSGR BH23 ..... 59 E1
CHCH/BSGR BH23 ...... 63 E4
LYMN SO41 ...... 48 C4
Mallard Rd CHAR BH8 ...... 59 F1

WIMB BH21 ...... 17 C2
Mallory Cl CHCH/BSGR BH23 ..... 62 D2
Mallow Cl BDST BH18 ...... 34 C4
The Mallows NMIL/BTOS BH25.... 47 H3
Malmesbury Ct CHAR BH8 ...... 59 E4
Malmesbury Park Rd CHAR BH8 .. 58 D4
Malmesbury Rd RGWD BH24 ..... 11 C3
Maloren Wy FERN BH22 ...... 10 C5
Malthouse PLE BH15 ...... 72 C3
Malvern Cl MOOR/WNTN BH9 .... 39 G4
Malvern Rd MOOR/WNTN BH9.... 39 C5
Mandale Cl BWD BH11 ...... 38 A3
Mandale Rd BWD BH11 ...... 37 H4
Manderley LYMN SO41 ...... 82 C5
Manning Av CHCH/BSGR BH23 ... 63 G1
Mannings Heath Rd
BKME/WDN BH12 ...... 36 D5
Mannington Pl WCLF BH2 ...... 2 E4
Manor Av BKME/WDN BH12 ...... 56 A1
Manor Cl FERN BH22 ...... 20 A4
LYMN SO41 ...... 68 B5
Manor Ct RGWD BH24 ...... 8 B3
VWD BH31 ...... 4 B2
Manor Farm Cl
NMIL/BTOS BH25 ...... 65 H1
Manor Farm Rd NBNE BH10 ...... 38 C1
Manor Gdns RGWD BH24 ...... 8 B3
VWD BH31 ...... 4 B2
Manor La VWD BH31 ...... 4 B3
Manor Rd BMTH BH1 ...... 77 E2
CHCH/BSGR BH23 ...... 61 G4
LYMN SO41 ...... 68 B4
NMIL/BTOS BH25 ...... 47 F4
RGWD BH24 ...... 8 C4
VWD BH31 ...... 4 B2
Manor Wy VWD BH31 ...... 4 B1
Mansel Cl BKME/WDN BH12 ...... 57 C3
Mansfield Cl FERN BH22 ...... 27 H2
Mansfield Rd MOOR/WNTN BH9 .. 58 A1
PSTN BH14 ...... 74 A1
RGWD BH24 ...... 8 B4
Manton Rd PLE BH15 ...... 71 G2
Maple Cl CHCH/BSGR BH23 ...... 64 B3
NMIL/BTOS BH25 ...... 66 B3
Maple Dr FERN BH22 ...... 19 G1
Maple Rd MOOR/WNTN BH9...... 58 C2
PLE BH15 ...... 72 D2
Mapperton Cl CFDH BH17 ...... 36 C5
Marabout Cl CHCH/BSGR BH23 ... 62 B3
Marchwood Rd NBNE BH10 ...... 38 C4
Margards La VWD BH31 ...... 4 A3
Marian Cl WIMB BH21 ...... 34 A3
Marianne Rd BKME/WDN BH12 ... 57 C2
WIMB BH21 ...... 17 C2
Marian Rd WIMB BH21 ...... 34 A3
Marie Cl BKME/WDN BH12 ...... 56 B3
Marina Dr PSTN BH14 ...... 73 H4
The Marina BOSC BH5 ...... 77 C2
Marine Dr NMIL/BTOS BH25 ...... 65 G3
Marine Dr East
NMIL/BTOS BH25 ...... 66 A4
Marine Dr West
...... 65 F3
Marine Prospect
...... 65 H3
Marine Rd SBNE BH6 ...... 78 D2
Market Cl PLE BH15 ...... 72 C4
Market Pl RGWD BH24 ...... 8 B4
Market St PLE BH15 ...... 72 B4
Market Wy WIMB BH21 ...... 16 D5
Markham Av NBNE BH10 ...... 38 D1
Markham Cl NBNE BH10 ...... 27 H5
Markham Rd MOOR/WNTN BH9 .. 38 D5
Mark's La NMIL/BTOS BH25 ...... 47 E1
Marks Rd MOOR/WNTN BH9 ..... 39 F4
Marlborough Pl LYMN SO41 ...... 50 D2
WBNE BH4 ...... 2 B4
Marlborough Rd PSTN BH14 ...... 74 A1
WBNE BH4 ...... 2 B4
Marley Av NMIL/BTOS BH25 ...... 46 C5
Marley Cl NMIL/BTOS BH25 ...... 46 D4
Marline Rd BKME/WDN BH12 ..... 56 B4
Marlott Rd PLE BH15 ...... 54 C5
Marlow Dr CHCH/BSGR BH23 .... 42 A4
Marlpit Dr CHCH/BSGR BH23 .... 45 C5
Marmion Gn CHCH/BSGR BH23 .. 62 D3
Marnhull Rd PLE BH15 ...... 72 D1
Marpet Cl BWD BH11 ...... 37 H1
Marquis Wy BWD BH11 ...... 37 F2
Marram Cl LYMN SO41 ...... 51 E1
Marryat Rd NMIL/BTOS BH25 ..... 46 D4
Marshal Rd CFDH BH17 ...... 54 B1
Marshfield WIMB BH21 ...... 17 F2
Marsh La CHCH/BSGR BH23 ...... 42 B5
LYMN SO41 ...... 51 E1
UPTN BH16 ...... 52 C3
Marshwood Av CFDH BH17 ...... 36 B5
Marston Cl NMIL/BTOS BH25 ..... 47 F2

Marston Gv *CHCH/BSGR* BH23 ...... 64 A1
Marston Rd *NMIL/BTOS* BH25 ...... 47 F2
  PLE BH15 .... 72 B3 ▣
Martello Pk *CCLF* BH13 .... 85 H1
Martello Rd *CCLF* BH13 .... 74 D4
The Martells *NMIL/BTOS* BH25 .... 66 B3
Martin Cl *CFDH* BH17 .... 53 G3
Martindale Av *WIMB* BH21 .... 17 H4
Martingale Cl *UPTN* BH16 .... 53 F3
Martins Cl *FERN* BH22 .... 20 A2
Martins Dr *FERN* BH22 .... 20 A2
Martins Hill Cl *CHCH/BSGR* BH23 .. 62 A1
Martins Hill La
  CHCH/BSGR BH23 .... 62 B1 ▣
Martin's Rd *BROC* SO42 .... 15 G2
Martins Wy *FERN* BH22 .... 20 A2
Marwell Cl *LTDN* BH7 .... 60 A3
Maryland Rd *UPTN* BH16 .... 71 E1
Matchams La *CHCH/BSGR* BH23 .. 30 B5
  RGWD BH24 .... 22 B4
Matlock Rd *FERN* BH22 .... 27 G1
Maturin Cl *LYMN* SO41 .... 50 D4
Maundeville Crs
  CHCH/BSGR BH23 .... 61 G2
Maundeville Rd
  CHCH/BSGR BH23 .... 61 E2
Maureen Cl *BKME/WDN* BH12 ..... 55 H2
Mavis Rd *MOOR/WNTN* BH9 .... 58 D1
Maxwell Rd *BDST* BH18 .... 34 B4
  CCLF BH13 .... 85 H1
  MOOR/WNTN BH9 .... 58 C3
May Av *LYMN* SO41 .... 50 D2
Mayfair Gdns *BWD* BH11 .... 38 A3
Mayfield Av *PSTN* BH14 .... 74 C2
Mayfield Cl *FERN* BH22 .... 19 G3
Mayfield Dr *FERN* BH22 .... 19 G3
Mayfield Rd *MOOR/WNTN* BH9 .... 39 G5
Mayfield Wy *FERN* BH22 .... 19 G3
Mayflower Cl *LYMN* SO41 .... 51 G4
Mayford Rd *BKME/WDN* BH12 ..... 57 F4
May Gdns *BWD* BH11 .... 37 G4
  CHCH/BSGR BH23 .... 45 H5
Mcintyre Rd *CHCH/BSGR* BH23 ... 29 H4
Mckinley Rd *WBNE* BH4 .... 2 A6
Mcwilliam Cl *BKME/WDN* BH12 ... 57 C2
Mcwilliam Rd
  MOOR/WNTN BH9 .... 39 G5 ▣
Mead Cl *CFDH* BH17 .... 54 A1
Meadow Cl *CHCH/BSGR* BH23 ..... 31 H5
  CHCH/BSGR BH23 .... 33 E5 ▣
  FERN BH22 .... 27 H3
  RGWD BH24 .... 8 D3
Meadow Court Cl
  MOOR/WNTN BH9 .... 39 G4
Meadow Gv *VWD* BH31 .... 4 D3
Meadowland *CHCH/BSGR* BH23 .. 62 C4
Meadowlands *LYMN* SO41 .... 50 C3
Meadow La *CHCH/BSGR* BH23 .... 43 E5
Meadow Ri *BDST* BH18 .... 34 D2
Meadow Rd *LYMN* SO41 .... 50 C5
  NMIL/BTOS BH25 .... 47 F3
  RGWD BH24 .... 8 D3
Meadows Cl *UPTN* BH16 .... 53 E2 ▣
Meadows Dr *UPTN* BH16 .... 53 E3 ▣
Meadowsweet Rd *CFDH* BH17 .... 53 G2
Meadow View Rd *BWD* BH11 ...... 37 G2
Meadow Wy *NMIL/BTOS* BH25 .... 66 A3
  RGWD BH24 .... 8 D3
  VWD BH31 .... 4 D4
Mead Rd *LYMN* SO41 .... 50 B5
The Meadway *CHCH/BSGR* BH23 . 64 C4
Medina Wy *CHCH/BSGR* BH23 ..... 63 G4
Medlar Cl *CHCH/BSGR* BH23 ...... 62 B1
Medway Rd *FERN* BH22 .... 20 C3
Meerut Rd *BROC* SO42 .... 14 D2
Meeting House La *RGWD* BH24 ... 8 B4 ▣
Melbourne Rd *CHAR* BH8 .... 59 E4 ▣
  CHCH/BSGR BH23 .... 61 E1
Melbury Av *BKME/WDN* BH12 ..... 56 C2
Melbury Cl *FERN* BH22 .... 19 H5
  LYMN SO41 .... 50 D4 ▣
Mellstock Rd *PLE* BH15 .... 54 C5
Melrose Ct *NMIL/BTOS* BH25 ..... 47 G4 ▣
Melverley Gdns *WIMB* BH21 .... 16 D4
Melville Rd *MOOR/WNTN* BH9 .... 58 A2
Mendip Cl *NMIL/BTOS* BH25 .... 47 F5
  VWD BH31 .... 4 B3 ▣
Mendip Rd *VWD* BH31 .... 4 B2
Mentone Rd *PSTN* BH14 .... 73 G2 ▣
Meon Rd *LTDN* BH7 .... 60 B3
Meredith Cl *CHCH/BSGR* BH23 ... 62 B3
Meriden Cl *CCLF* BH13 .... 85 H1
The Meridians *CHCH/BSGR* BH23.. 61 F5
Merino Wy *FERN* BH22 .... 10 B5
Merley Dr *CHCH/BSGR* BH23 ...... 64 C2
Merley Gdns *WIMB* BH21 .... 24 D3
Merley La *WIMB* BH21 .... 24 D3
Merley Park Rd *WIMB* BH21........ 24 C4

Merley Ways *WIMB* BH21 .... 24 D1
Merlin Rd *RGWD* BH24 .... 9 E5
Merlin Wy *CHCH/BSGR* BH23 ...... 63 E5
Merriefield Cl *BDST* BH18 .... 35 G1 ▣
Merriefield Dr *BDST* BH18 .... 35 F1
Merrifield *WIMB* BH21 .... 17 E2
Merrifield Cl *BDST* BH18 .... 35 F1
Merritown La *CHCH/BSGR* BH23 . 29 F5
Merrivale Av *SBNE* BH6 .... 61 E5
Merrow Av *BKME/WDN* BH12 ...... 57 F4
Merryfield Cl *CHCH/BSGR* BH23 .. 33 E4
Merryfield La *NBNE* BH10 .... 38 C3 ▣
Methuen Rd *CFDH* BH17 .... 35 F5
  CHAR BH8 .... 58 D5
Meyrick Cl *CHCH/BSGR* BH23 ..... 33 E5
Meyrick Park Crs *TWDS* BH3 .... 58 B4
Michelgrove Rd *BOSC* BH5 .... 77 G2 ▣
Michelmersh Gn *CHAR* BH8 .... 40 B5 ▣
Mickleham Cl *BKME/WDN* BH12 .. 57 F2
Middlebere Crs *UPTN* BH16 .... 71 E1
Middle Common Rd *LYMN* SO41 .. 49 H4
Middlehill Dr *WIMB* BH21 .... 17 H3
Middlehill Rd *WIMB* BH21 .... 17 G2
Middle La *RGWD* BH24 .... 8 C4
Middle Rd *LYMN* SO41 .... 50 D4
  NBNE BH10 .... 38 C2
  PLE BH15 .... 55 E4
Middleton La *NBNE* BH10 .... 39 E5
  RGWD BH24 .... 8 C3
Midland Rd *MOOR/WNTN* BH9 .... 58 B1
Midwood Av *CHAR* BH8 .... 59 H1
Milborne Crs *BKME/WDN* BH12 .. 56 D2
Milbourne Rd *FERN* BH22 .... 19 G3
Milburn Cl *WBNE* BH4 .... 2 A2
Milburn Rd *WBNE* BH4 .... 75 F1
Milestone Rd *PLE* BH15 .... 54 D4
Milford Cl *FERN* BH22 .... 10 B4
Milford Ct *LYMN* SO41 .... 82 C1
Milford Crs *LYMN* SO41 .... 82 C1
Milford Dr *BWD* BH11 .... 37 H2
Milford Rd *LYMN* SO41 .... 68 D1
  NMIL/BTOS BH25 .... 66 C2
Miller Cl *NMIL/BTOS* BH25 .... 47 G3
Miller Rd *CHCH/BSGR* BH23 .... 62 B3
Millfield *CFDH* BH17 .... 54 A3
Millhams Rd *NBNE* BH10 .... 27 E5
Millhams St *CHCH/BSGR* BH23 ... 61 H4
Millhams St North
  CHCH/BSGR BH23 .... 61 H4
Mill Hill La *PSTN* BH14 .... 73 H2
Mill La *BROC* SO42 .... 15 F3
  CHCH/BSGR BH23 .... 41 F1
  CHCH/BSGR BH23 .... 64 D2
  LYMN SO41 .... 51 F3 ▣
  PSTN BH14 .... 73 H2
  WIMB BH21 .... 16 B4
Mill Meadow *LYMN* SO41 .... 68 A5
Mill Rd *CHCH/BSGR* BH23 .... 61 G2
Mill Rd (North) *CHAR* BH8 .... 40 B4
Mill Rd (South) *CHAR* BH8 .... 40 B5
Millstream Cl *CFDH* BH17 .... 54 A3
  WIMB BH21 .... 16 C5
Millyford Cl *NMIL/BTOS* BH25..... 65 F2
Milne Rd *CFDH* BH17 .... 54 B1
Milner Rd *WBNE* BH4 .... 2 B6
Milton Cl *PSTN* BH14 .... 74 B2
Milton Gv *NMIL/BTOS* BH25 .... 47 F5
Milton Md *NMIL/BTOS* BH25 ...... 46 D5
Milton Rd *BMTH* BH1 .... 58 C5
  PSTN BH14 .... 74 B2
  WIMB BH21 .... 16 B4
Milverton Cl *CHCH/BSGR* BH23 .. 64 A1 ▣
Mimosa Av *WIMB* BH21 .... 24 D4
Minstead Rd *NBNE* BH10 .... 38 C4
Minster Vw *WIMB* BH21 .... 16 C4
Minster Wy *UPTN* BH16 .... 52 D3
Minterne Rd *CHCH/BSGR* BH23 .. 62 C5
  MOOR/WNTN BH9 .... 39 G5 ▣
  PSTN BH14 .... 85 E1
Mission Rd *BDST* BH18 .... 35 E5
Mitchell Cl *NMIL/BTOS* BH25...... 66 A3
Mitchell Rd *CFDH* BH17 .... 55 F2
  WIMB BH21 .... 19 E2
Moat La *NMIL/BTOS* BH25 .... 65 H1
Moffat Rd *CHCH/BSGR* BH23 ..... 62 B3
Molyneux Rd *NMIL/BTOS* BH25 .. 47 H4
Moneyfly Rd *VWD* BH31 .... 4 D3
Monks Cl *FERN* BH22 .... 20 C1
Monkshood Cl
  CHCH/BSGR BH23 .... 63 F1 ▣
Monks Wy *WIMB* BH21 .... 37 E2
Monkswell Gn *CHCH/BSGR* BH23.. 62 B4
Monkton Cl *FERN* BH22 .... 19 H3
Monkton Crs *BKME/WDN* BH12 .. 56 B1
Monkworthy Dr *RGWD* BH24 ...... 11 H1
Monmouth Cl *VWD* BH31 .... 4 D4
Monmouth Dr *VWD* BH31 .... 4 D4
Monsal Av *FERN* BH22 .... 27 G1

Montacute Wy *WIMB* BH21 .... 25 E4
Montague Rd *BOSC* BH5 .... 78 B1
Montagu Rd *CHCH/BSGR* BH23 .. 64 D3
Monteray Dr *LYMN* SO41 .... 48 B3
Montgomery Av *BWD* BH11 .... 38 B4
Montrose Cl *VWD* BH31 .... 4 B2
Montrose Dr *NBNE* BH10 .... 38 D5
Monument La *LYMN* SO41 .... 51 G2
Moonrakers Wy
  CHCH/BSGR BH23 .... 64 A1
Moorcroft Av *CHCH/BSGR* BH23 .. 43 E5
Moordown Cl *MOOR/WNTN* BH9.. 39 G4
Moore Av *BWD* BH11 .... 38 A4
Moore Cl *NMIL/BTOS* BH25 .... 65 H1 ▣
Moorfield Gv *MOOR/WNTN* BH9 .. 39 F5
Moorfields Rd *CCLF* BH13 .... 74 D5 ▣
Moorland Av *NMIL/BTOS* BH25 ... 65 H2
Moorland Crs *UPTN* BH16 .... 52 D5
Moorland Ga *RGWD* BH24 .... 13 C1
Moorland Rd *BMTH* BH1 .... 77 F1
Moorlands Cl *BROC* SO42 .... 14 B3
Moorlands Ri *FERN* BH22 .... 10 A4
Moorlands Rd *FERN* BH22 .... 10 A4
  VWD BH31 .... 4 B1
Moorland Wy *UPTN* BH16 .... 52 D3
Moor Rd *BDST* BH18 .... 35 F2
Moors Cl *CHCH/BSGR* BH23 ...... 30 B5
Moorside Cl *BWD* BH11 .... 38 B4 ▣
Moorside Rd *BWD* BH11 .... 38 A4
  FERN BH22 .... 10 A4
  WIMB BH21 .... 34 B2
Moortown Dr *WIMB* BH21 .... 25 H3
Moortown La *RGWD* BH24 .... 13 H2
Moorvale Rd *MOOR/WNTN* BH9 .. 39 C5
Moor View Rd *PLE* BH15 .... 55 C4
Morant Rd *RGWD* BH24 .... 8 D2
Morden Av *FERN* BH22 .... 10 B4
Morden Rd *MOOR/WNTN* BH9 .. 58 B1 ▣
Moreton Rd *MOOR/WNTN* BH9 ... 39 H3
Morley Cl *BOSC* BH5 .... 60 A5
  CHCH/BSGR BH23 .... 43 E4
Morley Rd *BOSC* BH5 .... 60 A5 ▣
Mornish Rd *CCLF* BH13 .... 74 D3
Morrison Av *BKME/WDN* BH12 ... 56 D4
Mortimer Cl *CHCH/BSGR* BH23 .. 63 E4
Mortimer Rd *CHAR* BH8 .... 58 D1
Mossley Av *BKME/WDN* BH12 .... 56 D1
Motcombe Rd *CCLF* BH13 .... 75 E4
Mount Av *NMIL/BTOS* BH25 .... 66 A1
Mountbatten Cl
  CHCH/BSGR BH23 .... 63 E5 ▣
Mountbatten Dr *FERN* BH22 ...... 19 G4
Mountbatten Rd *CCLF* BH13 .... 75 E4
  CHAR BH8 .... 40 D5 ▣
Mount Cl *NMIL/BTOS* BH25 .... 66 A1
Mount Grace Dr *PSTN* BH14 .... 85 E1
Mountjoy Cl *WIMB* BH21 .... 25 F2
Mount Pleasant *RGWD* BH24 ..... 8 C4 ▣
Mount Pleasant Dr *CHAR* BH8 .... 59 H1
  CHCH/BSGR BH23 .... 33 G3 ▣
Mount Pleasant Rd *PLE* BH15 ..... 72 D3
Mount Rd *BWD* BH11 .... 38 A3
  PSTN BH14 .... 55 H5
The Mount *RGWD* BH24 .... 9 F3
Mudeford *CHCH/BSGR* BH23 ..... 62 D5
Mudeford Green Cl
  CHCH/BSGR BH23 .... 62 D5 ▣
Mudeford La *CHCH/BSGR* BH23 .. 62 D4
Mude Gdns *CHCH/BSGR* BH23 ... 63 E5
Mullins Cl *BKME/WDN* BH12 ...... 57 C2
Munster Rd *PSTN* BH14 .... 74 B2
Murley Rd *MOOR/WNTN* BH9 ..... 58 C2
Muscliffe La *MOOR/WNTN* BH9 .. 39 E4
Muscliffe Pk *MOOR/WNTN* BH9 .. 40 A3
Muscliffe Rd *MOOR/WNTN* BH9 .. 39 F4
Myrtle Cl *LYMN* SO41 .... 48 B3 ▣
Myrtle Rd *CHAR* BH8 .... 59 E4

N

Nada Rd *CHCH/BSGR* BH23 .... 63 H1
Nairn Rd *CCLF* BH13 .... 85 G1
  TWDS BH3 .... 58 A4
Naish Rd *NMIL/BTOS* BH25 .... 65 F3
Namu Rd *MOOR/WNTN* BH9 .... 58 A1
Nansen Av *PLE* BH15 .... 54 D5
Napier Rd *PLE* BH15 .... 71 E2
Narrow La *RGWD* BH24 .... 9 F2
Naseby Rd *MOOR/WNTN* BH9 .... 58 C1
Nathen Gdns *PLE* BH15 .... 71 F2 ▣
Nea Cl *CHCH/BSGR* BH23 .... 63 H2
Neacroft Cl *NMIL/BTOS* BH25..... 65 F2
Nea Rd *CHCH/BSGR* BH23 .... 64 A2
Needles Point *LYMN* SO41 .... 82 B1
Nelson Cl *CHCH/BSGR* BH23 ...... 62 D4
Nelson Dr *CHCH/BSGR* BH23 ...... 62 D4

Nelson Pl *LYMN* SO41 .... 51 F4
Nelson Rd *BKME/WDN* BH12 ...... 75 F1
Netherhall Gdns *WBNE* BH4 .... 2 B3
Netherwood Pl *WIMB* BH21 .... 16 A4
Netley Cl *PLE* BH15 .... 55 C3
Nettleton Cl *CFDH* BH17 .... 55 E3
New Borough Rd *WIMB* BH21 ..... 24 C1
Newbridge Wy *LYMN* SO41 .... 69 C1
Newbury Dr *NBNE* BH10 .... 57 H1 ▣
Newcombe Rd *SBNE* BH6 .... 61 E4
Newcroft Gdns
  CHCH/BSGR BH23 .... 61 G2
Newenham Rd *LYMN* SO41 .... 51 G5
New Forest Dr *BROC* SO42 .... 14 B3
Newfoundland Dr *PLE* BH15 .... 72 D4
New Harbour Rd South
  PLE BH15 .... 72 B4
Newlands Rd *CHCH/BSGR* BH23 .. 62 D3
  LTDN BH7 .... 60 A4
  NMIL/BTOS BH25 .... 66 B1
Newlands Wy *BDST* BH18 .... 34 B4
New La *LYMN* SO41 .... 82 D2
  NMIL/BTOS BH25 .... 46 D1
Newlyn Wy *BKME/WDN* BH12 .... 56 C3
Newmans Cl *WIMB* BH21 .... 10 A1 ▣
New Merrifield *WIMB* BH21 .... 17 F2 ▣
Newmorton Rd
  MOOR/WNTN BH9 .... 39 C3
New Orch *PLE* BH15 .... 72 B3
New Park Rd *SBNE* BH6 .... 78 C1
New Quay Rd *PLE* BH15 .... 72 A4
New Rd *BKME/WDN* BH12 .... 56 B4
  FERN BH22 .... 28 A4
  LYMN SO41 .... 83 E1
  NBNE BH10 .... 39 E2
Newstead Rd *SBNE* BH6 .... 78 D1
New St *LYMN* SO41 .... 51 E3
  PLE BH15 .... 72 B4 ▣
  RGWD BH24 .... 8 C5
Newton Morrell *PSTN* BH14 ...... 74 B2 ▣
Newton Rd *CCLF* BH13 .... 74 C5
  NMIL/BTOS BH25 .... 66 B2
Newtown Rd *VWD* BH31 .... 4 C4
New Valley Rd *LYMN* SO41 .... 82 A4
Nicholas Cl *CHCH/BSGR* BH23 ... 45 H5 ▣
Nicholas Gdns *NBNE* BH10 .... 38 C5
Nicholson Cl *CFDH* BH17 .... 55 E2 ▣
Nightingale Cl *VWD* BH31 .... 4 C3 ▣
Nightjar Cl *CFDH* BH17 .... 53 G2
Nimrod Wy *WIMB* BH21 .... 18 D3
Noble Cl *BWD* BH11 .... 56 D1
Noel Cl *BROC* SO42 .... 15 E3
Noel Rd *NBNE* BH10 .... 57 F1
Noon Gdns *VWD* BH31 .... 4 D2
Noon Hill Dr *VWD* BH31 .... 4 D2 ▣
Noon Hill Rd *VWD* BH31 .... 4 D2
Norcliffe Cl *BWD* BH11 .... 38 B4
Norfolk Av *CHCH/BSGR* BH23 ..... 61 F1
Norleywood *CHCH/BSGR* BH23 . 64 D2 ▣
Norman Av *BKME/WDN* BH12 .... 56 D4
Normandy La *LYMN* SO41 .... 51 F5
Normandy Dr *CHCH/BSGR* BH23 .. 62 D4
Normandy Wy *PLE* BH15 .... 71 F3
Norman Gdns *BKME/WDN* BH12 .. 57 E4
Normanhurst Av *CHAR* BH8 .... 59 F1
Normanton Cl *CHCH/BSGR* BH23.. 61 F1
Norris Cl *RGWD* BH24 .... 11 G2
Norris Gdns *NMIL/BTOS* BH25 ... 66 A4
Norrish Rd *BKME/WDN* BH12 ..... 56 A5
North Av *NBNE* BH10 .... 38 D1
Northbourne Av *NBNE* BH10 ...... 38 D2
Northbourne Gdns *NBNE* BH10... 39 E2
Northbourne Pl *NBNE* BH10 ...... 38 D2 ▣
Northbrook Rd *BDST* BH18 .... 35 E5
North Cl *LYMN* SO41 .... 51 E3
Northcote Rd *BMTH* BH1 .... 77 E1
Northey Rd *SBNE* BH6 .... 61 E4
Northfield Rd *LYMN* SO41 .... 68 C5
  RGWD BH24 .... 8 C2
North Greenlands *LYMN* SO41 ... 50 C5
North Head *LYMN* SO41 .... 67 G5
Northleigh La *WIMB* BH21 .... 17 E5
North Lodge Rd *PSTN* BH14 .... 74 C1
Northmead Dr *CFDH* BH17 .... 53 H2
Northmere Dr *BKME/WDN* BH12 .. 56 D5
Northmere Rd
  BKME/WDN BH12 .... 56 D5
Northover Rd *LYMN* SO41 .... 50 A3
North Poulner Rd *RGWD* BH24 ... 8 D2
North Rd *BROC* SO42 .... 15 E3
  LTDN BH7 .... 59 G5
  PLE BH15 .... 72 A3
  PSTN BH14 .... 73 G2
North St *LYMN* SO41 .... 50 C5
  PLE BH15 .... 72 C1
North Weirs *BROC* SO42 .... 14 B3
Nortoft Rd *CHAR* BH8 .... 59 E4 ▣
Norton Cl *CHCH/BSGR* BH23....... 62 D4

Norton Rd *MOOR/WNTN* BH9...... 58 A1
Norwich Av *WCLF* BH2 .... 2 D3
Norwich Av West *WBNE* BH4....... 2 C3
Norwich Rd *WCLF* BH2 .... 2 C3
Norwood Pl *BOSC* BH5 .... 60 B5
Nouale La *RGWD* BH24 .... 9 F4
Noyce Gdns *SBNE* BH6 .... 41 F5
Nuffield Rd *CFDH* BH17 .... 54 D2
Nugent Rd *SBNE* BH6 .... 79 F1
Nursery Rd *MOOR/WNTN* BH9 ... 39 G4
   RGWD BH24 .... 8 C5 🔲
Nursling Gn *CHAR* BH8 .... 40 B5
Nuthatch Cl *CFDH* BH17 .... 53 H3
   FERN BH22 .... 19 F1
Nutley Cl *BWD* BH11 .... 37 H3
Nutley Wy *BWD* BH11 .... 37 H4

O

Oak Av *CHCH/BSGR* BH23 .... 60 D2
Oak Cl *FERN* BH22 .... 28 A3
   WIMB BH21 .... 34 A2
Oakdale Rd *PLE* BH15 .... 55 E4
Oakdene Cl *WIMB* BH21 .... 16 D4 🔲
Oakfield Rd *PLE* BH15 .... 54 C4
Oak Gdns *LYMN* SO41 .... 68 D2 🔲
Oakhurst Cl *FERN* BH22 .... 10 B4
Oakhurst La *FERN* BH22 .... 10 B4
Oakhurst Rd *FERN* BH22 .... 10 B5
Oaklands *LYMN* SO41 .... 51 F5
Oaklands Cl *VWD* BH31 .... 4 A2
Oakland Wk *FERN* BH22 .... 28 A3
Oak La *RGWD* BH24 .... 8 D3
Oakleigh Wy *CHCH/BSGR* BH23 .. 64 B3
Oakley Gdns *UPTN* BH16............ 52 C3
Oakley Hl *WIMB* BH21 .... 24 D1
Oakley La *WIMB* BH21 .... 24 D2
Oakley Rd *WIMB* BH21 .... 24 D2
Oakley Straight *WIMB* BH21 ...... 25 E3
Oakmead Gdns *BWD* BH11 .... 37 H3
Oakmead Rd *CFDH* BH17 .... 54 A3 🔲
Oak Rd *CHAR* BH8 .... 59 E4
   NMIL/BTOS BH25 .... 47 G4
   UPTN BH16 .... 53 E4
Oaks Dr *RGWD* BH24 .... 11 F3
Oaks Md *VWD* BH31 .... 4 C2 🔲
The Oaks *VWD* BH31 .... 4 A2
Oakwood Av *NMIL/BTOS* BH25 .... 47 G3
Oakwood Cl
   MOOR/WNTN BH9 .... 39 H5 🔲
Oakwood Rd *CHCH/BSGR* BH23... 64 A1
   MOOR/WNTN BH9 .... 39 G5
Oates Rd *MOOR/WNTN* BH9 ...... 58 A4
Oban Rd *TWDS* BH3 .... 58 A3
Oberfield Rd *BROC* SO42 .... 14 B2
Ober Rd *BROC* SO42 .... 14 C2
Ockeford Rd *BDST* BH18 .... 35 F5
Old Barn Cl *CHCH/BSGR* BH23 .... 41 H5 🔲
   RGWD BH24 .... 8 D4
Old Barn Farm Rd *WIMB* BH21 ... 10 C1
Old Barn Rd *CHCH/BSGR* BH23... 41 H5
Old Bound Rd *UPTN* BH16 .... 53 E4
Old Bridge Rd *LTDN* BH7 .... 60 D2
Old Christchurch Rd *BMTH* BH1 ... 3 J3
   LYMN SO41 .... 68 B1
Old Coastguard Rd *CCLF* BH13 ... 84 D4
Old Farm Cl *RGWD* BH24 .... 9 F1
Old Farm Rd *PLE* BH15 .... 55 E4
Old Farm Wk *LYMN* SO41 .... 50 D4
Old Forge Rd *WIMB* BH21........... 18 D3
Old Ham La *WIMB* BH21 .... 18 B5
Old Kiln Rd *UPTN* BH16 .... 53 E3
Old Manor Cl *WIMB* BH21 .... 17 E5
Old Milton Gn *NMIL/BTOS* BH25... 65 H1
Old Milton Rd *NMIL/BTOS* BH25... 65 H1
Old Mulberry Cl *NBNE* BH10 ... 57 E1 🔲
Old Orch *PLE* BH15..................... 72 C4
Old Orchards *LYMN* SO41 .... 51 F5
Old Pines Cl *FERN* BH22 .... 20 A5
Old Priory Rd *SBNE* BH6 .... 79 F1
Old Rd *WIMB* BH21 .... 16 B5
Old Rope Wk *PLE* BH15 .... 71 H4
Old Sawmill Cl *VWD* BH31 .... 4 A2
Old School Cl *FERN* BH22 .... 19 G4 🔲
Old Stacks Gdns *RGWD* BH24 ..... 9 E5 🔲
Old St John's Ms *NBNE* BH10 .... 39 F4 🔲
Old Vicarage Rd *NBNE* BH9 ...... 39 E1 🔲
Old Wareham Rd
   BKME/WDN BH12 .... 55 G3
Oliver Rd *LYMN* SO41 .... 50 C4
Olivers Rd *WIMB* BH21 .... 17 G3
Olivers Wy *WIMB* BH21 .... 17 G3 🔲
Onslow Gdns *WIMB* BH21 .... 16 D3
Ophir Gdns *CHAR* BH8 .... 58 D5
Ophir Rd *CHAR* BH8 .... 58 D5
Oratory Gdns *CCLF* BH13 .... 74 D5

Orchard Av *PSTN* BH14 .... 73 F3
Orchard Cl *CHCH/BSGR* BH23 .... 61 G4
   FERN BH22 .... 20 A4
   RGWD BH24 .... 8 C3
Orchard Ct *VWD* BH31 .... 4 C3 🔲
Orchard Gv *NMIL/BTOS* BH25..... 66 A1
Orchard St *WCLF* BH2 .... 3 F4
The Orchard *BWD* BH11 .... 37 F1
   CHCH/BSGR BH23 .... 33 G4 🔲
   LYMN SO41 .... 82 B1
Orcheston Rd *CHAR* BH8............ 59 E4
Orford Cl *CHCH/BSGR* BH23 ...... 41 H3
Ormonde Rd *CCLF* BH13 .... 75 E3
Osborne Rd *MOOR/WNTN* BH9 ... 58 A2
   NMIL/BTOS BH25................ 47 F4
   PSTN BH14 .... 73 H2
   WIMB BH21 .... 16 D5
Osprey Cl *CHCH/BSGR* BH23 ..... 63 E5
Oswald Cl *MOOR/WNTN* BH9 ..... 39 E5
Oswald Rd *MOOR/WNTN* BH9 .... 39 E5
Otter Cl *UPTN* BH16 .... 52 D4
   VWD BH31 .... 4 C3
Otter Rd *PLE* BH15 .... 55 F4
Otters Wk *NMIL/BTOS* BH25....... 47 G1
Overbury Rd *PSTN* BH14 .... 74 A2
Overcombe Cl *CFDH* BH17 .... 36 A5
Over Links Dr *PSTN* BH14 .... 74 B3
Overstand Crs *LYMN* SO41 .... 82 B2
Ovington Av *LTDN* BH7 .... 60 C3
Ovington Gdns *LTDN* BH7 .... 60 C3
Owls Rd *BOSC* BH5 .... 77 G2
   VWD BH31 .... 4 C3
Oxford Av *SBNE* BH6 .... 60 B5
Oxford La *BWD* BH11.................. 38 B1

P

Paddington Gv *BWD* BH11........... 37 F1
Paddock Cl *BKME/WDN* BH12 .... 55 H3 🔲
   RGWD BH24 .... 11 H2
   WIMB BH21 .... 19 E3
Paddock Gdns *LYMN* SO41 .... 50 D2
Paddock Gv *VWD* BH31 .... 4 C3
The Paddock *BROC* SO42 .... 14 D3 🔲
Padfield Cl *SBNE* BH6 .... 61 E4
Padget Rd *RGWD* BH24 .... 9 E2 🔲
Paget Cl *WIMB* BH21 .... 17 G2
Paget Rd *BWD* BH11 .... 38 A3
Paisley Rd *SBNE* BH6 .... 60 C5
Palfrey Rd *NBNE* BH10 .... 38 D3
Palmer Pl *NMIL/BTOS* BH25........ 47 E3
Palmer Rd *PLE* BH15 .... 54 C5
Palmerston Av
   CHCH/BSGR BH23 .... 62 B4
Palmerston Cl *UPTN* BH16 ...... 53 F3 🔲
Palmerston Ms *BMTH* BH1 ...... 59 C5 🔲
Palmerston Rd *BMTH* BH1 .... 59 G5
   BOSC BH5 .... 77 G1 🔲
   PSTN BH14 .... 74 B1
   UPTN BH16 .... 53 E3
Pamplyn Cl *LYMN* SO41 .... 50 C3
Panorama Rd *CCLF* BH13 .... 84 C5
Paradise St *PLE* BH15 .... 72 B4 🔲
Parham Rd *NBNE* BH10 .... 38 C5
Parish Rd *PLE* BH15 .... 73 E2
Park Av *LYMN* SO41 .... 50 D3
   NBNE BH10 .... 38 C1
Park Cl *BROC* SO42 .... 15 E2
   CHCH/BSGR BH23 .... 43 E4
   LYMN SO41 .... 68 C5
   NMIL/BTOS BH25................ 47 G2
Park Dr *VWD* BH31 .... 4 A3
Parker Rd *MOOR/WNTN* BH9 ..... 58 B3
Park Homer Dr *WIMB* BH21 .... 17 F3
Park Homer Rd *WIMB* BH21 ... 17 F2 🔲
Park Lake Rd *PLE* BH15 .... 73 E3
Parkland *VWD* BH31 .... 5 F4
Parkland Dr *NMIL/BTOS* BH25 .... 65 H4
Park La *LYMN* SO41 .... 82 A1
   NBNE BH10 .... 39 F3
   WIMB BH21 .... 16 C5
Park Rd *BMTH* BH1 .... 3 K1
   LYMN SO41 .... 50 D3
   LYMN SO41 .... 82 C1
   NMIL/BTOS BH25................ 47 G2
   NMIL/BTOS BH25................ 65 H1
   PLE BH15 .... 73 F2
Parkside *CHCH/BSGR* BH23 .... 63 H1
   RGWD BH24 .... 8 D1
Parkside Gdns *NBNE* BH10 ..... 39 E5 🔲
Parkside Rd *PSTN* BH14 .... 74 A1
Parkstone Av *PSTN* BH14 .... 74 B1
Parkstone Hts *PSTN* BH14 .... 55 H5
Parkstone Rd *PLE* BH15 .... 73 E2
The Park *NMIL/BTOS* 65 E3
Park Wy *FERN* BH22 .... 10 A4 🔲

Parkway Dr *CHAR* BH8 .... 59 G2
Parkwood Rd *BOSC* BH5............. 78 B1
   WIMB BH21 .... 16 C5
Parley Cl *CHCH/BSGR* BH23 ...... 28 B3
Parley La *CHCH/BSGR* BH23 ...... 28 D4
Parley Rd *MOOR/WNTN* BH9 ..... 39 G5
Parmiter Dr *WIMB* BH21 .... 17 E5
Parmiter Rd *WIMB* BH21 .... 17 E5
Parmiter Wy *WIMB* BH21 .... 17 E5
Parr St *PSTN* BH14 .... 73 G1
Parsonage Barn La *RGWD* BH24 ... 8 C3
Parsonage Rd *BMTH* BH1 .... 3 J4
Partridge Cl *CHCH/BSGR* BH23 .. 63 E5 🔲
Partridge Dr *PSTN* BH14............. 73 H4
Partridge Gn *NMIL/BTOS* BH25 ... 47 F1
Partridge Rd *BROC* SO42 .... 14 D4
Partridge Wk *PSTN* BH14 .... 74 A4 🔲
Pascoe Cl *PSTN* BH14................. 73 G1
Patchins Rd *PLE* BH15 .... 70 D1
Pauncefote Rd *BOSC* BH5 ...... 60 A5 🔲
Pauntley Rd *CHCH/BSGR* BH23 ... 62 C5
Pavan Gdns *NBNE* BH10 .... 38 C4
Payne Cl *WIMB* BH21.................. 10 A1
Peace Cl *CHCH/BSGR* BH23........ 33 E4
Pearce Av *PSTN* BH14 .... 73 G4
Pearce Rd *UPTN* BH16 .... 52 C3
Pear Cl *BKME/WDN* BH12 .... 75 F1
Pearl Gdns *NBNE* BH10 .... 38 C3
Pearl Rd *NBNE* BH10 .... 38 C3
Pearson Av *PSTN* BH14 .... 55 H5
Pearson Gdns *NBNE* BH10 .... 38 D1
Peartree *LYMN* SO41 .... 51 E5 🔲
Pear Tree Cl *CHCH/BSGR* BH23... 33 E4
Peartree Ct *LYMN* SO41 .... 51 E5 🔲
Peckham Av *NMIL/BTOS* BH25..... 47 E5
Peel Cl *BKME/WDN* BH12 .... 56 A5
Pegasus Av *LYMN* SO41 .... 48 C5
Pelham Cl *CHCH/BSGR* BH23 ..... 62 B4
Pelican Md *RGWD* BH24 .... 9 E5
Pembroke Cl *BKME/WDN* BH12 .. 56 B3
   WBNE BH4 .... 75 F3
Pengelly Av *NBNE* BH10............. 39 E2
Pennant Wy *CHCH/BSGR* BH23 .. 62 D3
Penn Cl *NMIL/BTOS* BH25 .... 65 G1
Penn Hill Av *PSTN* BH14 .... 74 B2
Pennine Wy *VWD* BH31 .... 4 B2 🔲
Pennington Cl *LYMN* SO41 ...... 50 C5 🔲
Pennington Ov *LYMN* SO41 .... 50 C5
Penny Hedge *NMIL/BTOS* BH25... 66 B2
Pennywell Gdns
   NMIL/BTOS BH25................ 47 H3
Penrith Cl *VWD* BH31.................. 4 A3
Penrith Rd *BOSC* BH5 .... 78 A1
Penrose Rd *FERN* BH22 .... 19 H3
Percy Rd *BOSC* BH5 .... 77 G2
Peregrine Rd *CHCH/BSGR* BH23 .. 63 E4
Pergin Crs *CFDH* BH17 .... 54 B3
Pergin Wy *CFDH* BH17 .... 54 B3
Perryfield Gdns *LTDN* BH7 ...... 60 B2 🔲
Perry Gdns *PLE* BH15 .... 72 C4
Persley Rd *NBNE* BH10............... 38 D1
Perth Cl *CHCH/BSGR* BH23 .... 61 E1
Peter Grant Wy *FERN* BH22 .... 19 G4
Peters Cl *UPTN* BH16 .... 53 E4
Petersfield Pl *LTDN* BH7 .... 60 B3 🔲
Petersfield Rd *LTDN* BH7 .... 60 A4
Petersham Rd *CFDH* BH17 .... 53 H2
Petit Rd *MOOR/WNTN* BH9 .... 39 G4
Petwyn Cl *FERN* BH22 .... 20 C3
Peverell Rd *UPTN* BH16 .... 70 D1 🔲
Peveril Cl *RGWD* BH24 .... 6 D5
Phelipps Rd *WIMB* BH21 .... 34 B1
Phyldon Cl *BKME/WDN* BH12...... 55 H5
Phyldon Rd *BKME/WDN* BH12 .... 55 H4
Pickard Rd *FERN* BH22 .... 20 B2
Pickering Cl *BDST* BH18 .... 35 E5
Pickford Rd *MOOR/WNTN* BH9 ... 58 A4
Pig Shoot La *CHCH/BSGR* BH23 ... 40 D3
Pilford Heath Rd *WIMB* BH21 ..... 17 G2
Pilgrim Cl *NMIL/BTOS* BH25 .... 47 G3 🔲
Pilgrim Pk *RGWD* BH24 .... 12 B1
Pilgrims Wy *CFDH* BH17 .... 54 A3 🔲
Pilot Hight Rd *BWD* BH11 .... 38 A4
Pilsdon Dr *CFDH* BH17............... 36 A5
Pimpern Cl *CFDH* BH17 .... 36 A5
Pine Av *BKME/WDN* BH12........... 56 C1
   SBNE BH6 .... 78 C1
Pinecliffe Av *SBNE* BH6 .... 78 C1
Pinecliffe Rd *NMIL/BTOS* BH25 ... 65 E5
Pinecliff Rd *CCLF* BH13 .... 75 E5
Pine Cl *FERN* BH22 .... 19 G2
   NMIL/BTOS 65 G2
Pine Crs *CHCH/BSGR* BH23 .... 64 A2
Pine Dr *CCLF* BH13 .... 74 D2
   RGWD BH24 .... 11 H2
Pine Glen Av *FERN* BH22 .... 19 H3
Pineholt Cl *RGWD* BH24 .... 12 A1
Pinehurst Av *CHCH/BSGR* BH23 .. 62 D5

Pinehurst Rd *FERN* BH22 .... 10 B5
Pine Manor Rd *RGWD* BH24 .... 11 F1
Pine Rd *MOOR/WNTN* BH9 .... 58 B1
Pinesprings Dr *BDST* BH18 .... 34 C5
Pinetops Cl *LYMN* SO41 .... 50 A4
Pine Tree Cl *WIMB* BH21 .... 16 D4
Pine Tree Gln *WBNE* BH4 .... 2 A3
Pinetree Wk *CFDH* BH17 .... 53 H2
Pine Vale Crs *NBNE* BH10 .... 39 F4
Pine View Cl *UPTN* BH16 .... 53 E4
Pine Wk *VWD* BH31 .... 4 D3
Pinewood Av *NBNE* BH10 .... 38 D2
Pinewood Cl *CHCH/BSGR* BH23 .. 64 C1
   NBNE BH10 .... 38 D2 🔲
   UPTN BH16 .... 52 C3 🔲
Pinewood Gdns *FERN* BH22........ 19 H2
Pinewood Rd *CCLF* BH13 .... 75 F4
   CHCH/BSGR BH23 .... 64 D1
   FERN BH22 .... 19 C2
   LYMN SO41 .... 48 B4
   RGWD BH24 .... 11 H2
Pinewood Rd West *UPTN* BH16... 52 C3
Pipers Ash *RGWD* BH24 .... 9 E5 🔲
Pipers Dr *CHCH/BSGR* BH23 ...... 63 E3
Pippin Cl *CHCH/BSGR* BH23 ...... 42 A5
   LYMN SO41 .... 51 E5
Pithouse La *CHCH/BSGR* BH23 ... 30 D4
Pittmore Rd *CHCH/BSGR* BH23 .. 43 F4 🔲
Pitts Pl *NMIL/BTOS* BH25 .... 47 H5
Pitwines Cl *PLE* BH15 .... 72 D3
Plantaganet Crs *BWD* BH11........ 37 F2
Plantation Dr *CHCH/BSGR* BH23 .. 45 C5
Plantation Rd *CFDH* BH17 .... 54 C1
   CHCH/BSGR BH23 .... 22 B5
Plant Park Rd *RGWD* BH24 .... 12 C3
Plassey Crs *BWD* BH11 .... 38 B2
Playfields Dr *BKME/WDN* BH12 ... 56 C4
Pleasance Wy *NMIL/BTOS* BH25 .. 46 D4
Plecy Cl *FERN* BH22 .... 27 H1
Piemont Cl *BKME/WDN* BH12 ..... 56 C1
Pless Rd *LYMN* SO41 .... 67 G5
Plover Dr *LYMN* SO41................. 82 D1
Plumer Rd *CFDH* BH17 .... 54 A1
Policemans La *UPTN* BH16 .... 52 B3
Pomona Cl *FERN* BH22 .... 19 H3
Pompeys La *FERN* BH22 .... 19 E5
Pond Cl *NMIL/BTOS* BH25 .... 47 E4
Ponsonby Rd *PSTN* BH14 .... 74 B1
Pony Dr *UPTN* BH16 .... 53 F3
Poole Hl *WCLF* BH2 .... 2 D4
Poole La *BWD* BH11 .... 37 H3
Poole Rd *CCLF* BH13 .... 74 D1
   UPTN BH16 .... 53 E3
   WBNE BH4 .... 75 F2
   WCLF BH2 .... 2 D4
   WIMB BH21 .... 16 C5
Popes Rd *PLE* BH15 .... 54 D4
Poplar Cl *CHCH/BSGR* BH23 ...... 33 G4
   CHCH/BSGR BH23 .... 64 D2
   WIMB BH21 .... 16 D4
Poplar Crs *RGWD* BH24 .... 8 D4
Poplar La *CHCH/BSGR* BH23 ...... 33 G3
Poplar Rd *NMIL/BTOS* BH25 .... 47 H3
Poplar Wy *RGWD* BH24 .... 8 D4
Poppy Cl *CHCH/BSGR* BH23 ...... 63 F2
Portarlington Cl *WBNE* BH4 .... 2 C5
Portarlington Rd *WBNE* BH4 .... 2 B4
Portchester Pl *BMTH* BH1 .... 58 D5
Portchester Rd *CHAR* BH8 .... 58 C4
Portelet Cl *BKME/WDN* BH12...... 56 B1
Porter Rd *CFDH* BH17 .... 54 B3
Porters La *WIMB* BH21 .... 18 A3
Portesham Gdns
   MOOR/WNTN BH9 .... 39 H3
Portesham Wy *CFDH* BH17 .... 36 A4
Portfield Cl *CHCH/BSGR* BH23 ... 61 F3
Portfield Rd *CHCH/BSGR* BH23 ... 61 F3
Portland Rd *MOOR/WNTN* BH9 ... 58 C2
Portman Crs *SBNE* BH6 .... 78 B2
Portman Rd *LTDN* BH7 .... 59 H3
Portmore Cl *BDST* BH18 .... 35 G2
Portswood Dr
   MOOR/WNTN BH9 .... 39 G3 🔲
Post Office La *RGWD* BH24 .... 12 A1
Post Office Rd *WCLF* BH2 .... 3 G4
Potterne Wy *WIMB* BH21 .... 4 C4
Potters Wy *PSTN* BH14 .... 74 A3
Pottery Rd *PSTN* BH14 .... 73 G3
Poulner Hl *RGWD* BH24 .... 9 F5
Poulner Pk *RGWD* BH24 .... 9 F4
Pound Cl *PSTN* BH14 .... 55 F5 🔲
   RGWD BH24 .... 8 C3
Pound La *PLE* BH15 .... 55 E5
Pound Rd *LYMN* SO41 .... 50 B4
Powell Rd *PSTN* BH14 .... 73 H2
Powerscourt Rd
   NMIL/BTOS 65 F3
Powis Cl *NMIL/BTOS* BH25 .... 47 F4

Preston Cl UPTN BH16 ...... 53 E3
Preston La CHCH/BSGR BH23...... 43 F4
Preston Rd PLE BH15 ...... 54 C4
Preston Wy CHCH/BSGR BH23...... 63 H2
Prestwood Cl
  NMIL/BTOS BH25 ...... 65 H1
Priestlands La LYMN SO41 ...... 50 C4
Priestlands Rd LYMN SO41 ...... 50 C4
Priest La CHCH/BSGR BH23...... 31 H5
Priestley Rd NBNE BH10 ...... 57 F1
Primrose Gdns CFDH BH17 ...... 53 H1
Primrose Wy CHCH/BSGR BH23... 63 G2
Prince of Wales Rd WBNE BH4 ... 75 F1
Prince's Pl NMIL/BTOS BH25 ...... 47 G3
Princes Rd FERN BH22 ...... 19 H3
Princess Av CHCH/BSGR BH23 ... 61 H4
Princess Rd BKME/WDN BH12 ... 75 F1
  WBNE BH4 ...... 75 F1
Pringles Cl FERN BH22 ...... 20 A4
Pringles Dr FERN BH22 ...... 20 A4
Priors Cl CHCH/BSGR BH23 ...... 63 G3
Priors Rd CFDH BH17 ...... 53 H2
Priors Wk WIMB BH21 ...... 16 B4
Priory Rd FERN BH22...... 20 C1
  WCLF BH2 ...... 3 G5
Priory View Pl
  MOOR/WNTN BH9 ...... 39 G4
Priory View Rd
  CHCH/BSGR BH23 ...... 43 E5
  MOOR/WNTN BH9 ...... 39 G4
Privet Rd MOOR/WNTN BH9 ... 58 A2
Promenade CCLF BH15 ...... 85 H1
Prosperous Rd PLE BH15 ...... 72 C4
Prunus Cl FERN BH22 ...... 19 F2
Prunus Dr FERN BH22 ...... 19 F2
Puddletown Crs CFDH BH17 ...... 36 B5
Pullman Wy RGWD BH24 ...... 8 C5
Purbeck Av PLE BH15 ...... 71 G4
Purbeck Cl UPTN BH16 ...... 52 D3
Purbeck Dr VWD BH31 ...... 4 B5
Purbeck Rd NMIL/BTOS BH25 ... 65 F3
  WCLF BH2 ...... 2 E4
Purchase Rd BKME/WDN BH12 ... 57 G2
Purewell CHCH/BSGR BH23 ...... 62 B4
Purewell Cl CHCH/BSGR BH23 ... 62 C4
Purewell Cross Rd
  CHCH/BSGR BH23 ...... 62 B3
Pussex La CHCH/BSGR BH23 ... 30 A4
Pye La WIMB BH21 ...... 16 B5
Pyrford Ms LYMN SO41 ...... 51 E5

Q

Quarry Rd WIMB BH21 ...... 17 C2
Quayle Dr BWD BH11 ...... 37 H1
Quay Rd CHCH/BSGR BH23...... 61 H5
Quay St LYMN SO41 ...... 51 F3
The Quay PLE BH15 ...... 72 C4
Queen Anne Dr WIMB BH21...... 25 E5
Queen Elizabeth Av
  LYMN SO41 ...... 50 D3
Queen Katherine Rd LYMN SO41.. 51 F4
Queen Mary Av
  MOOR/WNTN BH9 ...... 39 F5
Queen's Av CHCH/BSGR BH23 ... 61 H5
Queens Gdns WBNE BH4...... 2 C2
Queens Gv NMIL/BTOS BH25 ...... 47 G3
Queensland Rd LTDN BH7...... 60 A5
Queensmead
  CHCH/BSGR BH23 ...... 61 G1
Queen's Park Av CHAR BH8 ...... 59 E2
Queen's Park Gdns CHAR BH8 ... 59 F3
Queen's Park Rd CHAR BH8 ...... 59 F3
Queen's Park South Dr
  CHAR BH8 ...... 59 F3
Queen's Park West Dr
  CHAR BH8 ...... 59 E3
Queen's Rd CHCH/BSGR BH23 ... 62 C4
  FERN BH22 ...... 19 H2
  PSTN BH14 ...... 74 B1
  WBNE BH4 ...... 2 C3
  WIMB BH21 ...... 34 B2
Queensmead RGWD BH24...... 8 D4
Queenswood Av CHAR BH8 ...... 59 G1
Queenswood Dr FERN BH22 ...... 19 H2
Quince La WIMB BH21 ...... 16 D3
Quintin Cl CHCH/BSGR BH23 ... 64 B2
The Quomp RGWD BH24 ...... 8 C4

R

Radipole Rd CFDH BH17 ...... 36 B5
Raglan Gdns BWD BH11 ...... 38 A5
Raleigh Cl CHCH/BSGR BH23 ... 62 D5

NMIL/BTOS BH25...... 46 D4
  RGWD BH24...... 9 E3
Ramley Rd LYMN SO41 ...... 49 H2
The Rampart LYMN SO41 ...... 50 D2
Randalls Hl UPTN BH16 ...... 52 B2
Randolph Rd BOSC BH5 ...... 77 G1
  PSTN BH14 ...... 56 A5
Ranelagh Rd CHCH/BSGR BH23...64 B3
Ravenscourt Rd LYMN SO41 ...... 50 D4
  SBNE BH6 ...... 60 C5
Ravensdale Cl
  BKME/WDN BH12 ...... 56 A4
Ravens Wy LYMN SO41 ...... 82 B1
Raven Wy CHCH/BSGR BH23 ... 63 E5
Ravine Rd BOSC BH5 ...... 78 B1
  CCLF BH13 ...... 74 D5
Raymond Cl VWD BH31...... 4 D2
Rebbeck Rd LTDN BH7 ...... 60 A5
Recreation Rd
  BKME/WDN BH12 ...... 56 C4
Rectory Rd PLE BH15 ...... 54 C4
Redan Cl CHCH/BSGR BH23 ...... 64 B3
Redbreast Rd BWD BH9.. 39 G4
Redbreast Rd North
  MOOR/WNTN BH9 ...... 39 G4
Redcliffe Cl CHCH/BSGR BH23 ... 43 E5
Redcotts La WIMB BH21 ...... 16 B4
Redcotts Rd WIMB BH21 ...... 16 B4
Redhill Av NBNE BH10 ...... 39 E5
Redhill Cl NBNE BH10 ...... 39 E5
Redhill Ct MOOR/WNTN BH9 ... 39 G3
Redhill Crs MOOR/WNTN BH9 ... 39 F4
Redhill Dr NBNE BH10 ...... 39 E5
Redhoave Rd CFDH BH17 ...... 35 H5
Redhorn Cl UPTN BH16 ...... 71 E1
Redlands BKME/WDN BH12 ...... 56 D5
Red Oaks Cl FERN BH22 ...... 19 F2
Redshank Cl CFDH BH17 ...... 53 H1
Redvers Rd CHCH/BSGR BH23 ... 62 C3
Redwood Cl LYMN SO41 ...... 50 C2
  RGWD BH24 ...... 8 D4
Redwood Dr FERN BH22...... 19 C1
Redwood Rd UPTN BH16 ...... 52 C2
Regency Crs CHCH/BSGR BH23 .. 61 F2
Regent Dr LTDN BH7 ...... 59 H2
Regent Wy CHCH/BSGR BH23 ... 61 H4
Reid St CHCH/BSGR BH23 ...... 61 G3
Rempstone Rd WIMB BH21 ...... 24 D3
Renault Dr BDST BH18 ...... 54 A1
Renouf Cl LYMN SO41 ...... 50 C4
Retreat Rd WIMB BH21 ...... 16 D5
Reuben Dr PLE BH15 ...... 71 F3
Rhinefield Cl BROC SO42...... 14 C2
Ribble Cl BDST BH18 ...... 35 E5
Ricardo Crs CHCH/BSGR BH23 ... 63 E4
Rice Gdns UPTN BH16 ...... 71 F1
Richard Cl UPTN BH16 ...... 52 D3
Richmond Gdns WCLF BH2...... 3 G3
Richmond Hl WCLF BH2...... 3 G3
Richmond Hill Dr WCLF BH2...... 3 G3
Richmond Park Av CHAR BH8 ... 58 D3
Richmond Park Cl BMTH BH1 ... 59 F4
Richmond Park Crs CHAR BH8 ... 58 D3
Richmond Park Rd BMTH BH1 ... 59 F4
  CHAR BH8 ...... 58 D3
Richmond Rd PSTN BH14 ...... 74 A1
Richmond Wood Rd CHAR BH8 ... 58 D3
Ridgefield Gdns
  CHCH/BSGR BH23 ...... 63 H2
Ridgemount Gdns PLE BH15 ... 71 G2
  FERN BH22 ...... 28 A4
Ridgeway La LYMN SO41 ...... 50 D5
Ridley Rd MOOR/WNTN BH9 ... 58 B2
Ridout Cl NBNE BH10 ...... 57 F1
Riggs Gdns BWD BH11 ...... 37 H5
Rigler Rd PLE BH15 ...... 72 A4
Rimbury Wy CHCH/BSGR BH23 ... 61 G2
Ringbury LYMN SO41 ...... 50 D1
Ringwood Rd BKME/WDN BH12 .. 56 A1
  BWD BH11 ...... 37 G3
  CHCH/BSGR BH23 ...... 31 G4
  CHCH/BSGR BH23 ...... 33 E3
  FERN BH22 ...... 20 D1
  PSTN BH14 ...... 55 F4
  RGWD BH24 ...... 11 F4
  VWD BH31 ...... 4 B1
Ripon Rd MOOR/WNTN BH9 ... 58 C2
The Rise BROC SO42...... 14 D3
Ritchie Rd BWD BH11 ...... 38 B3
River Cl WIMB BH21 ...... 16 C3
Riverdale La CHCH/BSGR BH23 ... 61 G4
River Gdns LYMN SO41 ...... 82 C1
Riverlea Rd CHCH/BSGR BH23 ... 61 G4
Rivermead Gdns
  CHCH/BSGR BH23 ...... 42 A5
Riversdale Rd SBNE BH6 ...... 79 G1

Riverside RGWD BH24 ...... 8 B5
Riverside Av LTDN BH7 ...... 60 C1
Riverside La SBNE BH6 ...... 61 F5
Riverside Rd SBNE BH6 ...... 61 F5
River Wy CHCH/BSGR BH23 ...... 41 H5
R L Stevenson Av WBNE BH4 ... 75 F2
Roberts Cl LYMN SO41 ...... 68 C1
Roberts La CFDH BH17 ...... 54 A3
Roberts Rd CFDH BH17 ...... 54 B1
  LTDN BH7 ...... 60 A4
Robin Crs NMIL/BTOS BH25 ...... 46 B2
Robin Gv NMIL/BTOS BH25 ...... 46 D5
Robins Wy CHCH/BSGR BH23 ... 63 F5
Robinswood Dr FERN BH22 ...... 19 H1
Rochester Rd BWD BH11 ...... 38 B3
Rockbourne Gdns
  NMIL/BTOS BH25 ...... 65 F2
Rockford Cl SBNE BH6 ...... 79 E1
Rockley Rd PLE BH15 ...... 71 G3
Rodbourne Cl LYMN SO41...... 68 B1
Rodney Cl BKME/WDN BH12 ... 57 E2
Rodney Dr CHCH/BSGR BH23 ... 62 D4
Rodway WIMB BH21 ...... 16 C5
Rodwell Cl NBNE BH10 ...... 38 C1
Roebuck Cl NMIL/BTOS BH25...... 47 F4
Roeshot Crs CHCH/BSGR BH23 ... 64 A1
Rolls Dr SBNE BH6 ...... 79 H1
Roman Rd BDST BH18 ...... 34 C3
Romney Cl NBNE BH10 ...... 39 E4
Romney Rd NBNE BH10 ...... 39 E3
Rookcliff Wy LYMN SO41 ...... 82 A1
Rookes La LYMN SO41 ...... 50 D5
Rook Hill Rd CHCH/BSGR BH23 ... 63 F4
Roosevelt Crs BWD BH11 ...... 38 B1
Ropers La UPTN BH16 ...... 53 F3
Ropley Rd LTDN BH7 ...... 60 C3
Rosamund Av WIMB BH21 ...... 25 E3
Roscrea Cl SBNE BH6 ...... 79 H1
Roscrea Dr SBNE BH6 ...... 79 H1
Rosebery Cl VWD BH31...... 5 E3
Rosebery Rd BOSC BH5 ...... 77 H2
Rosebud Av MOOR/WNTN BH9 .. 39 G5
Rosecrae Cl NMIL/BTOS BH25 ... 46 D3
Rose Crs PLE BH15...... 55 F4
Rosedale Cl CHCH/BSGR BH23 .. 62 C4
Rose Gdns MOOR/WNTN BH9...... 39 G5
Rosehill Cl CHCH/BSGR BH23 ... 33 F3
Rosehill Dr CHCH/BSGR BH23...... 33 F3
Rosemary Gdns
  BKME/WDN BH12 ...... 55 H3
Rosemary Rd BKME/WDN BH12 .. 56 A3
Rosemount Rd WBNE BH4 ...... 75 F3
Rosewood Gdns
  NMIL/BTOS BH25...... 46 D3
Roslin Rd TWDS BH3 ...... 58 A3
Roslin Rd South TWDS BH3 ...... 57 H3
Ross Gdns WIMB BH21 ...... 37 E2
Rossley Cl CHCH/BSGR BH23 ... 45 E5
Rossmore Rd BKME/WDN BH12 .. 56 A2
Ross Rd RGWD BH24 ...... 9 E2
Rotary Cl WIMB BH21 ...... 17 F2
Rothbury Pk NMIL/BTOS BH25 .. 47 F5
Rotherfield Rd
  CHCH/BSGR BH23 ...... 64 C1
  SBNE BH6 ...... 78 B2
Rothesay Dr CHCH/BSGR BH23 .. 64 A3
Rothesay Rd TWDS BH3 ...... 57 G4
Rotterdam Dr CHCH/BSGR BH23.. 62 B3
Roumelia La BOSC BH5 ...... 77 G1
Roundhaye Rd BWD BH11 ...... 37 H2
Rowan Cl CHCH/BSGR BH23 ... 63 H2
  RGWD BH24 ...... 11 F2
Rowan Dr CFDH BH17 ...... 53 C1
  CHCH/BSGR BH23 ...... 63 H2
  VWD BH31 ...... 4 D4
Rowans Pk LYMN SO41 ...... 50 D4
Rowbarrow Cl CFDH BH17 ...... 36 A5
Rowena Rd SBNE BH6 ...... 78 B5
Rowland Av PLE BH15 ...... 55 E5
Rowlands Hl WIMB BH21 ...... 16 C4
Rowlett Rd LYMN SO41 ...... 51 E4
Rownhams Rd CHAR BH8 ...... 40 A4
Royal Oak Rd NBNE BH10 ...... 38 C2
Royster Cl CFDH BH17 ...... 54 C1
Royston Dr WIMB BH21 ...... 16 D4
Royston Pl NMIL/BTOS BH25 ... 66 B2
Rozelle Rd PSTN BH14 ...... 74 A1
Rubens Cl NMIL/BTOS BH25 ...... 47 E3
Rufford Gdns SBNE BH6 ...... 61 E5
Rugby Rd CFDH BH17 ...... 54 B1
Runnymede Av BWD BH11 ...... 37 F1
Runton Rd BKME/WDN BH12 ... 56 D5
The Runway CHCH/BSGR BH23 .. 63 F3
  WIMB BH21 ...... 34 B1
Rushcombe Wy WIMB BH21 ... 34 C1
Rushford Warren
  CHCH/BSGR BH23 ...... 80 D1
Rushmere Rd SBNE BH6 ...... 60 C3

Rushton Crs TWDS BH3 ...... 58 B4
Ruskin Av MOOR/WNTN BH9 ... 39 H4
Russell Cotes Rd BMTH BH1...... 3 J5
Russell Dr CHCH/BSGR BH23 ... 62 B4
Russell Gdns RGWD BH24 ...... 12 B1
  UPTN BH16 ...... 71 E1
Russel Rd NBNE BH10 ...... 38 C1
Russet Cl FERN BH22 ...... 19 H3
  LYMN SO41 ...... 51 F5
Rutland Rd CHCH/BSGR BH23 ... 61 F1
  MOOR/WNTN BH9 ...... 58 D2
Ryall Dr CFDH BH17 ...... 54 D1
Ryan Cl FERN BH22 ...... 19 G2
Ryan Gdns FERN BH22 ...... 19 G2
Rydal Cl CHCH/BSGR BH23 ...... 41 H3
Ryecroft Av BWD BH11 ...... 37 G2

S

Saddle Cl WIMB BH21 ...... 18 A3
Saffron Dr CHCH/BSGR BH23 ... 63 F2
Saffron Wy BWD BH11 ...... 37 F4
St Alban's Av CHAR BH8 ...... 58 D3
St Alban's Crs CHAR BH8...... 58 D3
St Alban's Rd CHAR BH8 ...... 58 D3
St Aldhelm's Cl CCLF BH13 ...... 74 D2
St Aldhelm's Rd CCLF BH13 ...... 74 D1
St Andrews Rd WIMB BH21 ...... 35 E2
St Anne's Av SBNE BH6 ...... 61 E5
St Annes Gdns LYMN SO41 ...... 50 D4
St Anne's Rd UPTN BH16 ...... 52 D3
St Anthony's Rd WCLF BH2 ...... 58 B5
St Aubyns Ct PLE BH15 ...... 72 B3
St Aubyns La RGWD BH24...... 9 G2
St Augustin's Rd WCLF BH2 ...... 58 B5
St Brelades Av
  BKME/WDN BH12 ...... 56 B1
St Catherines WIMB BH21 ...... 16 C5
St Catherine's Rd SBNE BH6 ... 79 E2
St Catherines's Wy LTDN BH7 ... 41 H4
St Clair Rd CCLF BH13 ...... 85 G2
St Clements Gdns BMTH BH1 ... 59 F5
St Clement's Rd BMTH BH1 ...... 59 F5
  PLE BH15 ...... 55 H3
St David's Rd UPTN BH16 ...... 52 D3
St George's Av
  BKME/WDN BH12 ...... 55 H2
  CHAR BH8 ...... 59 E2
St George's Cl CHAR BH8 ...... 59 E2
  CHCH/BSGR BH23 ...... 33 F4
  CHCH/BSGR BH23 ...... 63 H2
St George's Dr FERN BH22 ...... 19 G5
St Helier Rd BKME/WDN BH12 ... 56 B1
St Ives End La RGWD BH24 ...... 12 A1
St Ives Gdns WCLF BH2 ...... 58 B5
St Ives Pk RGWD BH24 ...... 12 A1
St Ives Wd RGWD BH24 ...... 12 B1
St James Cl PLE BH15 ...... 72 B4
St James Rd WIMB BH21 ...... 19 E3
St James's Sq BOSC BH5 ...... 60 A5
St John's Cl WIMB BH21 ...... 16 D5
St John's Gdns
  MOOR/WNTN BH9 ...... 58 B1
St John's Hl WIMB BH21 ...... 16 D4
St John's Rd BOSC BH5 ...... 77 H2
  CHCH/BSGR BH23 ...... 61 G4
  PLE BH15 ...... 72 D1
St Just Cl FERN BH22 ...... 27 F4
St Ledger's Pl BMTH BH1 ...... 59 F4
St Ledger's Rd CHAR BH8 ...... 59 F3
St Leonard's Rd CHAR BH8 ...... 58 D4
St Leonards Wy RGWD BH24 ... 11 F1
St Luke's Rd TWDS BH3 ...... 58 B3
St Margaret's Av
  CHCH/BSGR BH23 ...... 61 G0
St Margarets Cl WIMB BH21 ...... 16 A4
St Margaret's Hl WIMB BH21 ... 16 A4
St Margaret's Rd NBNE BH10 ... 38 B5
  PLE BH15 ...... 72 C1
St Mark's Rd BWD BH11 ...... 38 B4
  LYMN SO41 ...... 50 B4
St Martins Rd UPTN BH16 ...... 52 C4
St Mary Gv LYMN SO41 ...... 48 C3
St Mary's Cl CHCH/BSGR BH23 ... 33 F4
St Mary's Rd CHAR BH8 ...... 59 F4
  FERN BH22 ...... 19 G5
  PLE BH15 ...... 73 E2
St Merrin's Cl NBNE BH10 ...... 38 C3
St Michaels Cl PLE BH15 ...... 71 G2
  VWD BH31 ...... 4 B5
St Michaels Rd VWD BH31...... 4 B4
  WCLF BH2 ...... 2 E5
St Osmund's Rd PSTN BH14 ... 74 A3
St Paul's La BMTH BH1 ...... 76 D3
St Pauls Rd CHAR BH8 ...... 76 D3
St Pauls Rbt BMTH BH1 ...... 3 K

St Peter's Rd *BMTH* BH1 .... 3 H3
PSTN BH14 .... 73 G1 🔲
St Peters Rbt *BMTH* BH1 .... 3 J4
St Stephens La *VWD* BH31 .... 4 C2
St Stephen's Rd *WCLF* BH2 .... 2 C1
St Stephen's Wy *WCLF* BH2 .... 3 C2
St Swithun's Rd South
BMTH BH1 .... 76 D1
St Thomas Pk *LYMN* SO41 .... 50 D3
St Thomas's Cl *NBNE* BH10 .. 38 D5 🔲
St Thomas's St *LYMN* SO41 .... 50 C4
St Valerie Rd *WCLF* BH2 .... 58 B5
St Winifred's Rd *WCLF* BH2 .... 58 B5
Salerno Pl *PLE* BH15 .... 71 F3 🔲
Salisbury Rd *BOSC* BH5 .... 77 G1 🔲
CHCH/BSGR BH23 .... 42 D1
PSTN BH14 .... 56 A5
RGWD BH24 .... 8 B3
Salterns Rd *PSTN* BH14 .... 73 G2
Salterns Wy *PSTN* BH14 .... 73 H5
Salter Rd *CCLF* BH13 .... 84 D5
Saltgrass La *LYMN* SO41 .... 83 E3
Saltings Rd *UPTN* BH16 .... 52 D4
Samber Cl *LYMN* SO41 .... 50 D3
Samples Wy *CFDH* BH17 .... 55 F2 🔲
Samson Pl *PLE* BH15 .... 71 F2
Sancreed Rd *BKME/WDN* BH12 ... 56 C3
Sandbanks Rd *PLE* BH15... .... 73 F2
PSTN BH14 .... 73 G2
Sandbourne Rd *CCLF* BH13 .... 73 G2
PLE BH15 .... 72 D1
WBNE BH4 .... 75 G4
Sandecotes Rd *PSTN* BH14... .... 74 A2
Sanderlings *RGWD* BH24 .... 9 E5 🔲
Sandford Cl *MOOR/WNTN* BH9 ..... 40 A4
Sandford Wy *BDST* BH18 .... 34 D4
Sandhills Cl *CFDH* BH17 .... 35 H5
Sandmartin Rd *NMIL/BTOS* BH25 .. 65 H3
Sandown Rd *CHCH/BSGR* BH23 .... 62 C4
Sandpiper Cl *CFDH* BH17 .... 53 H1
Sandringham Cl
MOOR/WNTN BH9 .... 39 H3
Sandringham Gdns
MOOR/WNTN BH9 .... 39 H3
Sandringham Rd *PSTN* BH14 ...... 73 F2
Sandy Cl *WIMB* BH21 .... 17 G1
Sandyhurst Cl *CFDH* BH17 .... 54 C1
Sandy La *CHCH/BSGR* BH23 ...... 42 A5
RGWD BH24 .... 11 H2
SBNE BH6 .... 60 B5
UPTN BH16 .... 52 C4
VWD BH31 .... 4 C2
WIMB BH21 .... 4 C2
Sandy Mead Rd *CHAR* BH8 .... 59 H1
Sandy Plot *CHCH/BSGR* BH23... .. 62 A1
Sandy Wy *NBNE* BH10... .... 39 G4
Saracen Cl *LYMN* SO41 .... 69 G1 🔲
Sarah Cl *LTDN* BH7 .... 60 B2
Sarah Sands Cl
CHCH/BSGR BH23 .... 62 B2 🔲
Sark Rd *BKME/WDN* BH12 .... 56 B2
Sarum Av *FERN* BH22 .... 10 A2
Sarum St *PLE* BH15 .... 72 B4 🔲
Sarum Wk *LYMN* SO41 .... 50 D1 🔲
Saulfland Dr *CHCH/BSGR* BH23 .. 63 H2
Saulfland Pl *CHCH/BSGR* BH23 .. 63 H2 🔲
Saxonbury Rd *SBNE* BH6 .... 61 E4
Saxonford Rd
CHCH/BSGR BH23 .... 63 G3 🔲
Saxonhurst Cl *NBNE* BH10 .... 39 E3 🔲
Saxonhurst Gdns *NBNE* BH10 .. 39 E3 🔲
Saxonhurst Rd *NBNE* BH10 ...... 38 D3
Saxon King Gdns *SBNE* BH6....... 79 H1
Saxon Pl *LYMN* SO41 .... 50 D1
Scarf Rd *CFDH* BH17 .... 55 F3
School Cl *LYMN* SO41 .... 50 C5
School La *BWD* BH11 .... 38 B2
LYMN SO41 .... 51 E3
LYMN SO41 .... 68 C4
PLE BH15 .... 54 C5
RGWD BH24 .... 8 C4
RGWD BH24 .... 12 A1
WIMB BH21 .... 16 B4
Scott Cl *BKME/WDN* BH12 .... 56 D1
Scotter Rd *LTDN* BH7 .... 60 B5
Scott Rd *BKME/WDN* BH12.... .... 56 D2
Scott's Gn *CHCH/BSGR* BH23 ...... 62 B4
Scotts Hills La *CHCH/BSGR* BH23.. 62 B4
Seabank Cl *UPTN* BH16 .... 52 C3
Seabourne Pl *BOSC* BH5 .... 60 B5 🔲
Seabourne Rd *BOSC* BH5 .... 60 B5
BOSC BH5 .... 78 B1 🔲
Seabreeze Wy *LYMN* SO41 .... 67 G4
Seacombe Rd *CCLF* BH13 .... 84 A5
Seacroft Av *NMIL/BTOS* BH25 ...... 65 G3
Seafield Cl *NMIL/BTOS* BH25 ...... 65 H3
Seafield Dr *SBNE* BH6 .... 61 E4
Seafield Rd *CHCH/BSGR* BH23 .... 63 G4

NMIL/BTOS BH25 .... 65 G2
SBNE BH6 .... 78 D1
Seagull Rd *CHAR* BH8 .... 59 E1
Seamoor La *CCLF* BH13 .... 75 F2 🔲
Seamoor Rd *CCLF* BH13 .... 75 F2
WBNE BH4 .... 75 F2
Sea Rd *BOSC* BH5 .... 77 G1
LYMN SO41 .... 82 C1
NMIL/BTOS BH25 .... 65 G2
SBNE BH6 .... 79 F2
Seaton Cl *CHCH/BSGR* BH23 ...... 64 D2
LYMN SO41 .... 51 E2 🔲
Seaton Rd *CHCH/BSGR* BH23 ...... 64 D2
Seatown Cl *CFDH* BH17 .... 55 G1
Sea View Rd *BKME/WDN* BH12 ... 55 G5
UPTN BH16 .... 52 C3
Seaview Rd *CHCH/BSGR* BH23 .... 65 F3
NMIL/BTOS BH25 .... 65 G3
SBNE BH6 .... 78 D1
Seaward Av *NMIL/BTOS* BH25 ..... 65 G3
SBNE BH6 .... 78 B1
Seaway *NMIL/BTOS* BH25 .... 66 B2 🔲
Seaway Av *CHCH/BSGR* BH23 ..... 63 G4
Seawinds Dr *LYMN* SO41 .... 67 G5 🔲
Second Marine Av
NMIL/BTOS BH25 .... 66 A4
Sedgley Rd *MOOR/WNTN* BH9 ...... 58 A2
Selby Cl *BDST* BH18 .... 35 E4
Seldown Pl *PLE* BH15 .... 72 D2 🔲
Seldown Br *PLE* BH15 .... 72 D3
Seldown La *PLE* BH15 .... 72 D2
Seldown Rd *PLE* BH15 .... 72 D2
Selfridge Av *SBNE* BH6 .... 79 H2 🔲
Selfridge Cl *SBNE* BH6 .... 79 H2 🔲
Seliot Cl *PLE* BH15 .... 54 D5
Selkirk Cl *WIMB* BH21 .... 25 E3
Sellwood Wy *NMIL/BTOS* BH25 .. 65 F2 🔲
Selworthy Cl *PSTN* BH14 .... 73 G3
Serpentine Rd *PLE* BH15... .... 72 C2
Setley Gdns *CHAR* BH8 .... 40 C4
Sevenoaks Dr *LTDN* BH7 .... 60 A2
Severn Rd *FERN* BH22 .... 20 C3 🔲
Seymour Rd *RGWD* BH24 .... 8 D2
Shackleton Sq
CHCH/BSGR BH23 .... 33 F3 🔲
Shaftesbury Cl *FERN* BH22........ 10 B4
Shaftesbury Rd *CHAR* BH8 .... 59 E4
FERN BH22 .... 10 B5 🔲
PLE BH15 .... 72 D2 🔲
Shakespeare Rd *SBNE* BH6 ... 60 D3 🔲
WIMB BH21 .... 16 C3
Shapland Av *BWD* BH11 .... 37 G2
Shapwick Rd *PLE* BH15 .... 72 A4
Shard Cl *VWD* BH31 .... 4 C2
Sharf Rd *BKME/WDN* BH12.... .... 57 E3
Sharlands Cl *BDST* BH18 .... 35 F4
Sharvells Rd *LYMN* SO41 .... 68 A5
Shaves La *NMIL/BTOS* BH25 ...... 47 E2
Shawford Gdns *CHAR* BH8 .... 40 B5 🔲
Shawford Rd *CHAR* BH8 .... 40 B4
Shaw Rd *RGWD* BH24 .... 9 E1
Shears Brook Cl
CHCH/BSGR BH23 .... 33 F3 🔲
Shelbourne Cl *CHAR* BH8 .... 59 E4 🔲
Shelbourne Rd *CHAR* BH8 .... 59 E4
Sheldrake Gdns *LYMN* SO41 ...... 48 D3
Sheldrake Rd *CHCH/BSGR* BH23 .. 63 E5
Shelley Cl *BMTH* BH1 .... 59 G5 🔲
CHCH/BSGR BH23 .... 63 G3
RGWD BH24 .... 11 G1
Shelley Gdns *BMTH* BH1 .... 59 G5
Shelley Rd *BMTH* BH1 .... 59 G5
PSTN BH14 .... 56 B5
Shelley Rd East *BMTH* BH1........ 59 G5
Shelton Rd *SBNE* BH6 .... 60 C4
Shepherd Cl *CHCH/BSGR* BH23 .. 64 B1
Shepherds Wy *LTDN* BH7 .... 60 A3
Sheppards Fld *WIMB* BH21 ...... 16 B3 🔲
Sherborn Crs *CFDH* BH17 .... 55 F1
Sherborne Dr *FERN* BH22 .... 19 H5
Sherfield Cl *CHAR* BH8 .... 40 B5 🔲
Sheringham Rd
BKME/WDN BH12 .... 56 D5
Shermin's Bank
CHCH/BSGR BH23 .... 62 C5
Sherrin Cl *PLE* BH15 .... 54 D5
Sherwood Av *FERN* BH22 .... 27 G1
PSTN BH14 .... 73 F3
Sherwood Cl *CHCH/BSGR* BH23 .. 61 F3
Sherwood Dr *VWD* BH31... .... 4 D2
Shillingstone Dr
MOOR/WNTN BH9 .... 39 H4 🔲
Shillito Rd *BKME/WDN* BH12 ...... 56 B5
Shingle Bank Dr *LYMN* SO41 ...... 82 B3
Shipstal Cl *UPTN* BH16 .... 71 E1
Shires Cl *RGWD* BH24 .... 13 G2
Shires Copse *SBNE* BH6 .... 79 F2 🔲
Shires Md *VWD* BH31 .... 4 C2 🔲
Shirley Cl *CHCH/BSGR* BH23 ...... 33 F3

FERN BH22 .... 10 A4
Shirley Rd *BKME/WDN* BH12 ...... 55 H4
MOOR/WNTN BH9 .... 58 C1
Shore Av *UPTN* BH16 .... 53 E4
Shore Cl *UPTN* BH16 .... 53 E4
Shorefield Crs *LYMN* SO41 .... 68 A5
Shorefield Rd *LYMN* SO41 .... 68 A5
Shorefield Wy *LYMN* SO41 .... 68 A5
Shore Gdns *UPTN* BH16 .... 52 D4 🔲
Shore La *UPTN* BH16 .... 52 D5
Shore Rd *CCLF* BH13 .... 85 F2
PSTN BH14 .... 85 F1
Short Cl *BKME/WDN* BH12 .... 57 E2
Shorts Cl *CHCH/BSGR* BH23 ...... 62 A1
Shottsford Rd *PLE* BH15 .... 55 E3
Shrubb's Av *LYMN* SO41 .... 51 E3
Silchester Cl *WCLF* BH2 .... 58 B5
Silver Birch Cl *BKME/WDN* BH12 .. 75 E1
Silverdale *NMIL/BTOS* BH25 ...... 66 B3 🔲
Silverdale Cl *BDST* BH18 .... 34 C3
Silver St *CHCH/BSGR* BH23 ...... 61 H4 🔲
LYMN SO41 .... 48 B3
Silver Wy *CHCH/BSGR* BH23 ...... 64 A2
Silverwood Cl *WIMB* BH21 .... 24 D2
Simmonds Cl *PLE* BH15 .... 54 D5 🔲
Singleton Dr *NBNE* BH10 .... 38 C5
Siskin Cl *FERN* BH22 .... 19 F2
Sixpenny Cl *BKME/WDN* BH12 ... 56 D3
Skinner St *PLE* BH15 .... 72 C4
Skipton Cl *BDST* BH18 .... 35 E5
Sky End La *LYMN* SO41 .... 48 C5
Slade Cl *LYMN* SO41 .... 48 C4
Slades Farm Rd *NBNE* BH10...... 57 G1
Slade's La *NBNE* BH10 .... 57 G2
Sleepbrook Cl *VWD* BH31 .... 4 A2
Slepe Crs *BKME/WDN* BH12 ...... 56 D2
Slinn Rd *CHCH/BSGR* BH23 ...... 62 C3
Slip Wy *PLE* BH15 .... 72 B3
Slough La *UPTN* BH16 .... 52 B4
Smithfield Pl
MOOR/WNTN BH9 .... 58 B1 🔲
Smithson Cl *BKME/WDN* BH12 .. 57 G2 🔲
Smithy La *NMIL/BTOS* BH25 ...... 46 D1
Smugglers La North
CHCH/BSGR BH23 .... 63 G2
Smugglers La South
CHCH/BSGR BH23 .... 64 A2
Smugglers Wood Rd
CHCH/BSGR BH23 .... 63 G1
Snail's La *RGWD* BH24 .... 8 C1
Snooks La *LYMN* SO41 .... 51 H1
Snowdon Rd *WBNE* BH4 .... 2 A2
Snowdrop Gdns
CHCH/BSGR BH23 .... 63 F1
Soberton Rd *CHAR* BH8 .... 59 F3
Solent Av *LYMN* SO41 .... 51 F4
Solent Cl *LYMN* SO41 .... 51 F4
Solent Dr *NMIL/BTOS* BH25 ...... 66 A3
Solent Rd *CHCH/BSGR* BH23 ...... 45 H5
SBNE BH6 .... 79 G2
Solent Wy *LYMN* SO41 .... 82 D1
LYMN SO41 .... 82 D3
Solly Cl *BKME/WDN* BH12 .... 56 C3
Solomon Wy *PLE* BH15 .... 71 F3
Somerby Rd *PLE* BH15 .... 54 D4
Somerford Av *CHCH/BSGR* BH23.. 63 F2
Somerford Rd *CHCH/BSGR* BH23.. 62 D3
Somerford Wy
CHCH/BSGR BH23 .... 62 D3
Somerley Rd *MOOR/WNTN* BH9 .. 58 C3
Somerley Vw *RGWD* BH24 .... 8 C3 🔲
Somerset Rd *CHCH/BSGR* BH23 .. 61 E3
LTDN BH7 .... 59 H5
Somerton Cl *NMIL/BTOS* BH25 .. 47 H4 🔲
Somerville Rd *RGWD* BH24 .... 9 E3
WCLF BH2 .... 2 D4
Sopers La *CFDH* BH17 .... 54 A1
CHCH/BSGR BH23 .... 61 G4
Sopley Cl *NMIL/BTOS* BH25........ 65 F2
Sopwith Cl *CHCH/BSGR* BH23 .. 63 F4 🔲
Sopwith Crs *WIMB* BH21 .... 25 F3
Sorrel Gdns *WIMB* BH21 .... 34 D5
Sorrell Wy *CHCH/BSGR* BH23 ...... 63 F1
Southampton Rd *LYMN* SO41 ...... 50 D2
RGWD BH24 .... 8 C3
South Av *NMIL/BTOS* BH25 ...... 47 F5
South Baddesley Rd *LYMN* SO41 .. 51 H3
Southbourne Coast Rd
SBNE BH6 .... 79 G2
Southbourne Gv *SBNE* BH6 .... 78 B1
Southbourne Overcliff Dr
SBNE BH6 .... 78 C2
Southbourne Rd *LYMN* SO41 ...... 50 C4
SBNE BH6 .... 78 C1
Southbrook Cl *CFDH* BH17 .... 36 C5
Southcliffe Rd
CHCH/BSGR BH23 .... 63 F4

NMIL/BTOS BH25 .... 65 F2
South Cliff Rd *WCLF* BH2 .... 3 C6
Southcote Rd *BMTH* BH1 .... 77 E1
Southdown Wy *FERN* BH22 .... 10 B5
Southern Av *FERN* BH22 .... 10 C5
Southernhay Rd *VWD* BH31......... 4 H2
Southern La *NMIL/BTOS* BH25 ... 65 H2
Southern Oaks
NMIL/BTOS BH25 .... 65 H1
Southern Rd *LYMN* SO41 .... 50 D3
SBNE BH6 .... 78 C1
Southey Rd *CHCH/BSGR* BH23 .. 62 D3 🔲
Southfield *RGWD* BH24 .... 8 C5 🔲
Southfield Ms *RGWD* BH24 .... 8 C5 🔲
South Gv *LYMN* SO41 .... 51 F4
South Haven Cl *UPTN* BH16 ...... 70 C1
Southill Av *BKME/WDN* BH12 ...... 56 A4
Southill Gdns *MOOR/WNTN* BH9 .. 58 C1
Southill Rd *BKME/WDN* BH12..... 56 A4
MOOR/WNTN BH9 .... 58 C1
South Kinson Dr *BWD* BH11 ...... 38 A3
Southlands *LYMN* SO41 .... 50 C5
Southlands Av *SBNE* BH6 .... 79 F1
WIMB BH21 .... 34 B1
Southlawns Wk
NMIL/BTOS BH25 .... 65 H1
Southlea Av *SBNE* BH6 .... 61 F5
South Park Rd
BKME/WDN BH12 .... 57 E2
South Rd *BMTH* BH1 .... 59 G5
South St *LYMN* SO41 .... 50 C5
South View Pl *WCLF* BH2 .... 2 C1
South View Rd
CHCH/BSGR BH23 .... 61 G4
Southville Rd *BOSC* BH5 .... 60 B5 🔲
South Weirs *BROC* SO42 .... 14 B5
South Western Crs *PSTN* BH14 .... 73 H2
Southwick Pl *SBNE* BH6 .... 60 C5 🔲
Southwick Rd *SBNE* BH6 .... 60 C4
Southwood Av
CHCH/BSGR BH23 .... 64 C1
SBNE BH6 .... 78 C1
Southwood Cl *CHCH/BSGR* BH23.. 64 C1
FERN BH22 .... 19 G4
Sovereign Cl *LTDN* BH7 .... 59 H2 🔲
Sparkford Cl *LTDN* BH7 .... 60 B2 🔲
Spartina Dr *LYMN* SO41 .... 51 F1
Speedwell Dr
CHCH/BSGR BH23 .... 63 F2 🔲
Spencer Rd *BMTH* BH1 .... 77 E1 🔲
CCLF BH13 .... 74 C5
NMIL/BTOS BH25 .... 47 E4
Spetisbury Cl *MOOR/WNTN* BH9 .. 39 H4
Spicer La *BWD* BH11 .... 38 C2
Spinacre *NMIL/BTOS* BH25 ...... 66 B2
Spindle Cl *WIMB* BH21 .... 34 D5
Spindlewood Cl
NMIL/BTOS BH25 .... 66 A1 🔲
Spinners Cl *FERN* BH22 .... 10 A5 🔲
Spinney Cl *RGWD* BH24 .... 11 F2
Spinneys La *FERN* BH22 .... 19 H4
The Spinney *RGWD* BH24 .... 6 D5
Spinney Wy *NMIL/BTOS* BH25 ... 47 E1
Spittlefields *RGWD* BH24 .... 8 D4
Springbank Rd *LTDN* BH7 .... 59 H2
Spring Cl *VWD* BH31 .... 4 B3
Springdale Av *BDST* BH18 .... 34 C3
Springdale Gv *WIMB* BH21 .... 34 C3
Springdale Rd *BDST* BH18 .... 35 E2 🔲
WIMB BH21 .... 34 B3
Springfield Av *CHCH/BSGR* BH23.. 41 H5
SBNE BH6 .... 79 C1
Springfield Cl *LYMN* SO41 .... 51 G4
VWD BH31 .... 4 B3
Springfield Crs *PSTN* BH14 .... 73 H1
Springfield Gdns
NMIL/BTOS BH25 .... 47 H5 🔲
Springfield Rd *PSTN* BH14 .... 55 G5
VWD BH31 .... 4 B3
Spring Gdns *BKME/WDN* BH12 .. 56 B5
Spring La *NMIL/BTOS* BH25 ...... 47 H5
Spring Rd *BMTH* BH1... .... 59 E5
LYMN SO41 .... 51 G4
Springvale Av *LTDN* BH7 .... 59 H2
Springwater Cl *BWD* BH11 .... 38 A4 🔲
Springwater Rd *BWD* BH11 .... 38 A4
Spruce Cl *CFDH* BH17 .... 53 C1
Spur Cl *WIMB* BH21 .... 18 A3 🔲
Spurgeon Rd *LTDN* BH7 .... 60 B4
Spur Hill Av *PSTN* BH14 .... 74 B2
Spur Rd *PSTN* BH14 .... 74 B1
The Square *LYMN* SO41 .... 50 C4
Squirrels Cl *CHCH/BSGR* BH23 .. 41 H5 🔲
Stacey Cl *BKME/WDN* BH12 ...... 56 A3
Stacey Gdns *CHAR* BH8............. 40 D5
Stafford Rd *BMTH* BH1 .... 3 K3
Stag Cl *NMIL/BTOS* BH25............ 46 C3
Stalbridge Dr *FERN* BH22 .... 19 H5

Stalbridge Rd CFDH BH17	54	A5
Stalham Rd BKME/WDN BH12	56	D4
Stallards La RGWD BH24	8	B4
Stamford Rd SBNE BH6	60	D5
Stanfield Rd BKME/WDN BH12	56	B3
FERN BH22	19	C3
MOOR/WNTN BH9	58	A2
Stanley Cl VWD BH31	4	C3
Stanley Green Rd PLE BH15	54	C5
Stanley Rd BMTH BH1	3	H5
CHCH/BSGR BH23	64	C2
LYMN SO41	51	F5
PLE BH15	72	C4
Stannington Cl NMIL/BTOS BH25	47	F5 ⬛
Stanpit CHCH/BSGR BH23	62	C5
Stanton Rd NBNE BH10	38	C5
Stapehill Crs WIMB BH21	17	H4
Stapehill Rd WIMB BH21	26	C2
Staple Close La PLE BH15	54	C4
Staplecross La CHCH/BSGR BH23	62	B2
Stapleford Av FERN BH22	20	B3
Starlight Farm Cl VWD BH31	4	C1 ⬛
Station Ap BDST BH18	35	E3
Station Rd CHCH/BSGR BH23	45	E4
CHCH/BSGR BH23	61	G3
NMIL/BTOS BH25	47	E5
PSTN BH14	73	H2
WIMB BH21	24	D1
Station St LYMN SO41	51	F3
Station Ter WIMB BH21	16	D5
Stedman Rd BOSC BH5	60	B5 ⬛
Steepdene PSTN BH14	73	H2
Steeple Cl CFDH BH17	35	H4
Steepleton Rd BDST BH18	35	E4
Stem La NMIL/BTOS BH25	46	C2
Stenhurst Rd PLE BH15	55	E4 ⬛
Stephen Langton Dr BWD BH11	37	F2 ⬛
Sterte Av PLE BH15	72	C1
Sterte Cl PLE BH15	72	C1
Sterte Rd PLE BH15	72	C1
Stevenson Crs PSTN BH14	74	B2
Stevenson Rd SBNE BH6	79	G2 ⬛
Stevensons Cl WIMB BH21	16	C5
Stewart Rd CHAR BH8	58	D4
Stewarts Wy FERN BH22	20	A3
Stibbs Wy CHCH/BSGR BH23	33	G3
Stillmore Rd BWD BH11	37	F4
Stinsford Cl MOOR/WNTN BH9	39	H3
Stinsford Rd CFDH BH17	54	D1
Stirling Cl NMIL/BTOS BH25	47	F4
Stirling Rd MOOR/WNTN BH9	58	A3
Stirling Wy CHCH/BSGR BH23	63	F4
Stirrup Cl UPTN BH16	53	F3
WIMB BH21	18	A3
Stoborough Dr BDST BH18	35	E5 ⬛
Stockbridge Cl CFDH BH17	36	D5 ⬛
Stokes Av PLE BH15	72	C1
Stoke Wood Rd TWDS BH3	58	B3
Stonechat Cl FERN BH22	19	F1
Stonecrop Cl WIMB BH21	34	C5 ⬛
Stone Gdns CHAR BH8	41	E5
Stone La WIMB BH21	16	A3
Stoneleigh Av LYMN SO41	48	B4
Stony La CHCH/BSGR BH23	42	D5
Stony La South CHCH/BSGR BH23	62	A4
Stopples La LYMN SO41	48	B3
Story La BDST BH18	35	F3
Stourbank Rd CHCH/BSGR BH23	61	G4
Stourcliffe Av SBNE BH6	78	C1
Stour Cl WIMB BH21	18	B5
Stourcroft Dr CHCH/BSGR BH23	41	H5
Stourfield Rd BOSC BH5	78	B1
Stourpaine Rd CFDH BH17	35	H5
Stour Rd CHAR BH8	59	F4
CHCH/BSGR BH23	61	G3
Stourvale Av CHCH/BSGR BH23	60	D2
Stourvale Pl BOSC BH5	60	B5 ⬛
Stourvale Rd SBNE BH6	60	B5
Stour Valley Wy FERN BH22	27	H4
MOOR/WNTN BH9	40	A1
SBNE BH6	61	E3
WIMB BH21	16	A3
Stour Wy CHCH/BSGR BH23	41	H5
Stourwood Av SBNE BH6	78	C1
Stouts La CHCH/BSGR BH23	33	F3
Strand St PLE BH15	72	B4
Stratfield Pl NMIL/BTOS BH25	46	C4 ⬛
Stratford Pl LYMN SO41	50	D2
Strathmore Dr VWD BH31	4	D2
Strathmore Rd NBNE BH10	39	G3
Stratton Rd MOOR/WNTN BH9	40	A3
Strides La RGWD BH24	8	B4
Strode Gdns RGWD BH24	12	B1
Stroud Cl WIMB BH21	17	G3
Strouden Av CHAR BH8	58	D1
Strouden Rd MOOR/WNTN BH9	58	C1
Stroud Gdns CHCH/BSGR BH23	62	C4 ⬛
Stroud La CHCH/BSGR BH23	62	C4
Stroud Park Av CHCH/BSGR BH23	62	C3
Struan Cl RGWD BH24	7	E5
Struan Dr RGWD BH24	7	E5
Struan Gdns RGWD BH24	6	D5
Stuart Cl UPTN BH16	52	D3
Stuart Rd CHCH/BSGR BH23	64	D2
Studland Dr LYMN SO41	67	H5
Studland Rd WBNE BH4	2	A7
Studley Cl CHCH/BSGR BH23	65	E2
Studley Ct NMIL/BTOS BH25	65	F2 ⬛
Sturminster Rd MOOR/WNTN BH9	39	H3 ⬛
Suffolk Av CHCH/BSGR BH23	63	F4
Suffolk Cl WIMB BH21	18	A3 ⬛
Suffolk Rd WCLF BH2	2	C3
Suffolk Rd South WBNE BH4	2	C2
Summercroft Wy FERN BH22	10	A3
Summer Fld WIMB BH21	17	G5
Summerfield Cl CHCH/BSGR BH23	43	E5 ⬛
Summerfields LTDN BH7	59	H3
Summer Flds VWD BH31	4	B4
Summers Av BWD BH11	38	B1
Summers La CHCH/BSGR BH23	62	B1
Summertrees Ct NMIL/BTOS BH25	47	H3
Sunderland Dr CHCH/BSGR BH23	63	F3 ⬛
Sundew Cl CHCH/BSGR BH23	63	G1
NMIL/BTOS BH25	47	H3 ⬛
Sundew Rd WIMB BH21	34	C5
Sunningdale Crs NBNE BH10	38	C3
Sunnybank Rd WIMB BH21	17	H3
Sunnyfield Rd NMIL/BTOS BH25	66	A2
Sunny Hill Rd BKME/WDN BH12	56	B5
Sunnyhill Rd SBNE BH6	60	B5
Sunnylands Av SBNE BH6	79	F1
Sunnymoor Rd BWD BH11	57	E1
Sunnyside Rd BKME/WDN BH12	56	B4
Sunridge Cl BKME/WDN BH12	57	E4
Surrey Cl CHCH/BSGR BH23	42	B5
Surrey Gdns WBNE BH4	2	B2
Surrey Rd BKME/WDN BH12	57	E5
WBNE BH4	2	B2
Surrey Rd South WBNE BH4	2	B2
Sussex Cl MOOR/WNTN BH9	39	H3
Sutherland Av BDST BH18	34	C2
Sutton Cl CFDH BH17	36	C5
Sutton Pl BROC SO42	15	E3 ⬛
Sutton Rd MOOR/WNTN BH9	58	D1
Swallow Cl CFDH BH17	53	H2
Swallow Dr LYMN SO41	82	D1
Swallow Wy WIMB BH21	17	G1
Swan Md RGWD BH24	8	B4
Swanmore Cl LTDN BH7	60	B3 ⬛
Swanmore Rd LTDN BH7	60	B4
Swansbury Dr CHAR BH8	41	E5
Sway Gdns CHAR BH8	40	B5
Sway Rd BROC SO42	14	C5
LYMN SO41	49	G2
NMIL/BTOS BH25	47	F1
The Sweep RGWD BH24	8	B4 ⬛
Swift Cl CFDH BH17	53	H2
Swordfish Dr CHCH/BSGR BH23	63	F3 ⬛
Sycamore Cl CFDH BH17	53	H1
CHCH/BSGR BH23	60	D2 ⬛
LYMN SO41	68	A5
Sycamore Rd LYMN SO41	48	B3
Sydling Cl CFDH BH17	36	D5
Sydney Rd BDST BH18	35	E4
CHCH/BSGR BH23	61	E1
Sylmor Gdns MOOR/WNTN BH9	39	G5
Sylvan Cl LYMN SO41	48	D5
Sylvan Ct LYMN SO41	48	D5 ⬛
RGWD BH24	11	F2
Sylvan Rd BKME/WDN BH12	55	H4
Symes Rd PLE BH15	71	G1

T

Tadden Wk BDST BH18	34	D5
Tait Cl CFDH BH17	55	H3
Talbot Av TWDS BH3	58	A3
Talbot Dr BKME/WDN BH12	57	F2
CHCH/BSGR BH23	45	F5
Talbot Hill Rd MOOR/WNTN BH9	57	H2
Talbot Mdw BKME/WDN BH12	57	F2
Talbot Ms NBNE BH10	57	H1 ⬛
Talbot Ri NBNE BH10	57	H1
Talbot Rd MOOR/WNTN BH9	57	H2

Tamar Cl FERN BH22	20	C4
Tamworth Rd LTDN BH7	59	H5 ⬛
Tangmere Cl CHCH/BSGR BH23	63	F4
Tan Howse Cl LTDN BH7	60	B2
Tarn Dr CFDH BH17	53	H1
Tarrant Cl CFDH BH17	36	A5
Tarrant Rd MOOR/WNTN BH9	39	H4
Tasman Cl CHCH/BSGR BH23	61	F2
Tatnam Rd PLE BH15	72	C1
Tattenham Rd BROC SO42	14	D4
Taverner Cl PLE BH15	72	D5 ⬛
Taylor Dr CHAR BH8	40	B3
Taylor's Buildings PLE BH15	72	C4 ⬛
Teasel Wy FERN BH22	10	A5
Tedder Cl BWD BH11	38	B4
Tedder Gdns BWD BH11	38	B4
Tedder Rd BWD BH11	38	B4
Telford Rd WIMB BH21	19	E1
Templar Cl BKME/WDN BH12	56	B2
Tennyson Rd MOOR/WNTN BH9	39	F5
PSTN BH14	73	G2
WIMB BH21	16	C3
Tensing Rd CHCH/BSGR BH23	62	C3
Terence Av CFDH BH17	54	C1 ⬛
Terence Rd WIMB BH21	34	A2
Tern Ct SBNE BH6	60	D4
Terrace Rd WCLF BH2	3	F4
Terrington Av CHCH/BSGR BH23	64	A1
Thames Cl FERN BH22	20	C3
Thames Ms PLE BH15	72	B4 ⬛
Thames St PLE BH15	72	B4
Thatchers La CHCH/BSGR BH23	32	B3
Theobald Rd CHCH/BSGR BH23	30	A4
Thetchers Cl NMIL/BTOS BH25	47	H4
Thetford Rd BKME/WDN BH12	56	D5 ⬛
Thistlebarrow Rd LTDN BH7	59	H5 ⬛
Thoresby Ct NMIL/BTOS BH25	46	C4 ⬛
Thornbury Rd SBNE BH6	79	G1
Thorncombe Cl CFDH BH17	36	A5
Thorne Cl VWD BH31	4	A1
Thornfield Dr CHCH/BSGR BH23	64	B1
Thornham Rd NMIL/BTOS BH25	47	H4
Thornley Rd NBNE BH10	38	D3
Thorn Rd CFDH BH17	35	G4
Thornton Cl WIMB BH21	34	A2 ⬛
Three Acre Dr NMIL/BTOS BH25	65	H2
Throop Cl CHAR BH8	60	A1
Throop Rd CHAR BH8	40	C3
Throopside Av MOOR/WNTN BH9	40	B3
Thrush Rd BKME/WDN BH12	56	A1
Thursby Rd CHCH/BSGR BH23	45	F5
Thwaite Rd BKME/WDN BH12	56	B5
Tidemill Cl CHCH/BSGR BH23	61	G2
Tiffany Cl LYMN SO41	48	B3 ⬛
Tilburg Rd CHCH/BSGR BH23	62	A3
Tilebarn La BROC SO42	15	E5
Timothy Cl NBNE BH10	38	D2
Tincleton Gdns MOOR/WNTN BH9	39	H3
Tithe Barn LYMN SO41	51	E2
Todber Cl BWD BH11	37	H4 ⬛
Tollard Cl BKME/WDN BH12	56	C2
Tollerford Rd CFDH BH17	35	H5
Tolpuddle Gdns MOOR/WNTN BH9	39	H3
Tolstoi Rd PSTN BH14	72	B2
Tonge Rd BWD BH11	38	B1
Top La RGWD BH24	8	C4
Torbay Rd PSTN BH14	74	A2
Totmel Rd CFDH BH17	36	C5
Tourney Rd BWD BH11	37	F1
Tower La WIMB BH21	16	D3
Tower Rd BMTH BH1	59	G5
CCLF BH13	75	F4
Tower Rd West CCLF BH13	75	F4
Towngate Br PLE BH15	72	C3
Townsend Cl BWD BH11	38	B1 ⬛
Townsville Rd MOOR/WNTN BH9	39	H5
Tozer Cl BWD BH11	37	H5
Trafalgar Rd MOOR/WNTN BH9	58	B3
Tranmere Cl LYMN SO41	51	F5
Treebys Cl CHCH/BSGR BH23	62	B1
Treeside CHCH/BSGR BH23	44	C5
Trefoil Wy CHCH/BSGR BH23	63	G2
Tregonwell Rd WCLF BH2	3	F4
Trentham Av LTDN BH7	60	B4
Trentham Cl LTDN BH7	60	B2
Trent Wy FERN BH22	20	C3
Tresillian Wy CHCH/BSGR BH23	45	H5
The Triangle WCLF BH2	2	E4
Tricketts La FERN BH22	20	B3
Trigon Rd PLE BH15	54	D3
Trinidad Crs BKME/WDN BH12	56	A2
Trinity Rd BMTH BH1	3	K2
Troak Cl CHCH/BSGR BH23	63	G2
Troon Rd WIMB BH21	35	E2

Truman Rd BWD BH11	38	B1
Truscott Av MOOR/WNTN BH9	58	C3
Tuckers La PLE BH15	71	H4
Tucks Cl CHCH/BSGR BH23	33	E3
Tuckton Cl SBNE BH6	78	D1
Tuckton Rd SBNE BH6	78	D1
Tudor Ct PLE BH15	55	E4
Tudor Rd BDST BH18	35	F3
Turbary Cl BKME/WDN BH12	56	C2
Turbary Ct UPTN BH16	53	E2 ⬛
Turbary Park Av BWD BH11	37	H4
Turbary Rd BKME/WDN BH12	56	B3
FERN BH22	20	B2
Turks La PSTN BH14	73	G4
Turlin Rd UPTN BH16	71	E1
Turnberry Cl CHCH/BSGR BH23	61	G4 ⬛
Turners Farm Crs LYMN SO41	48	C5 ⬛
Turnworth Cl BDST BH18	35	G4
Tweedale Rd MOOR/WNTN BH9	40	A4
Twemlow Av PSTN BH14	73	F3
Twin Oaks Cl BDST BH18	35	F4
Twyford Cl CHAR BH8	40	B5
Twyford Wy CFDH BH17	36	C5
Twynham Av CHCH/BSGR BH23	61	G4
Twynham Rd SBNE BH6	79	F1 ⬛
Tylers Cl LYMN SO41	50	D2
Tynedale Cl MOOR/WNTN BH9	40	A3
Tyneham Av BKME/WDN BH12	55	H2
Tyrrell Gdns CHAR BH8	41	E5
Tyrrells Ct CHCH/BSGR BH23	33	F3
Tytherley Gn CHAR BH8	40	B5

U

Uddens Dr WIMB BH21	18	B1
Ullswater Rd WIMB BH21	24	C2
Undercliff Dr BMTH BH1	3	K5
Undercliff Rd BOSC BH5	77	F2
Undershore LYMN SO41	51	G2
Underwood Cl CFDH BH17	54	B1 ⬛
Uplands Av NMIL/BTOS BH25	66	A2
Uplands Cl FERN BH22	20	C1
Uplands Rd CHAR BH8	40	A5
FERN BH22	10	B4
Uplyme Cl CFDH BH17	36	C5
Upper Common Rd LYMN SO41	49	H3 ⬛
Upper Golf Links Rd BDST BH18	35	F2
Upper Gordon Rd CHCH/BSGR BH23	64	C1
Upper Hinton Rd BMTH BH1	3	H4
Upper Norwich Rd WCLF BH2	3	F4
Upper Rd BKME/WDN BH12	56	A4
Upper Terrace Rd WCLF BH2	3	F4
Uppleby Rd BKME/WDN BH12	56	A4
Upton Cl UPTN BH16	52	D3
Upton Ct UPTN BH16	53	E3 ⬛
Upton Heath Est UPTN BH16	53	F3
Upton Rd CFDH BH17	53	G3
Upton Wy BDST BH18	34	C4
Upwey Av PLE BH15	71	G2
Utrecht Ct CHCH/BSGR BH23	62	B3 ⬛

V

Vaggs La LYMN SO41	48	A3
Valencia Cl CHCH/BSGR BH23	41	H3 ⬛
Vale Rd BMTH BH1	77	F2
PSTN BH14	74	C4
Valette Rd MOOR/WNTN BH9	39	G4
Valiant Wy CHCH/BSGR BH23	63	F4
Valley Cl CHCH/BSGR BH23	42	A5
Valley Rd CHAR BH8	40	D3
Valley Vw BKME/WDN BH12	57	F2
Vallis Cl PLE BH15	72	D4
Vanguard Rd CHAR BH8	59	G4
PLE BH15	72	C3 ⬛
Vecta Cl CHCH/BSGR BH23	63	G4
Vectis Rd NMIL/BTOS BH25	65	F4
Velvet Lawn Rd NMIL/BTOS BH25	46	D4
Venator Pl WIMB BH21	16	C5
Venning Av BWD BH11	37	G4
Ventry Cl CCLF BH13	74	D4
Ventura Pl UPTN BH16	53	F4
Verity Crs CFDH BH17	55	G2
Vernalls Cl NBNE BH10	38	D3
Vernalls Gdns NBNE BH10	38	D2
Verne Rd VWD BH31	4	C4
Verney Cl BWD BH11	38	E4
Verney Rd BWD BH11	38	A4
Verno La CHCH/BSGR BH23	44	C1
Verona Av SBNE BH6	60	C2
Verulam Pl BMTH BH1	3	H4

Jerulam Rd PLE BH15 ... 73 F1
Jerwood Crs SBNE BH6 ... 79 G1
Jerwood Rd RGWD BH24 ... 7 E2
Jetch Cl CHCH/BSGR BH23 ... 63 F2
Vicarage Gdns LYMN SO41 ... 48 C5
Vicarage La WIMB SO41 ... 48 C5
Vicarage Rd MOOR/WNTN BH9 ... 58 A1
  PLE BH15 ... 54 C5
  VWD BH31 ... 4 B2
Vicarage Wy CHCH/BSGR BH23 ... 43 F5
Vickers Cl CHAR BH8 ... 41 F5
Vickery Wy CHCH/BSGR BH23 ... 62 C2
Victoria Av MOOR/WNTN BH9 ... 58 A1
Victoria Crs BKME/WDN BH12 ... 56 B4
Victoria Gdns FERN BH22 ... 19 H3
  RGWD BH24 ... 8 C5
Victoria Park Rd
  MOOR/WNTN BH9 ... 58 A1
Victoria Pl BMTH BH1 ... 59 E5
  LYMN SO41 ... 51 E5
  WIMB SO41 ... 16 B4
Victoria Rd BKME/WDN BH12 ... 56 A5
  BMTH BH1 ... 59 E5
  CHCH/BSGR BH23 ... 62 C5
  FERN BH22 ... 19 H3
  LTDN BH7 ... 16 A4
Viewside Cl WIMB BH21 ... 34 A2
Viking Cl SBNE BH6 ... 79 H1
Viking Wy CHCH/BSGR BH23 ... 63 E5
  SBNE BH6 ... 79 G1
Villette Cl CHCH/BSGR BH23 ... 61 G1
Vince Cl BWD BH11 ... 38 B2
Vincent Cl NMIL/BTOS BH25 ... 47 F2
Vincent Rd NMIL/BTOS BH25 ... 46 D4
Vine Cl LTDN BH7 ... 60 A3
Vine Farm Cl
  BKME/WDN BH12 ... 57 G2
Vine Farm Rd BKME/WDN BH12 ... 57 F2
Vinegar Hl LYMN SO41 ... 68 B5
Vineries Cl WIMB BH21 ... 17 F3
The Vineries WIMB BH21 ... 17 F3
Vinneys Cl CHCH/BSGR BH23 ... 43 E5
Violet La NMIL/BTOS BH25 ... 47 E3
Virginia Cl BKME/WDN BH12 ... 56 A3
Viscount Dr CHCH/BSGR BH23 ... 63 F4
Viscount Wk BWD BH11 ... 37 F1
  WIMB BH21 ... 37 E2
Vitre Gdns LYMN SO41 ... 51 E5
Vixen Wk NMIL/BTOS BH25 ... 47 F2

W

Wagtail Dr NMIL/BTOS BH25 ... 46 D5
Wainford Cl LYMN SO41 ... 50 B4
Wainford Plantation
  LYMN SO41 ... 68 C2
Wainford Rd LYMN SO41 ... 49 G5
Wakefield La NBNE BH10 ... 39 E2
Wakely Gdns BWD BH11 ... 38 A2
Wakely Rd BWD BH11 ... 38 B2
Walcheren Pl PLE BH15 ... 71 E2
Walcott Av CHCH/BSGR BH23 ... 61 F1
Walditch Gdns CFDH BH17 ... 36 A5
Waldren Cl PLE BH15 ... 72 D3
Walford Cl WIMB BH21 ... 16 C3
Walford Gdns WIMB BH21 ... 16 B3
Walhampton Hl LYMN SO41 ... 51 F2
Walkford La NMIL/BTOS BH25 ... 46 B4
Walkford Rd CHCH/BSGR BH23 ... 46 A5
Walkford Wy
  CHCH/BSGR BH23 ... 64 D1
Walkwood Av LTDN BH7 ... 60 C4
Wallace Rd BDST BH18 ... 35 E4
Walliscott Rd BWD BH11 ... 57 E1
Wallisdown Rd
  BKME/WDN BH12 ... 37 F5
  NBNE BH10 ... 57 F1
Walnut Cl WIMB BH21 ... 46 D4
Walpole Rd BMTH BH1 ... 59 F5
Walsford Rd WBNE BH4 ... 57 G5
Walsingham Dene LTDN BH7 ... 59 H2
Waltham Rd LTDN BH7 ... 60 B3
Walton Rd NBNE BH10 ... 38 C5
  PLE BH15 ... 55 G4
Wanstead Cl RGWD BH24 ... 8 D3
Warbler Cl UPTN BH16 ... 52 D2
Warburton Rd CFDH BH17 ... 55 E2
Wareham Rd WIMB BH21 ... 34 B2
Warmwell Cl CFDH BH17 ... 36 B5
Warnford Rd LTDN BH7 ... 60 B3
Warren Av CHCH/BSGR BH23 ... 62 D5
Warren Cl RGWD BH24 ... 12 D1
Warren Ct RGWD BH24 ... 7 H5
Warren Edge Cl SBNE BH6 ... 79 H2
Warren Edge Rd SBNE BH6 ... 79 F2

Warren La RGWD BH24 ... 12 D1
Warren Pk LYMN SO41 ... 67 G4
Warren Rd PSTN BH14 ... 74 B1
  WBNE BH4 ... 75 F3
Warwick Av NMIL/BTOS BH25 ... 47 F4
Warwick Rd LTDN BH7 ... 60 A5
  PSTN BH14 ... 74 A2
Washington Av BMTH BH1 ... 59 F4
Watcombe Rd SBNE BH6 ... 60 D5
Waterditch Rd
  CHCH/BSGR BH23 ... 43 H4
Waterford Cl LYMN SO41 ... 51 F4
Waterford Cl PSTN BH14 ... 73 G3
Waterford Gdns
  CHCH/BSGR BH23 ... 64 C3
Waterford La LYMN SO41 ... 51 F4
Waterford Pl
  CHCH/BSGR BH23 ... 64 C3
Waterford Rd CHCH/BSGR BH23 ... 64 C2
  NMIL/BTOS BH25 ... 47 G4
Water La SBNE BH6 ... 60 D3
Waterloo Rd CFDH BH17 ... 54 C2
  LYMN SO41 ... 51 F3
  MOOR/WNTN BH9 ... 58 B3
Waterloo Wy RGWD BH24 ... 8 C5
Watermain Rd RGWD BH24 ... 22 A4
Watermill Rd CHCH/BSGR BH23 ... 61 G2
Waters Gn BROC SO42 ... 15 E2
Waters Green Ct BROC SO42 ... 15 E2
Watership Dr RGWD BH24 ... 9 F5
Waterside CHCH/BSGR BH23 ... 80 D1
Waterside Rd RGWD BH24 ... 8 D2
Waterston Rd CFDH BH17 ... 54 D1
Water Tower Rd BDST BH18 ... 35 G3
Watery La CHCH/BSGR BH23 ... 63 E1
  UPTN BH16 ... 52 B3
Watkin Rd BOSC BH5 ... 77 H1
Watton Cl CHAR BH8 ... 41 E5
Wavell Av CFDH BH17 ... 54 A1
Wavell Rd BWD BH11 ... 38 B3
Wavendon Av NMIL/BTOS BH25 ... 65 G2
Waverley Crs PLE BH15 ... 54 D5
Waverley Rd NMIL/BTOS BH25 ... 47 F5
Wayman Rd WIMB BH21 ... 34 C1
Wayne Rd BKME/WDN BH12 ... 55 H4
Wayside Cl LYMN SO41 ... 68 B5
Wayside Rd RGWD BH24 ... 11 C5
  SBNE BH6 ... 79 E1
Waytown Cl CFDH BH17 ... 54 D1
Weavers Cl FERN BH22 ... 10 A5
Webbs Cl RGWD BH24 ... 8 D2
Webster Rd MOOR/WNTN BH9 ... 39 C4
Wedgewood Gdns
  CHCH/BSGR BH23 ... 33 G3
Wedgwood Dr PSTN BH14 ... 73 G3
Weldon Av BWD BH11 ... 37 G2
Welland Rd WIMB BH21 ... 16 D5
Well Cl NMIL/BTOS BH25 ... 65 H1
Wellesley Av CHCH/BSGR BH23 ... 63 G3
Wellington Av CHCH/BSGR BH23 ... 63 G3
Wellington Rd CHAR BH8 ... 58 C5
  PSTN BH14 ... 74 A2
Well La PLE BH15 ... 72 C1
Wendover Cl NMIL/BTOS BH25 ... 65 H1
Wentwood Gdns
  NMIL/BTOS BH25 ... 47 H5
Wentworth Av BOSC BH5 ... 78 A1
Wentworth Cl BOSC BH5 ... 78 A2
Wentworth Dr BDST BH18 ... 35 E2
  CHCH/BSGR BH23 ... 61 F4
Wescott Wy BWD BH11 ... 37 G3
Wesley Cl CHAR BH8 ... 59 E5
Wesley Rd PSTN BH14 ... 56 A5
  WIMB BH21 ... 16 D4
Wessex Av NMIL/BTOS BH25 ... 47 E5
Wessex Cl CHCH/BSGR BH23 ... 63 G3
Wessex Est RGWD BH24 ... 8 D3
Wessex Rd PSTN BH14 ... 73 G2
  RGWD BH24 ... 8 D3
Wessex Wy WBNE BH4 ... 75 F1
  WCLF BH2 ... 2 E2
West Borough WIMB BH21 ... 16 B4
Westbourne Cl WBNE BH4 ... 2 A3
Westbourne Park Rd
  WBNE BH4 ... 75 F1
Westbury Cl CHCH/BSGR BH23 ... 33 G3
  CHCH/BSGR BH23 ... 63 H1
  NMIL/BTOS BH25 ... 66 A2
Westbury Rd RGWD BH24 ... 8 D4
West Butts St PLE BH15 ... 72 B3
Westby Rd BOSC BH5 ... 77 G1
West Cliff Gdns WCLF BH2 ... 2 E6
West Cliff Rd WBNE BH4 ... 2 A5
  WCLF BH2 ... 2 E5
West Cl LYMN SO41 ... 50 B5
Westcroft Pk BDST BH18 ... 35 G3
Westdown Rd BWD BH11 ... 38 A2
Westerham Rd CCLF BH13 ... 75 F2

Western Av CCLF BH13 ... 74 C3
  NBNE BH10 ... 38 D3
  NMIL/BTOS BH25 ... 65 F2
Western Cl NBNE BH10 ... 38 D2
Western Rd CCLF BH13 ... 74 D5
  LYMN SO41 ... 50 D3
Westfield Cl WIMB BH21 ... 16 B4
Westfield Gdns
  CHCH/BSGR BH23 ... 63 F1
Westfield Rd LYMN SO41 ... 51 F5
  SBNE BH6 ... 79 E1
Westgate Pk WBNE BH4 ... 75 F2
Westham Cl CFDH BH17 ... 36 A4
West Hayes LYMN SO41 ... 51 F4
Westheath Rd BDST BH18 ... 35 F3
West Hill Pl WCLF BH2 ... 2 E4
West Hill Rd WCLF BH2 ... 2 E5
West Howe Cl BWD BH11 ... 38 A3
Westlands Ct CHCH/BSGR BH23 ... 33 E4
West La LYMN SO41 ... 68 C1
Westminster Rd CCLF BH13 ... 75 F4
Westminster Rd East CCLF BH13 ... 75 F4
West Moors Rd FERN BH22 ... 19 H2
Weston Rd WIMB BH21 ... 17 F2
West Overcliff Dr WBNE BH4 ... 2 A6
Westover La RGWD BH24 ... 7 H5
Westover Rd BMTH BH1 ... 3 H4
  LYMN SO41 ... 82 B1
West Quay Rd PLE BH15 ... 72 B3
West Rd BOSC BH5 ... 60 A5
  BOSC BH5 ... 78 B1
  CHCH/BSGR BH23 ... 33 G4
  LYMN SO41 ... 67 G5
West Rw WIMB BH21 ... 16 B5
West St PLE BH15 ... 72 B3
  RGWD BH24 ... 8 A4
  WIMB BH21 ... 16 B5
West Undercliff Prom
  WBNE BH4 ... 75 G4
West View Rd CHCH/BSGR BH23 ... 62 C4
  PLE BH15 ... 72 C1
West Wy BDST BH18 ... 35 E4
  LYMN SO41 ... 50 C5
  MOOR/WNTN BH9 ... 39 H5
West Way Cl
  MOOR/WNTN BH9 ... 58 D1
Westwood Av FERN BH22 ... 19 C3
Wetherby Cl CFDH BH17 ... 35 E5
Weyman's Av NBNE BH10 ... 38 C1
Weymans Dr NBNE BH10 ... 38 C1
Weymouth Rd PSTN BH14 ... 56 A5
Wharf Cl BKME/WDN BH12 ... 56 C4
Wharfdale Rd BKME/WDN BH12 ... 56 B4
  WBNE BH4 ... 2 B2
Wharncliffe Gdns
  CHCH/BSGR BH23 ... 64 C3
Wharncliffe Rd BMTH BH1 ... 77 F1
  CHCH/BSGR BH23 ... 64 C3
Whatleigh Cl PLE BH15 ... 72 C2
Wheaton Rd LTDN BH7 ... 60 A5
Wheelers La BWD BH11 ... 37 E2
Whincroft Cl FERN BH22 ... 20 A2
Whincroft Dr FERN BH22 ... 20 A3
Whistlers Cl CHCH/BSGR BH23 ... 33 F3
Whitaker Crs LYMN SO41 ... 50 C4
Whitby Av BDST BH18 ... 35 E5
Whitby Cl CHCH/BSGR BH23 ... 41 H3
Whitby Crs BDST BH18 ... 35 E5
Whitchurch Av BDST BH18 ... 35 G4
White Barn Crs LYMN SO41 ... 48 C4
Whitebeam Wy VWD BH31 ... 4 D3
Whitecliff Crs PSTN BH14 ... 73 G3
White Cliff Rd PSTN BH14 ... 73 F3
White Cl PLE BH15 ... 55 G3
Whitecross Cl CFDH BH17 ... 36 A4
White Farm Cl NBNE BH10 ... 57 H2
Whitefield Rd NMIL/BTOS BH25 ... 47 E4
  PSTN BH14 ... 73 G3
Whitehall CHCH/BSGR BH23 ... 61 H5
Whitehart Flds RGWD BH24 ... 9 E3
Whitehayes Cl
  CHCH/BSGR BH23 ... 43 F5
Whitehayes Rd
  CHCH/BSGR BH23 ... 62 A1
White Horse Dr PLE BH15 ... 54 C5
Whitehouse Rd WIMB BH21 ... 24 C3
White Knights NMIL/BTOS BH25 ... 65 H3
Whitelands CHCH/BSGR BH23 ... 33 H1
Whitelegg Wy NBNE BH10 ... 39 E4
Whitemoor Rd BROC SO42 ... 14 B2
Whiteways WIMB BH21 ... 17 E3
Whitfield Pk RGWD BH24 ... 12 B1
Whitley Wy NMIL/BTOS BH25 ... 47 F2
Whitsbury Cl CHAR BH8 ... 40 B5
Whittle Rd WIMB BH21 ... 18 D2
Whittles Wy PLE BH15 ... 72 B3
Wick Cl NMIL/BTOS BH25 ... 46 C5

Wick Dr NMIL/BTOS BH25 ... 46 C5
Wicket Rd NBNE BH10 ... 38 C2
Wickfield Av CHCH/BSGR BH23 ... 61 H4
Wickfield Cl CHCH/BSGR BH23 ... 61 H4
Wickham Dr WIMB BH21 ... 34 B3
Wick La CHCH/BSGR BH23 ... 61 H5
  SBNE BH6 ... 61 H5
Wicklea Rd SBNE BH6 ... 79 H1
Wickmeads Rd SBNE BH6 ... 61 G5
Widbury Rd LYMN SO41 ... 50 C5
Widdicombe Av PSTN BH14 ... 74 C3
Wide Lane Cl BROC SO42 ... 14 D3
Widget Cl BWD BH11 ... 38 B5
Widworthy Dr BDST BH18 ... 34 D2
Wight Wk FERN BH22 ... 28 A2
Wilderton Rd CCLF BH13 ... 74 D1
Wilderton Rd West CCLF BH13 ... 74 D1
Wildfell Cl CHCH/BSGR BH23 ... 61 G1
Wildown Gdns SBNE BH6 ... 79 F2
Wildown Rd SBNE BH6 ... 79 G2
Wilfred Rd BOSC BH5 ... 77 H1
Wilkinson Dr CHAR BH8 ... 41 E5
Willett Rd WIMB BH21 ... 24 A2
William Cl CHCH/BSGR BH23 ... 45 G5
William Rd LTDN BH7 ... 59 H3
  LYMN SO41 ... 51 E2
Willis Wy CFDH BH17 ... 54 B4
Willow Cl RGWD BH24 ... 11 F2
  UPTN BH16 ... 53 F5
Willowdene Cl NMIL/BTOS BH25 ... 47 G4
Willow Dr CHCH/BSGR BH23 ... 61 G5
  RGWD BH24 ... 13 G1
  WIMB BH21 ... 18 A3
Willow La CHCH/BSGR BH23 ... 33 H1
Willow Md CHAR BH8 ... 40 B3
Willow Pk PSTN BH14 ... 73 F2
The Willows NMIL/BTOS BH25 ... 66 B2
Willow Tree Ri BWD BH11 ... 38 B5
Willow Wy CHCH/BSGR BH23 ... 61 G5
  FERN BH22 ... 19 H2
Wills Cl WIMB BH21 ... 34 B3
Wills Rd BKME/WDN BH12 ... 56 D2
Willwood Cl CFDH BH17 ... 36 A4
Wilmur Crs PLE BH15 ... 55 E4
Wilson Rd BMTH BH1 ... 59 F5
  PSTN BH14 ... 74 A1
Wilton Cl CHCH/BSGR BH23 ... 60 D1
Wilton Gdns NMIL/BTOS BH25 ... 46 D4
Wilton Rd LTDN BH7 ... 59 H5
Wiltshire Gdns
  CHCH/BSGR BH23 ... 32 D4
Wiltshire Rd CHCH/BSGR BH23 ... 32 D4
Wilverley Av CHAR BH8 ... 40 D5
Wilverley Rd BROC SO42 ... 14 D3
Wimborne Rd BWD BH11 ... 38 A1
  MOOR/WNTN BH9 ... 58 B2
  PLE BH15 ... 54 C4
  TWDS BH3 ... 58 B3
  WCLF BH2 ... 3 H1
  WIMB BH21 ... 16 B3
  WIMB BH21 ... 17 E3
Wimborne Rd East FERN BH22 ... 19 H3
  WIMB BH21 ... 19 E5
Wimborne Rd West WIMB BH21 ... 17 G5
Winchester Rd NMIL/BTOS BH25 ... 47 G2
Wincombe Cl FERN BH22 ... 27 H1
Wincombe Dr FERN BH22 ... 19 H5
Windermere Rd TWDS BH3 ... 58 C4
Windham Rd BMTH BH1 ... 59 E5
Windmill Cl LYMN SO41 ... 68 B5
  RGWD BH24 ... 12 D2
Windmill La RGWD BH24 ... 12 D2
Windsor Cl LYMN SO41 ... 48 A3
  RGWD BH24 ... 11 H1
Windsor Rd BOSC BH5 ... 77 G1
  CHCH/BSGR BH23 ... 61 E2
  PSTN BH14 ... 73 H2
Winfrith Crs BKME/WDN BH12 ... 56 C2
Wingfield Av CHCH/BSGR BH23 ... 63 H1
  PLE BH15 ... 54 D4
Winifred Rd PLE BH15 ... 55 E5
Winkton Cl CHCH/BSGR BH23 ... 43 E4
Winnards Cl FERN BH22 ... 24 A2
Winsford Cl NMIL/BTOS BH25 ... 63 H1
Winsley Av SBNE BH6 ... 78 C1
Winspit Cl PLE BH15 ... 71 E2
Winston Av BKME/WDN BH12 ... 57 E4
Winston Gdns BKME/WDN BH12 ... 57 E4
Winston Rd MOOR/WNTN BH9 ... 39 G4
Winston Wy RGWD BH24 ... 8 D3
Winterbourne Rd PLE BH15 ... 72 D1
Winterhayes Cl CFDH BH17 ... 35 H4
Winton Cl LYMN SO41 ... 51 F4
Winton Wy NBNE BH10 ... 57 H1
  NMIL/BTOS BH25 ... 47 F2
Wisbech Wy LYMN SO41 ... 48 B4
Wishart Gdns MOOR/WNTN BH9 ... 39 H2
Wisteria Dr VWD BH31 ... 5 E4

Witchampton Rd *DDST* DI I10....... 34 D3
Withermoor Rd
  MOOR/WNTN BH9...................... 58 A2
Withingham Rd *CCLF* BH13 .... 74 D2
Wiverley Cl *LYMN* SO41 .... 50 B5
Woking Rd *PSTN* BH14 .... 74 A1
Wolfe Cl *CHCH/BSGR* BH23 ...... 62 C3 🔢
Wollaston Rd *SBNE* BH6 .... 79 F2
Wollaton Rd *FERN* BH22 .... 27 G1
Wollstonecraft Rd *BOSC* BH5 .... 77 H2 🔢
Wolseley Rd *BKME/WDN* BH12 .. 56 B4
Wolsey Wy *LYMN* SO41 .... 68 B5
Wolterton Rd *BKME/WDN* BH12 .. 57 E5
Wolverton Rd *LTDN* BH7 .... 59 H5
Woodacre Gdns *FERN* BH22 ...... 20 A5
Woodbury Av *CHAR* BH8 .... 40 D5
Woodbury Cl *CHCH/BSGR* BH23... 42 A4
Woodcock La *LYMN* SO41 .... 48 C4
Woodcocks Crs *LTDN* BH7 .... 60 A3
Woodcote Dr *UPTN* BH16 .... 52 D4
Woodend Rd *MOOR/WNTN* BH9 .. 58 A3
Woodfield Gdns
  CHCH/BSGR BH23 .... 63 H1
Woodfield Rd *BWD* BH11 .... 38 A2
Woodford Cl *RGWD* BH24 .... 8 D4
Woodford Rd *BMTH* BH1 .... 77 E1
Woodgreen Dr *BWD* BH11 .... 37 F3
Woodhayes Av
  CHCH/BSGR BH23 .... 45 E5
Woodlake Cl *CFDH* BH17 .... 54 D1 🔢
Woodland Av *BOSC* BH5 .... 78 A1
Woodlands Av *PLE* BH15 .... 71 G2
Woodlands Cl
  CHCH/BSGR BH23 .... 33 E4 🔢
Woodlands Crs *PLE* BH15 .... 71 H2
Woodlands Rd *BROC* SO42 .... 14 D5
  NMIL/BTOS BH25................... 65 G3
Woodlands Wy
  NMIL/BTOS BH25................... 47 F1
  RGWD BH24 .... 11 H2
Woodland Wk *BOSC* BH5 .... 78 A1

FERN BH22 .... 20 B2
Woodland Wy *CHCH/BSGR* BH23.. 63 H2
  LYMN SO41 .... 82 A1 🔢
Wood La *BWD* BH11.................... 37 G1
  LYMN SO41 .... 82 A1
Wood Lawn Cl *NMIL/BTOS* BH25 .. 65 H2
Woodleaze Cl *BDST* BH18.......... 35 F1
Woodley Gdns *LYMN* SO41 .... 50 D2
Woodlinken Cl *VWD* BH31 .... 4 D3
Woodlinken Dr *VWD* BH31 .... 4 D4
Woodlinken Wy *VWD* BH31 .... 4 D3
Woodpecker Cl *VWD* BH31 .... 4 B3 🔢
Woodpecker Dr *CFDH* BH17....... 53 G2
Woodside Cl *FERN* BH22 .... 20 A3
Woodside La *LYMN* SO41 .... 51 F5
Woodside Rd *BOSC* BH5 .... 78 B1
  FERN BH22 .... 20 A3
  PSTN BH14 .... 74 A2
Woodstock La *RGWD* BH24 .... 8 C5 🔢
Woodstock Rd
  CHCH/BSGR BH23 .... 43 F5 🔢
  PSTN BH14 .... 73 G3 🔢
Woods View Rd
  MOOR/WNTN BH9 .... 57 H2
Woodvale Gdns
  NMIL/BTOS BH25................... 47 G3
Wood Vw *WIMB* BH21............... 17 G1
Woolmer La *RGWD* BH24 .... 8 B1
Wool Rd *BKME/WDN* BH12 .... 55 H2
Wools Br *RGWD* BH24 .... 6 A5
Woolsbridge Rd *RGWD* BH24 .... 11 G2
Woolslope Cl *FERN* BH22 .... 10 A5 🔢
Woolslope Gdns *FERN* BH22 ..... 10 B5
Woolslope Rd *FERN* BH22......... 10 A5
Woolven Cl *PSTN* BH14 .... 55 G5 🔢
Wootton Gdns *BMTH* BH1 .... 3 J3
Wootton Mt *BMTH* BH1 .... 3 K3
Worbarrow Gdns
  BKME/WDN BH12 .... 56 A2
Worcester Pl *LYMN* SO41 .... 51 F5 🔢
Wordsworth Av *CHAR* BH8........ 59 G1

Worgret Rd *PLE* BH15 .... 54 D3
Worrell Dr *BKME/WDN* BH12 .... 56 A2
Worthington Crs *PSTN* BH14 ..... 73 G2
Worthy Rd *NMIL/BTOS* BH25 .... 47 E4
Wortley Rd *CHCH/BSGR* BH23 ... 64 C3
Wraxhall Cl *CFDH* BH17 .... 54 D1
Wren Cl *CHCH/BSGR* BH23 .... 63 F5
  NMIL/BTOS BH25 .... 46 D5 🔢
  RGWD BH24 .... 9 E5 🔢
Wren Crs *BKME/WDN* BH12 ...... 57 F5
Wroxham Rd *BKME/WDN* BH12 .. 56 D5
Wyatts Cl *WIMB* BH21............... 34 B1
Wyatts La *WIMB* BH21............... 34 B1
Wychwood Cl *WCLF* BH2 .... 3 F1
Wychwood Dr *WCLF* BH2 .... 58 B5
Wycliffe Rd *MOOR/WNTN* BH9... 58 B2
Wyelands Av *WIMB* BH21 .... 18 B4
Wykeham Cl *CFDH* BH17 .... 55 E2 🔢
Wykeham Pl *LYMN* SO41 .... 51 E4
Wyncombe Rd *BOSC* BH5 .... 60 B5
Wyndham Cl
  CHCH/BSGR BH23 .... 45 H5 🔢
Wyndham Rd *CHCH/BSGR* BH23 .. 45 H5
  PSTN BH14 .... 73 H2
Wynford Rd *MOOR/WNTN* BH9 .. 39 C3
  PSTN BH14 .... 74 A2
Wynne Cl *BDST* BH18................ 34 D3
Wynter Cl *LTDN* BH7 .... 59 H3
Wyvern Cl *BKME/WDN* BH12 .... 56 B3

Yarrow Rd *BKME/WDN* BH12..... 55 G2
Yeatminster Rd *CFDH* BH17 ...... 36 B5
Yelverton Rd *WCLF* BH2 .... 3 G3
Yeomans Rd *CHAR* BH8............. 40 C4
Yeomans Wy *CHAR* BH8 .... 40 C4
Yeovilton Cl *LYMN* SO41 .... 68 C1
Yerville Gdns *LYMN* SO41 .... 48 B4 🔢
Yew La *NMIL/BTOS* BH25 .... 47 G3
Yew Tree Cl *WIMB* BH21 .... 16 C4
York Av *NMIL/BTOS* BH25 .... 47 F4
York Cl *BDST* BH18 .... 35 E5 🔢
  CHCH/BSGR BH23 .... 61 F3
York Pl *LTDN* BH7 .... 60 A5
York Rd *BMTH* BH1 .... 76 D1
  CFDH BH17 .... 54 A1
Youngs Rd *BWD* BH11............... 38 A2

Z

Zamek Cl *BWD* BH11 .... 38 A2
Zinnia Cl *NBNE* BH10 .... 39 E5

Y

Yaldhurst La *LYMN* SO41........... 50 B3
Yarmouth Cl *BKME/WDN* BH12 .. 57 E5 🔢
Yarmouth Rd *BKME/WDN* BH12 .. 56 D4
Yarrell Md *LYMN* SO41 .... 50 B3
Yarrells Cl *UPTN* BH16.............. 53 E4
Yarrells La *UPTN* BH16.............. 53 E4
Yarrow Cl *CHCH/BSGR* BH23...... 63 F2

Index - featured places

ABC Cinema
  BMTH BH1 .... 3 H4
Ad Astra County First School
  CFDH BH17 .... 55 E1
Adeline Road Surgery
  BOSC BH5 .... 77 G1
Alderney Middle School
  BKME/WDN BH12 .... 56 B1
Allenbourn County Middle School
  WIMB BH21 .... 16 B4
The Arnewood Practice
  NMIL/BTOS BH25................... 47 E4
Arnewood School
  NMIL/BTOS BH25................... 65 H1
Ashdown School
  CFDH BH17 .... 55 E1
Ashley County Infant School
  NMIL/BTOS BH25................... 47 H4
Ashley Heath Industrial Estate
  WIMB BH21 .... 6 A4
Ashley Junior School
  NMIL/BTOS BH25................... 47 G4
Avenue Shopping Centre
  WCLF BH2 .... 3 F3
Avonbourne Girls School
  LTDN BH7 .... 60 A3
Avon Castle
  RGWD BH24 .... 12 D3
Avonlea Preparatory School
  RGWD BH24 .... 8 D3
Baden Powell &
St Peters C of E (VC) School
  PSTN BH14 .... 73 H2
Ballard College
  NMIL/BTOS BH25................... 47 E4
Ballard Lake
Preparatory School
  NMIL/BTOS BH25................... 47 E3
Barton Surgery
  NMIL/BTOS BH25................... 66 A1
Bearwood County
Primary School
  WIMB BH21 .... 37 E1
Beaucroft School
  WIMB BH21 .... 17 E3
Beaufort Road Surgery
  SBNE BH6 .... 60 C5
Bethany C of E
(VA) Junior School
  BMTH BH1 .... 59 F5

Bicknell Boys
Residential School
  LTDN BH7 .... 60 A3
Birchwood Medical Centre
  CFDH BH17 .... 53 H2
Blue Fish Zoo
  BMTH BH1 .... 3 G4
The Bold Gallery
  CHCH/BSGR BH23 .... 61 H3
Boscombe Dental
Health Centre
  BOSC BH5 .... 59 H5
Boscombe Manor
Medical Centre
  BOSC BH5 .... 77 H1
Bournemouth College
  BMTH BH1 .... 77 E1
Bournemouth County Court
  BMTH BH1 .... 3 K2
Bournemouth
International Airport
  CHCH/BSGR BH23 .... 29 H4
Bournemouth
Magistrates Court
  BMTH BH1 .... 3 K3
Bournemouth Mosque
  MOOR/WNTN BH9 .... 58 B2
Bournemouth & Poole College
  BMTH BH1 .... 3 K3
Bournemouth & Poole College
  PSTN BH14 .... 55 F5
Bournemouth & Poole College of
Further Education
  PSTN BH14 .... 73 F1
Bournemouth School for Boys
  CHAR BH8 .... 59 E1
Bournemouth School for Girls
  CHAR BH8 .... 40 A5
Bournemouth Sports Club
  CHCH/BSGR BH23 .... 29 E3
Bournemouth University
  BKME/WDN BH12 .... 57 G2
Bournemouth University
  BMTH BH1 .... 76 D2
Branksome Heath
Middle School
  BKME/WDN BH12 .... 56 A4
Bransgore Primary School
  CHCH/BSGR BH23 .... 33 G4
Broadstone First School
  BDST BH18........................... 35 F3

Broadstone Middle School
  BDST BH18........................... 35 G2
Brockenhurst College
  BROC SO42 .... 15 E2
Brockenhurst Primary School
  BROC SO42 .... 14 D3
Brownsea Open Air Theatre
  CFDH BH17 .... 54 A2
Buckholme School
  PSTN BH14 .... 73 G1
Burton Primary School
  CHCH/BSGR BH23 .... 43 E4
Canada House Business Centre
  NMIL/BTOS BH25 .... 47 G5
Canford Heath First School
  CFDH BH17 .... 55 E3
Canford Heath Middle School
  CFDH BH17 .... 54 D3
Canford School
  WIMB BH21 .... 25 G2
The Carpet Gallery
  WBNE BH4 .... 2 A3
Carter Community School
  PLE BH15 .... 71 H3
Carvers Trading Estate
  RGWD BH24 .... 8 C4
Chawton House Surgery
  LYMN SO41 .... 51 E4
Christchurch Infant School
  CHCH/BSGR BH23 .... 61 G3
Christchurch Junior School
  CHCH/BSGR BH23 .... 61 F3
Christchurch Ski &
Leisure Centre
  CHCH/BSGR BH23 .... 30 B1
Christ the King RC
Primary School
  BWD BH11 .... 38 A2
Corfe Hills School
  WIMB BH21 .... 34 D1
Cornerways Surgery
  RGWD BH24 .... 11 G2
Corpus Christie School
  BOSC BH5 .... 59 H5
Courthill First School
  PSTN BH14........................... 74 B1
Crow Arch Lane Industrial Estate
  RGWD BH24 .... 13 G1
Cutlers Gallery
  BMTH BH1 .... 3 H3

Dawkins Business Centre
  PLE BH15 .... 71 F2
Dean Court (Bournemouth FC)
  LTDN BH7 .... 59 H4
Dorset County Council
  BMTH BH1 .... 3 K2
Dorset County Council
  FERN BH22 .... 19 H4
Dorset County Council
  WIMB BH21 .... 16 C4
Dorset County Council
  WIMB BH21 .... 18 D2
Dorset Health Authority
  FERN BH22 .... 19 H
Dorset Magistrates Court
  BMTH BH1 .... 3 J
Dr Hughes & Partners
  RGWD BH24 .... 8 B4
Dumpton School
  WIMB BH21 .... 16 D
Durlston Court School
  NMIL/BTOS BH25................... 66 A
Eagle House School
  PSTN BH14........................... 55 G
East Dorset Area
Health Authority
  FERN BH22 .... 19 H
East Dorset District Council
  WIMB BH21 .... 16 C
Ebblake Industrial Estate
  RGWD BH24.......................... 5 F
Elmrise Junior & Infant School
  BWD BH11 .... 37 H
The Epiphany School
  MOOR/WNTN BH9 .... 39 H
Ferndown First School
  FERN BH22 .... 19 G
Ferndown Medical Centre
  FERN BH22 .... 19 H
Ferndown Middle School
  FERN BH22 .... 19 F
Ferndown Sports Centre
  FERN BH22 .... 19 F
Ferndown Town Council
  FERN BH22 .... 19 G
Ferndown Upper School
  FERN BH22 .... 19 F
Fernside Business Park
  WIMB BH21 .... 19 E
Glenmoor School for Girls
  NBNE BH10 .... 57 H

ordleton Industrial Estate
　CHCH/BSGR BH23 .... 49 H2
range Comprehensive School
　CHCH/BSGR BH23 .... 62 C2
undrymoor Trading Estate
　WIMB BH21 .... 10 B1
adleigh Practice
　WIMB BH21 .... 34 A3
ampreston Primary School
　WIMB BH21 .... 26 C1
ampshire County Council
　LYMN SO41 .... 51 E3
ampshire County Council
　RGWD BH24 .... 8 C5
ampshire Gallery
　BMTH BH1 .... 3 K2
amworthy Community Clinic
　PLE BH15 .... 71 G2
amworthy First School
　PLE BH15 .... 71 H4
amworthy Middle School
　PLE BH15 .... 71 H4
ayeswood County First School
　WIMB BH21 .... 17 C3
aymoor Middle School
　CFDH BH17 .... 55 E1
eadlands Business Park
　RGWD BH24 .... 8 C1
eatherlands First School
　BKME/WDN BH12 .... 56 B5
eathlands Primary School
　BWD BH11 .... 38 A4
enbury View First School
　WIMB BH21 .... 34 A1
ghcliffe Castle Golf Club
　CHCH/BSGR BH23 .... 64 A3
ghcliffe County Junior School
　CHCH/BSGR BH23 .... 64 C1
ghcliffe Gm
　Comprehensive School
　CHCH/BSGR BH23 .... 63 H1
ghcliffe Medical Centre
　CHCH/BSGR BH23 .... 64 B2
ghtown Industrial Estate
　RGWD BH24 .... 8 D5
lbourne First School
　CFDH BH17 .... 35 E5
lbourne Middle School
　CFDH BH17 .... 35 E5
lside County First School
　VWD BH31 .... 4 C1
l View First School
　NBNE BH10 .... 39 E4
l View Junior School
　NBNE BH10 .... 39 E4
M Coroners Court
　BMTH BH1 .... 3 K2
mefield School
　CHCH/BSGR BH23 .... 43 E3
meopathic Surgery
　NMIL/BTOS BH25 .... 65 H3
rdle C of E GM Primary School
　LYMN SO41 .... 48 C4
rdle House School
　LYMN SO41 .... 67 G5
nter Simmonds Gallery
　CCLF BH13 .... 75 F1
ax Cinema
　BMTH BH1 .... 3 H5
ernational Centre &
　Leisure Pool
　WCLF BH2 .... 3 G6
icoe Theatre
　PSTN BH14 .... 55 F5
gs Junior School
　SBNE BH6 .... 61 F5
gsleigh First School
　NBNE BH10 .... 38 C4
gsleigh Junior School
　NBNE BH10 .... 38 C4
gsleigh Secondary School
　NBNE BH10 .... 38 C4
gs Park Primary School
　BMTH BH1 .... 59 C4
son Primary School
　BWD BH11 .... 38 B2
gside School
　BKME/WDN BH12 .... 57 E2
out First School
　PSTN BH14 .... 74 A5
wood School
　MOOR/WNTN BH9 .... 58 C3
ledown Leisure Centre
　LTDN BH7 .... 60 A2
gfleet C of E VC
　Combined School
　PLE BH15 .... 73 E1
gspee School
　CFDH BH17 .... 54 D3
ington Community Hospitals
　LYMN SO41 .... 51 E3

Lymington County
　Junior & Infant School
　LYMN SO41 .... 50 D3
Lymington Hospital
　LYMN SO41 .... 50 D3
Lymington Recreation Centre
　LYMN SO41 .... 50 C4
Lytchett Minster Upper School
　UPTN BH16 .... 52 A2
Malmesbury Park School
　CHAR BH8 .... 58 D4
Manor Road Surgery
　VWD BH31 .... 4 A2
Maple Business Park
　WIMB BH21 .... 18 D2
The Martin Kemp Welch School
　BKME/WDN BH12 .... 56 B2
Mayfield Gallery
　MOOR/WNTN BH9 .... 39 F5
Milford C of E School
　LYMN SO41 .... 68 C4
Millstream Trading Estate
　RGWD BH24 .... 13 F1
M L S College
　BMTH BH1 .... 3 G3
Moordown C of E
　Primary School
　MOOR/WNTN BH9 .... 58 B1
Moorlands College
　CHCH/BSGR BH23 .... 42 D1
Mudeford County
　Primary School
　CHCH/BSGR BH23 .... 62 C4
Mudeford Junior School
　CHCH/BSGR BH23 .... 62 D4
Muscliff C Primary School
　MOOR/WNTN BH9 .... 40 A4
Music Gallery
　MOOR/WNTN BH9 .... 58 D2
New Forest District Council
　NMIL/BTOS BH25 .... 47 E5
New Forest District Council
　NMIL/BTOS BH25 .... 8 B5
New Milton Junior School
　NMIL/BTOS BH25 .... 66 A1
New Milton Recreation Centre
　NMIL/BTOS BH25 .... 46 D5
New Milton Sports Club
　NMIL/BTOS BH25 .... 47 G4
New Milton Town Council
　NMIL/BTOS BH25 .... 47 E5
Nova Business Park
　NMIL/BTOS BH25 .... 46 C5
Oakdale South Road
　Middle School
　PLE BH15 .... 54 D5
Oakmead College of Technology
　BWD BH11 .... 37 H2
Odeon Cinema
　BMTH BH1 .... 3 H4
Our Lady & St Joseph RC Primary
　School
　LYMN SO41 .... 51 F3
Parkstone Grammar School for
　Girls
　CFDH BH17 .... 54 B2
Parley First School
　FERN BH22 .... 27 H1
Pavilion
　BMTH BH1 .... 3 J1
Pavilion Theatre
　BMTH BH1 .... 3 G4
Pavillion Theatre
　BMTH BH1 .... 3 H5
Pennington County Junior &
　Infant School
　LYMN SO41 .... 50 C4
Pier Theatre
　WCLF BH2 .... 3 H6
Pokesdown Primary School
　BOSC BH5 .... 60 B5
Poole Grammar School
　CFDH BH17 .... 35 H5
Poole Road Medical Centre
　WBNE BH4 .... 2 C4
Poole Technical High School
　PLE BH15 .... 72 C1
Portcastrian R F C
　SBNE BH6 .... 61 E4
Portchester School
　LTDN BH7 .... 60 A3
Poulner Junior & Infant School
　RGWD BH24 .... 9 E1
Priestlands County
　Secondary School
　LYMN SO41 .... 50 C4
Priets House Museum
　WIMB BH21 .... 16 C5
Priory C of E VA Primary School
　CHCH/BSGR BH23 .... 61 H4
Private Medical Centre
　BMTH BH1 .... 3 J3

Red House Museum & Gardens
　CHCH/BSGR BH23 .... 61 H4
Ringwood C of E Infant School
　RGWD BH24 .... 8 C4
Ringwood County Junior School
　RGWD BH24 .... 8 C5
Ringwood Recreation Centre
　RGWD BH24 .... 8 C4
Ringwood School
　RGWD BH24 .... 8 C4
Ringwood Town Council
　RGWD BH24 .... 8 C5
Ringwood Trading Estate
　RGWD BH24 .... 8 C5
Ringwood Waldorf School
　RGWD BH24 .... 7 F5
Riverside Business Park
　LYMN SO41 .... 51 F3
Robert King Gallery
　LYMN SO41 .... 50 D4
Rushcombe County First School
　WIMB BH21 .... 34 B1
Russell Cotes Art
　Gallery & Museum
　BMTH BH1 .... 3 J5
St Aldhelms C of E
　Combined School
　BKME/WDN BH12 .... 57 E4
St Anns Hospital
　CCLF BH13 .... 85 G2
St Barbe Museum
　LYMN SO41 .... 51 E3
St Catherines RC Primary School
　BMTH BH1 .... 17 G3
St Clements C of E School
　BMTH BH1 .... 59 F5
St Edward Comprehensive
　School
　PLE BH15 .... 55 F3
St Georges Hospital
　LYMN SO41 .... 82 A1
St Ives CP School
　RGWD BH24 .... 12 A1
St James C of E Primary School
　LTDN BH7 .... 60 B5
St Johns School
　WIMB BH21 .... 16 D5
St Josephs RC School
　BKME/WDN BH12 .... 56 C5
St Josephs RC School
　CHCH/BSGR BH23 .... 63 E2
St Katherines C of E
　Primary School
　SBNE BH6 .... 79 H1
St Leonards Hospital
　RGWD BH24 .... 11 E5
St Lukes C of E School
　MOOR/WNTN BH9 .... 58 B2
St Marks C of E County
　Infant School
　CHCH/BSGR BH23 .... 64 B1
St Marks C of E Primary School
　NBNE BH10 .... 57 G1
St Marys RC School
　PLE BH15 .... 55 E5
St Michaels C of E School
　WCLF BH2 .... 2 D4
St Michaels Middle School
　WIMB BH21 .... 17 E2
St Peter's Church
　BMTH BH1 .... 3 H4
St Peters School
　LTDN BH7 .... 60 B2
St Peters School
　SBNE BH6 .... 79 F1
St Thomas Clinic
　LYMN SO41 .... 50 D4
St Walburgas RC Primary School
　MOOR/WNTN BH9 .... 39 H5
The Sanatorium Canford School
　WIMB BH21 .... 25 G3
Scaplens Court Museum
　PLE BH15 .... 72 B4
Shelley Museum
　BOSC BH5 .... 77 H1
Slades Farm Special School
　NBNE BH10 .... 57 H1
Somerford County
　Infant School
　CHCH/BSGR BH23 .... 62 C3
Somerford County
　Junior School
　CHCH/BSGR BH23 .... 62 C3
Sopley CP School
　CHCH/BSGR BH23 .... 32 A3
Southern Electric Museum
　CHCH/BSGR BH23 .... 61 H3
Spectrum Sports Club
　SBNE BH6 .... 78 C1
Springdale First School
　BDST BH18 .... 34 C3

Stag Business Park
　RGWD BH24 .... 13 G1
Stanley Green First School
　PLE BH15 .... 54 C1
Stapehill Abbey
　WIMB BH21 .... 18 C4
Stone Lane Industrial Estate
　WIMB BH21 .... 16 A3
Stourfield First School
　SBNE BH6 .... 60 D4
Summerbee First School
　CHAR BH8 .... 59 E1
Summerbee Junior School
　CHAR BH8 .... 59 E1
Summerbee Secondary School
　CHAR BH8 .... 59 F1
Super Bowl (Bournemouth)
　BMTH BH1 .... 3 J5
Sylvan First School
　BKME/WDN BH12 .... 55 H4
Synagogue
　BMTH BH1 .... 3 J3
Talbot Heath School
　WBNE BH4 .... 57 G5
Talbot House
　Preparatory School
　MOOR/WNTN BH9 .... 58 A2
Talbot School
　BKME/WDN BH12 .... 57 F2
Trinidad First School
　BKME/WDN BH12 .... 56 A2
Turlin Moor First School
　UPTN BH16 .... 71 E1
Turlin Moor Middle School
　UPTN BH16 .... 71 E1
Two Riversmeet Leisure Centre
　CHCH/BSGR BH23 .... 62 A4
Twynham
　Comprehensive School
　CHCH/BSGR BH23 .... 61 G4
Uplands School
　PSTN BH14 .... 74 A2
Upton Health Centre
　UPTN BH16 .... 53 E3
Upton Infant School
　UPTN BH16 .... 52 C3
Upton Junior School
　UPTN BH16 .... 52 C4
Verwood C of E First School
　VWD BH31 .... 4 A3
Verwood C of E School
　VWD BH31 .... 4 A3
Verwood Industrial Estate
　VWD BH31 .... 4 D2
Verwood Leisure Centre
　VWD BH31 .... 4 B2
Verwood Sports Centre
　VWD BH31 .... 4 C2
Verwood Town Council
　VWD BH31 .... 4 B1
Vintage Motorcycle Museum
　NMIL/BTOS BH25 .... 46 C2
Walford Mill Medical Centre
　WIMB BH21 .... 16 B3
War Memorial Hospital
　LYMN SO41 .... 82 C1
Waterfront Museum
　PLE BH15 .... 72 B4
Webb Peploe House Surgery
　LYMN SO41 .... 51 E4
Wentworth College
　BOSC BH5 .... 78 A1
Westbourne Galleries
　CCLF BH13 .... 75 F2
West Cliff Medical Centre
　WCLF BH2 .... 2 E6
West Moors Middle School
　FERN BH22 .... 10 B5
Westover Gallery
　BMTH BH1 .... 3 H4
Wick 1 Industrial Estate
　NMIL/BTOS BH25 .... 46 C4
Wick 2 Industrial Estate
　NMIL/BTOS BH25 .... 46 C5
Wimborne First School
　WIMB BH21 .... 16 B4
Wimborne Hospital
　WIMB BH21 .... 16 A4
Wimborne Industrial Estate
　WIMB BH21 .... 16 C4
Wimborne Town Football Club
　WIMB BH21 .... 16 A4
The Wishing Well Gallery
　CHCH/BSGR BH23 .... 33 F3
Yarrells Preparatory School
　UPTN BH16 .... 52 D3

Notes

Notes

Notes

Notes

Notes